The Emergence of Russian Foreign Policy

THE EMERGENCE of RUSSIAN FOREIGN POLICY

Leon Aron and
Kenneth M. Jensen, Editors

UNITED STATES INSTITUTE OF PEACE PRESS
Washington, D.C.

The views expressed in this book are those of the authors alone. They do not necessarily reflect views of the United States Institute of Peace.

United States Institute of Peace
1550 M Street, N.W.
Washington, D.C. 20005

First published 1994

Printed in the United States of America

The paper used in this publication meets the minimum requirements of American National Standard for Information Sciences—Permanence of Paper for Printed Library Materials, ANSI Z39.48-1984.

Library of Congress Cataloging-in-Publication Data
The emergence of Russian foreign policy / edited by Leon Aron and Kenneth M. Jensen.
    p. cm.
    "First presented at an international conference entitled 'The Emerging National Security Doctrine of a New Russia,' which was held March 17–19, 1993, in Washington, D.C."—CIP pref.
    ISBN 1-878379-36-4 (alk. paper)
    1. Russia (Federation)—Foreign relations—Forecasting. 2. Russia (Federation)—Defense—Forecasting. 3. National security—Russia (Federation)—Forecasting. I. Aron, Leon Rabinovich. II. Jensen, Kenneth M. (Kenneth Martin), 1944– . III. United States Institute of Peace.
    DK510.764.E46 1994
    327.47'09'049—dc20   94-3625
                                                                 CIP

Contents

Part III: Russia and the Far Abroad

Preface

With the exception of the editors' contributions, the ideas from which the essays in this volume originate were first presented at an international conference held March 17–19, 1993, in Washington, D.C. Entitled "The Emerging National Security Doctrine of a New Russia," the conference was sponsored by the United States Institute of Peace as part of its continuing efforts to monitor the dramatic changes in Eastern Europe and the former Soviet Union since 1989.

March 1993 was an important time for the United States, as a new administration was beginning its foreign policy work in a vastly complicated international atmosphere. One of the aims of the conference was to bring Russian parties to foreign policy debates into contact with the new policymakers of the Clinton administration, thereby improving understanding and cooperation on both sides. Accordingly, the event gathered together a wide variety of Russian and American policymakers, scholars, and other expert participants for a broad-ranging discussion of the development of Russian foreign policy.

On the Russian side, fortunate timing brought us such key players in that country's debates as Evgenii Ambartsumov, chairman of the Supreme Soviet's Committee on Foreign Affairs and member of the Presidential Council; Andranik Migranian, Presidential Council member, advisor to the Foreign Affairs Committee, and originator of the "Russian Monroe Doctrine"; Russian arms control expert Andrei Kortunov; and Vladimir Lukin, then ambassador to the United States and now chairman of the Committee on Foreign Affairs of the new Russian Parliament. On the American side, we were pleased to have the insights of former Defense Secretary Dick Cheney, Ambassador Max Kampelman, former UN ambassador Jeane Kirkpatrick, Policy Planning director Samuel W. Lewis, scholar Michael Mandelbaum, Ambassador Paul Nitze, Joseph Nye of the National

Intelligence Council, and scholar Peter Reddaway, among others. Needless to say, we were also pleased to have the analyses and views of all the Russian and U.S. authors whose contributions are gathered in this book.

Given the richness of the conference presentations, we determined that they should go into print in revised form to benefit a broader audience. What follows is a substantial primer on the developing foreign policy of a new Russia—a primer that, by dint of its Russian contributions in particular, also serves to document the substance and manner of the Russian debate both at the time and as it continues.

The editors owe a debt of gratitude to the many people who made this book possible. Charles E. Nelson, who was acting president of the Institute of Peace at the time of the conference, gave unqualified support to the conference and book projects. Without the support of the Institute's new president, Dr. Richard Solomon, our work would not have been completed.

We would like to thank Dr. Joseph Klaits of the Jennings Randolph Fellowship Program of the United States Institute of Peace for assistance rendered on the conference and book projects during, and beyond, Leon Aron's fellowship year at the Institute. We would also like to thank the staff of the Research and Studies Program of the Institute—Dr. Sheryl Brown, Dr. David Wurmser, Ms. Kimber Schraub, Ms. Shirley Bekins, and Ms. Victoria Sams—for their hard work in staging the conference on which this book is based. We also owe substantial thanks to the Publications and Marketing Department of the Institute for making this book possible. In particular, editorial manager Dan Snodderly and editor Nigel Quinney greatly eased our burden in bringing the book into its ultimate form.

A special note of gratitude must be made with regard to the contribution of Ms. Laura Libanati. As Dr. Aron's research assistant both during his fellowship year and since, Ms. Libanati rendered enormous assistance with the conference and with the preparation of the book manuscript. Not only did she keep the editors hard at their task, but also she played a significant part in making the essays accurate and readable. Dr. Jensen, in particular, would like to thank Ms. Libanati for her attempt to make his introduction an apt summary of the book's contents.

Needless to say, any deficiencies in this volume are fully the responsibility of the authors and editors. The views expressed in the following pages are those of the contributors and do not necessarily reflect those of the United States Institute of Peace.

Leon Aron
Kenneth M. Jensen

The Emergence of Russian
Foreign Policy

Introduction

Kenneth M. Jensen

This volume offers unusual access to the complexities of Russian foreign policy, both as it has emerged in the 13 months since March 1993 and as it continues to develop. Either implicitly or explicitly, the various contributions to this book affirm 1993 as the formative period of Russian foreign policy, that is to say, the period during which the essential issues of the debate were raised in durable form and during which the general structure of the debate—the principles, the rhetoric, if you will, the boundaries—attained a kind of permanence that will not be substantially altered for some time.

With the exception of Leon Aron's contribution, which was written in the fall of 1993, the essays in this book (although updated since) were originally conceived during the late winter and early spring of 1993—that is to say, during the critical stage in the conflict between President Boris Yeltsin and the Russian Parliament that ended temporarily with the referenda supporting Yeltsin in April and that ultimately culminated in the prorogation of parliament in September. Inasmuch as the parties to the struggle between Yeltsin and parliament held opposed views in the ongoing Russian foreign policy debate, the Russian contributors to this volume were bound to reflect them—or, if not *reflect* them, then reflect *on them*. Their essays and remarks here stand as documentation of the *manner* in which the Russian foreign policy debate was conducted in the spring of 1993.

The principal opposing views that obtained during 1993 surely still obtain. On the one side is the view that Russia's best interests lie in pursuing democratic internationalism and rapprochement with the West, as well as conciliation toward and accommodation with the former Soviet republics, collectively known as the "Near Abroad." On the other side is the view that Russia must find its way to being a strong presence internationally, take a "tougher" line toward the Near Abroad, pursue a more resolute defense of Russia's national interests, and conduct a more independent foreign policy, one that is at times even divergent from, if not hostile to, the United States. More often than not, these views are still articulated in very much the same manner in which they were articulated in 1993. They have developed—on their own and in response to events—to be sure. The "strong Russia" position is now nearly as well articulated as the more accommodationist view, which developed earlier. Such events as Russian intervention in the Georgian civil war and Russia's attempts to play a more forceful role in Bosnia in 1994 bring the meaning of "strong Russia" home to us. But for all that, the two positions remain fundamentally the same as they were in the spring of 1993.

Although the two views are seemingly further apart now, one has hardly overwhelmed the other. This fact suggests that they are inextricably bound to one another and that they are likely to remain so even as they develop and diverge further. In early 1993, the "derzhavniks," as the advocates of a strong Russia were known at the time, proceeded cautiously in their public statements. They most often couched their advocacy in the rhetoric of their opponents, giving more than a nod of support to the basic accommodationist premises of foreign policy as articulated by Yeltsin and Foreign Minister Andrei Kozyrev. Indeed, two of the most notable derzhavniks, Evgenii Ambartsumov and Andranik Migranian, had their feet planted firmly in both camps. In March 1993, Ambartsumov was chairman of the Supreme Soviet's Committee on Foreign Affairs and Migranian a senior advisor to that committee; at the same time, both sat on Yeltsin's 12-man Presidential Council. Interestingly, they remain in roughly the same position even now, more than a year later. Both are members of the [now 25-man] Presidential Council, and Ambartsumov has been elected to the new Duma and sits on its Committee on Foreign Affairs.

The reader will notice in the tone and substance of the essays by the Russians in this volume a reluctance to portray the various broad tendencies in Russian thinking as being fundamentally incompatible with one another. In proceeding, these authors show an inclination to regard domestic reform as Russia's key foreign policy problem. They also evince a marked preference to break foreign policy down into a series of discrete problems, each of which should be addressed in and for itself, rather than to focus on those problems as, for example, part of the larger problem of finding a strong Russian or accommodationist general course.

Apart from documenting the manner of the debate, perhaps the chief virtue of this volume is that it lays out in some detail most of the major problems to be faced in developing a foreign policy for the new Russia. Those issues addressed in the following essays include sorting out the sources and developing the mechanisms of foreign policy; determining Russia's relationship to the former Soviet states and to the Commonwealth of Independent States (CIS) as an institution; dealing with the problem of Russians outside the Russian Federation; establishing Russia's role in maintaining order in the former Soviet space; developing Russia's regional relationships in the Far East; determining a new role for Russia in international arms control; and developing new strategic and technical-intellectual relations with the United States.

Sources and Mechanisms of Russian Foreign Policy

We have organized the essays under three rubrics. Under the first—on the sources and mechanisms of Russian foreign policy—Leon Aron launches the volume with a look at what he calls "the Yeltsin revolution in foreign policy." In examining the priorities that have emerged from that revolution, Aron makes explicit the argument regarding the import of 1993 to the future of Russian foreign policy.

Aron argues, in effect, that 1993—as a discrete period in the development of Russian foreign policy—can be best understood by what occurred at its beginning, rather than by what occurred at the end (the victory of Zhirinovsky, the resurgence of Russian nationalism, and so forth). He tells us that the confusion that characterized the fall of the Soviet Union gave way to a clear and clearly meaningful government position on Russian foreign policy in early 1993. The basic international posture of the Yeltsin regime that had been articulated variously after the 1991 coup was pulled together in a systematic fashion by a cooperative effort of foreign policy agencies headed by the Foreign Ministry. Beginning in March 1992, this endeavor resulted in a 58-page report that was forwarded to parliament by Kozyrev on January 25, 1993. During the last week in April, after extensive review and redrafting in the National Security Council, Yeltsin signed into law a document (what in the United States would be called a National Security Directive) entitled "The Key Tenets of the Concept of Foreign Policy of the Russian Federation."

Aron examines the key elements of the Yeltsin revolution, which preceded the "Key Tenets" by almost two years: reversal of the relative priority assigned by the Moscow leadership to domestic versus national security/foreign concerns; the elimination of the "messianic" component in Russian foreign policy; weakening and destruction of the empire (as opposed to its strengthening and expansion); and drastic cutbacks in resources going to the military. He also details the difficulties that have attended the Yeltsin position, giving the responses to it that have helped to establish the "poles" of the Russian foreign policy debate. He argues that the debate should not be characterized solely by its potential extremes but also by the fact of the struggle itself. According to Aron, what has emerged from "a debate unprecedented in Russian history" is a consensus on "the fundamental priorities and concerns" of Russian foreign policy—a consensus that will "inform Russian foreign policy for years, if not decades, to come."

Aron breaks that consensus down into three national security priorities: Russia as regional superpower, Russia as nuclear superpower, and Russia as "great power." Inasmuch as Russia will propose to be all these things, it must discover what they mean. In Aron's view, the answer to this question depends upon how, in Russian thinking, the need for change posited in the Yeltsin revolution in foreign policy will be blended with the imperatives of continuity, which derive from a powerful tradition and geostrategic circumstances. In the last analysis, what Russia's foreign policy will become cannot be understood unless one recognizes the consensual priorities and the struggle between change and continuity.

The three essays by Martin Malia, Charles Fairbanks, Jr., and Mikhail Bezrukov, which follow Aron's, treat other sorts of sources and mechanisms of foreign policy. In contrast to analysts who treat in a broad geopolitical and historical fashion the problem of how its Soviet and pre-Soviet past will shape Russia's future international identity, these authors focus on specific parts of the legacy that will determine how the past will be distilled. In doing this, they offer fresh and unusually useful perspectives.

For his part, Martin Malia argues that the formation of any Russian, as opposed to Soviet, foreign policy cannot be properly understood without a proper perception of the tradition of Russian *government*. Malia contends that Russian despotism is not exceptional when viewed in the context of European history generally. Further, he argues that Russia's expansion was achieved in fits and spurts rather than, as is commonly believed, through a process of constant enlargement. If one studies the history of

Europe prior to World War I, one can only conclude that the liberal West was concerned not with Russia's expansion but with its autocratic form of government. Except for the Soviet interlude, Russia's foreign policy has historically been fueled more by pragmatic considerations than by ideology or tradition. Inasmuch as tradition has played a role, says Malia, its content and expression are by no means unusual when viewed in the context of Western history. Malia finds Russia in every important way comparable to Western states in exerting itself to establish a place in the world. Absent communism, one can expect a return to pragmatism and geopolitical considerations in Russia's search for a foreign policy. Finally, Malia argues that the outcome of that search will depend as much on the other countries of the former Soviet Union, which together constitute the region in which Russia must first exercise its pragmatic and geopolitical considerations, as on Russia itself.

In treating the legacy of Soviet policy as a source of Russian foreign policy, Charles Fairbanks, Jr., argues that there is a symmetry between communist and postcommunist attachments to the past. For him, the current Russian foreign policy debate may be characterized in part as a struggle to discover which policymaking practices of the Soviet period should be retained and which relegated to the past. Fairbanks focuses on two practices that have clearly survived the collapse of Soviet rule: shapelessness and *sviazy*. Shapelessness is the practice of dividing one task among several persons or government agencies without clearly defining the responsibilities of each. According to Fairbanks, despite the heavy price that shapelessness wrought from the Soviet system in terms of efficiency and hopes for a smooth transition to a market economy, it still seems to be regarded as desirable. *Sviazy*, the Russian term for the extensive use of personal contacts in order to get things done or procured, is also still regarded as desirable. The point of Fairbank's argument is not that it despairs at the presence of old habits in decision making, but that it exposes the fact that such habits may have to be accepted—by Russians and non-Russians alike—in effecting and dealing with change.

Shapelessness is also a focal point of Mikhail Bezrukov's essay on the institutional mechanisms of Russian foreign policy. In Bezrukov's formulation, a principal foreign relations legacy of the Soviet past is the tension among the main mechanisms for policy formation. Without the ultimate control and discipline previously exercised by the Politburo and the Central Committee, this tension no longer constitutes a fruitful way of developing foreign policy alternatives. Bezrukov not only points to the tension between the Foreign Ministry and the parliamentary Committee on Foreign Affairs, but also to the tension between these combatants and the Security Council, which at the time Bezrukov was writing was proceeding with undefined goals and means of influence. Shapelessness in Bezrukov's analysis is a means of "bypassing," that is, of keeping power over one or another area policy from residing for too long in any one place under any one individual's direction. If this was helpful in managing the Soviet elite, it is not helpful now, according to Bezrukov, as it is the principal factor slowing the development of effective institutions and structures of decision making. In a final point, Bezrukov argues that, above all, it is the Russian president who must support the development of proper institutions and structures.

The Near Abroad and Commonwealth of Independent States

This part of the book, which includes essays by Elizabeth Teague, Igor' Kliamkin, and Susan Clark, offers useful perspectives on the relationship between Russia and its nearest neighbors. Echoing Leon Aron's themes, these authors address both the matter of emerging priorities and the subject of continuity and change.

Elizabeth Teague offers a substantial primer on Russians outside Russia and a perspective on the problems involved that take the subject beyond the usual realm of discussion. Teague points out that the 25 million Russians living beyond the federation's borders do not everywhere conceive of themselves as linked to one another. This, however, is in contrast to the attitude of the Russian government, which regards Russians abroad as an undifferentiated mass, at least insofar as their existence presents the government with a formidable threat to the stability of the federation. If conflict develops between Russians and non-Russians in the Near Abroad, either the Russian government will have to exert itself to protect them or it will have to support a large migration "home." In either case, the government would be hard pressed to project force on their behalf or to provide the housing and infrastructure to accommodate them. Teague predicts that the evolution of policy regarding Russians outside of Russia will continue to be slow and painful. Originally drawn to foster strife among the peoples of the former Soviet Union, the borders that now separate Russians from Russians are sure to be debated and contested. The non-Russian parties to this debate will not be easy interlocutors and armed struggle may ensue. This problem of finding and securing its borders, of defining itself geographically, is the most basic problem faced by the Russian Federation.

In addressing in his own way the problem of Russia's definition, Igor' Kliamkin speaks to what has become in the period since he wrote his essay perhaps the most interesting and disturbing development in the former Soviet space: the development of "reintegration." For Kliamkin, the chief problem that exists in the former Soviet space is the potential for conflict among the former republics of the Soviet Union. While acknowledging such contributing factors as ethnic conflict, the struggle to control former Soviet nuclear weapons, and economic chaos, Kliamkin focuses on the plain fact that the states of the former USSR are not viable in isolation from one another. Depending on one's disposition and the assumptions one might make regarding for whom he speaks, Kliamkin's essay can be read in a number of ways, some of them distressing. The fact is, however, that Kliamkin's insight is valuable. If the former Soviet states are not viable, then the self-affirmation of their statehood through the pursuit of strict independence is apt to lead them from nonviability into a chaos of conflict. The reader will decide if Kliamkin's remedy—making a truly useful suprastate structure out of the CIS—could be a means to facilitate national self-affirmation without either reviving the Soviet Union or fostering Russian imperialism.

Looking at yet another aspect of the relations among the various parts of the former Soviet Union, Susan Clark discusses the troublesome and complicated matter of Russian peacekeeping. In an essay detailing the mechanisms in place and Russia's performance, Clark places matters within the larger international debate over peacekeeping and peacemaking, the former occurring with the blessing of the parties to a conflict after the cessation of hostilities, and the latter occurring to halt conflicts when they break out or when cease-fires fail. In contrast to the world of conflict as seen from a UN vantage point—where peacekeepers and peacemakers must intervene from the outside—Clark shows the world of the former Soviet Union to be one in which the Russian military intervenes from within and from a position that severely compromises its ability to serve as a neutral force. Clark brings home the reality that the Russian claim to peacekeeping in the territory of the former Soviet Union cannot be effectively disputed by an international community that lacks the means to offer an alternative. She calls for new, broadly based mechanisms of peacekeeping and peacemaking that will involve all of the appropriate countries of the former Soviet Union in any given case, as well as regional states outside the former USSR and the Western nations. Only in this way can Russia be a resource that does not dominate in peacekeeping and peacemaking. If Russian activities in Tajikistan, Azerbaijan, and Georgia in the time since Clark's essay was written complicate the picture of Russia's interventionist role outside the federation, they do not contradict the basic analysis of the essay.

Russia and the Far Abroad

Whereas Susan Clark asks us to address the problem of transforming Russia into a force for peace within the space of the former Soviet Union, Vladimir Ivanov invites us to consider assisting Russia in developing a positive role as a regional power—in this case, in Northeast Asia. Ivanov deplores the fact that outside of discussions of military power and strategic nuclear weapons Russia is rarely mentioned as a northern Pacific country despite its vast amount of territory there. Ivanov would have the United States and its friends in the region consider the opportunities to engage Russia internationally. Russian strategic and security postures with regard to the Pacific region are in transition and the opportunity to influence the process through cooperation must not be wasted. Ivanov argues that bringing Russia into security and development discussions could enhance the possibilities of resolving regional conflicts and disputes. Involving Russia in Asian-Pacific affairs could help it to develop economically, as similar involvement helped China. In this way, the United States and Japan could assist Russia in establishing a prosperous market democracy. If, however, Russia remains isolated, it could become an obstacle to the establishment of post–Cold War security and market economies in the region.

Surveying the general international response to emerging Russian foreign policies and the development of U.S.-Russian relations, Andrei Kortunov focuses on strategic issues and the nuclear world of the post–Cold War period. For Kortunov, Russia may have inherited from the Soviet Union a vast store of nuclear weapons and the role of chief negotiator in arms control agreements involving the former USSR, but both parts of this inheritance are rapidly becoming obsolete. Moreover, with Third World countries acquiring nuclear weapons, the dangers of proliferation may be greater today than they were during the Cold War. This fact of the new world order has made bilateral arms control negotiations a thing of the past. According to Kortunov, it is no longer realistic to pursue the goal of preserving the "nuclear club." Instead, the

United States and Russia should seek to engage other nuclear powers in the arms control process, thereby internationalizing arms control. Cooperation and leadership are key in this endeavor as there is no overarching authority in modern global politics and no way to enforce global law and order. A process must be devised to combine multilateral, bilateral, parallel, and unilateral actions for creative problem solving at each step of arms control negotiations.

If arms control and nuclear nonproliferation offer the United States important opportunities to influence the development of Russian foreign policy, they should not be regarded as the only subjects for joint U.S.-Russian consideration, according to Evgenii Volk. Western understanding of the formation of Soviet national security doctrine was always quite limited, he argues. In the Soviet Union, this was considered a strictly military affair rather than a broader issue of national defense requiring the participation of a wide variety of decision makers. As glasnost and "new thinking" began to permeate the Soviet Union, however, nonmilitary experts were permitted to contribute to national security discussions. "More mature and democratically oriented approaches toward arms control and disarmament" began to arise. The lack of a legitimate constitution had been an impediment to the construction, by democratic processes, of a broader-based national security doctrine. Although this is no longer the case, Volk says, Western analysts could be instrumental in locating the remaining contradictions and antagonisms that exist within the Russian political scene with regard to national security doctrine. Closer cooperation between Russian politicians and Western scholars could produce not only creative solutions to old problems but also new questions and answers.

The Future of Russian Foreign Policy

If Leon Aron is correct, it is extremely important for U.S. and other Western policymakers to study the substance and manner of the Russian foreign policy debate as it coalesced in 1993. The consensus wrought in 1993 has endured. The great priorities—Russia as regional superpower, nuclear superpower, and great power—continue to be raised and dealt with by crucially placed officials in the same manner, despite the surfacing of public xenophobia. The poles of the debate—traditionalist and accommodationist—remain fixed, the position—indeed, the very existence—of each extreme determined by its distance from the other.

Given the outcome of the December 1993 parliamentary elections, many observers might conclude that the consensus has broken down or been transcended. Looking back at the period since the fall of the Soviet Union, the temptation is very great to predict steady progress toward an aggressive new posture for Russia vis-à-vis its neighbors near and far. While it would be folly not to be wary of the disruptive potential of Russian nationalism, it would be equally imprudent not to assess the overall character of official Russian behavior and rhetoric.

How often during the past year or two did the official line swing from reform to retreat and back again? How often did the line in foreign policy swing from accommodationist to nationally assertive positions and back again? Frequently, toughness one day was followed by softness the next. Despite growing self-assertion, the rhetoric of democratic internationalism and rapprochement has hardly been abandoned. One might consider, for example, the late winter and spring of 1994 and the character of Russian involvement in Bosnia or Russia's restated interest in NATO's offer of a "Partnership for Peace." In both cases, there is an undeniable tentativeness of intention and a cautiousness to be seen as moderate that matches the cautiousness of the United States and Europe with regard to *their* intentions regarding these things. I would argue that this means that the consensus underlying, and boundaries delineating, the new Russian foreign policy remain intact.

An opinion piece by Russian Foreign Affairs Committee chairman Vladimir Lukin that appeared in *The Washington Post* in April 1994 seems to support this view.[1] Lukin devotes the first part of his remarks to U.S. and Russian delusions regarding the place of postcommunist Russia in the world. Although guilty of overstatement in claiming that U.S. policymakers expected Russia to be "a loyal junior partner of the United States" in foreign policy and that Russian policymakers expected America to be "eternally grateful to Russia for having done away with communism," Lukin argues persuasively that such expectations arose from a faulty analysis of Russia's circumstances and options. The reality, in his view, is that Russian reform has "turned out to be much more contradictory, painful, and slow than was generally expected"; that U.S. aid has been "too little and too late"; that Russia has a host of serious foreign policy problems, especially regarding other former Soviet states; and that the outside world has been reluctant to pursue "harmony in trade and economic relations or [to give] due regard for Russian traditional interests such as those in the Balkans." It should not be surprising, according to

Lukin, that Russia has taken "a more active role" within the CIS and has become "more serious about its reshaped national interests" and has "defend[ed] them more assertively." For him, "this has been a process of normalization of Russian foreign policy, proceeding in a fairly democratic way through public pressure, policy debates, and consensus building."

The foregoing is a reasonably clear statement of that part of the Russian foreign policy consensus that relates to Russia as a power (in this case, as a regional power and great power). The use of the word "normalization" is key: it suggests that Russia has a right to national interests and to use its power beyond its borders after the fashion of other "normal" (read "fairly democratic") states.

Lukin, however, does not leave the matter at this. His piece continues, and closes, with assertions fully in accord with the Yeltsin-Kozyrev language of democratic internationalism and rapprochement. "Russia today has neither aspirations nor resources to again become a global rival of the United States—not today and not tomorrow. In fact, my country is in the process of redefining its national interests in a democratic, nonexpansionist way." Lukin emphasizes the fact that "pre-Soviet Russia and the United States were among the very few great powers that never fought each other and cooperated more than they competed." Now that the Cold War is over: "We are returning to this historical norm. In fact, we can improve on it, since the new Russia is closer to the United States politically and culturally than its predecessor."

All this, the reader may fairly protest, is only rhetoric. Yet, notwithstanding evidence of growing xenophobic and imperialist tendencies in Russia, there is a marked correspondence between Russian official rhetoric and reality. The fact of the matter is that Russia cannot afford, at least for the moment, to abandon its push to join the community of democratic, free-market nations or to neglect its attempt to establish firm borders and power relations with other former Soviet states.

Additionally, one might keep in mind that Russia may not have shed a peculiarity of its Soviet past: the high level of discipline in political rhetoric. During the Soviet period, Western scholars and policy analysts labored constantly to detect new subtleties in what was said and by whom. When the rhetoric changed, so invariably did the political hierarchy and/or the political agenda. These days, the rhetoric shifts from self-assertive one day to accommodationist the next. As Lukin's piece illustrates, subtle adjustments are being made within the Russian foreign policy consensus. The fact that such adjustments are made as much in the rhetoric of rapprochement as in the rhetoric of national self-assertion supports the view that a meaningful balance still obtains in Russian foreign policy.

Whether or not that balance actually dictates the content and conduct of Russian foreign policy, we perhaps should treat it as though it does. Such an approach will help to foster a measured debate within Russia on how best to chart a moderate course—a course in which, to recall Leon Aron's formulation, the old and the new are blended to produce a Russia useful as an international citizen and restrained in response to geopolitical realities.

Noto

1. Vladimir Lukin, "No More Delusions," *The Washington Post,* April 3, 1994, p. C7.

PART I

Sources and Mechanisms of Russian Foreign Policy

1

The Emergent Priorities of Russian Foreign Policy

Leon Aron

On January 25, 1993, Minister of Foreign Affairs of the Russian Federation Andrei Kozyrev forwarded to Evgenii Ambartsumov, the chairman of the Committee on International Affairs and External Economic Relations of the Supreme Soviet, a 58-page document titled "The Concept of Foreign Policy of the Russian Federation" (*Kontseptsiia vneshnei politiki Rossiiskoi Federatsii*; hereafter "The Concept"). In a cover note, Kozyrev wrote that the text "reflected the result of the work conducted since March 1992 by the Ministry of Foreign Affairs, other government organizations, Committees of the Supreme Soviet, experts, and the public at large." "It seems," continued Kozyrev, "that the 'Concept' managed to combine the key directions of Russia's activity in the world arena and . . . presents a flexible system of coordinates for the day-to-day work in the field of foreign relations."

This was more than self-congratulation. "The Concept" embodied a year of intense work and often painful evolution of the Yeltsin administration's views on the most fundamental issues of the foreign policy of postcommunist Russia, the world's youngest nuclear superpower. Three months later, in the last week of April, after extensive review and redrafting in the National Security Council, President Boris Yeltsin signed into law—what in the United States would be called a National Security Directive—a leaner version of "The Concept" entitled "The Key Tenets of the Concept of Foreign Policy of the Russian Federation" (*Osnovnie polozhenia kontseptiia vneshnei politiki Rossiiskoi Federatsii*; hereafter, "The

Tenets"). The new, postcommunist Russia had finally received a new foreign policy doctrine.

The Yeltsin Revolution in Russian Foreign Policy

From Ivan the Terrible through Peter the Great and Catherine to Lenin and Stalin, the paradigm of Russian state-building always included four elements: the dominance of national security and foreign policy objectives over those of domestic economic, political, and social development; a strong, sometimes dominant, ideological messianic component (from Russia as a "Third Rome" to pan-Slavism to "world socialism"); expansion and strengthening of the empire; and military buildup. As he has proceeded with his own state-building, Boris Yeltsin has radically revised (indeed, in many respects, reversed) all four trends.

For the first time since 1914, Russia is not at war—real, "cold," or "class"—with anyone. "The Tenets" bear an unmistakably domestic, inward-looking, even isolationist imprint. Of the nine "vitally important interests" of Russia listed at the beginning of the document, only one (No. 3) pertains to the world outside the former Soviet border, and even this plank is distinctly defensive: "securing a reliable defense from any forms of external threat through the maintenance of a sufficient military potential of Russia and the existence of a stable system of international relations."

Three other interests that might be classified as belonging to the foreign policy realm are hardly indicative of aggressively ambitious designs: the strengthening of all manner of ties with the former Soviet republics, called the Near Abroad (No. 6); the protection of the rights of the members of the Russian Federation's ethnic groups in the Near Abroad (No. 7); and the protection of "rights and interests of citizens and organizations of the Russian Federation abroad" (No. 8).

All other vital interests of Russia are strictly domestic: "securing state sovereignty and territorial integrity" (No. 1); "maintenance of stability and strengthening of the constitutional order" (No. 2); "overcoming of the domestic crisis through deep socioeconomic and political reforms" (No. 4); "securing a stable progress in the economy and respectable standard of living for the people" (No. 5); and environmental protection (No. 9).

Russian foreign policy today appears to be shaped by national interests, not by a (nonexistent) dominant national ideology. Yeltsin is waking Russia up from the age-long solemn dream of "the mission" and is teaching it to speak prose. In the words of Foreign Minister Kozyrev: "The struggle of ideologies has ended. The time has come to take care of Russia's needs. . . . [It is] vitally important" that the foreign policy of Russia be determined not by "ideological dogmas" but by "fundamental national interests."[1]

Yeltsin is the first Russian leader who has not expanded, or at least strengthened, the domestic empire. When he hammered the last nail in the coffin of the Soviet Union in Belovezhskaia Pushcha in December 1991, he gave up all of the conquests of Peter the Great, Catherine, Alexander I, and Alexander II combined.[2] Yeltsin has reversed a 400-year-old political tradition in which the Russian national idea was identical with the Russian imperial idea. He has undertaken a historically unprecedented "uncoupling" of Russian national identity and Russian statehood from the Russian multinational empire. (The two were never separate before; the emergence of a modern Russian state under Ivan the Terrible coincided—after the conquest of the Kazan and Astrakhan Khanates in the 1550s —with the emergence of the Russian empire.)

Finally, in contravention of yet another historic tradition, Yeltsin's state-building has been accompanied by a dramatic shrinking of the military. The total procurement spending in fiscal year 1992 was 38 percent of the 1991 amount. The level of spending on conventional arms in 1992 was four times lower than it was in 1991.[3] All in all, defense expenditures are projected to fall to 5 percent of the gross domestic product (GDP), compared with at least 15 percent of the GDP in Soviet times. Troop reductions are projected to leave the armed forces with 1.5 million troops by 1995, down from 3.8 million in January 1992.

The Difficult Emergence of a Domestic Consensus on Foreign Policy

Given such dramatic revision of the key elements of the Russian national paradigm, the emergence of a politically sustainable foreign policy doctrine is somewhat of a miracle. Indeed, that such a doctrine could be forged at all seemed very unlikely in the late spring and summer of 1992.

At the time, the battle for the soul of the foreign policy of postcommunist Russia was at its peak. The seemingly irreconcilable combatants were, on the one hand, "liberals" and "internationalists" at the Foreign Ministry and, on the other, "neopatriots" or "derzhavniks" (from the Russian word *derzhava*, or great power), most of whom were to be found inside the Supreme Soviet but some of whom were in the Kremlin: Secretary of the Security Council Yurii Skokov, Advisor to the President Sergei Stankevich,

Minister of Security Viktor Barannikov, and, increasingly, Vice-President Aleksandr Rutskoi.

The internationalists advocated a conciliatory, noninterventionist, even isolationist stand vis-à-vis the Near Abroad and support for—if not, in fact, alliance with—the United States in world affairs. The derzhavniks demanded a tougher line on the Near Abroad states on most issues (nuclear weapons, conventional armaments, borders, the treatment of Russian-speaking minorities), and argued that what they saw as an automatic, knee-jerk support for the United States was a short-sighted and unprofitable strategy, unbecoming to a "great power."

In the late spring and early summer of 1992, the lines thus drawn hardened into opposite policy positions in the aftermath of the first serious crises that Russian foreign policy had to deal with: the declaration of independence by the "Dniester Republic," a Russo-Ukrainian enclave inside Moldova; the flare-up of tensions in the Baltic republics over the civil and political rights of the ethnic Russians and the withdrawal of Russian troops; and a Russian vote for the UN Security Council's resolution imposing economic sanctions on Serbia—a Slavic, Greek Orthodox nation fighting Muslim Bosnians and Catholic Croats, and a country in whose defense Russia had entered World War I.

In all three crises, the internationalists counseled and pursued gradualism, negotiations, accommodation, and support for the position of the U.S.-led "civilized world." The derzhavniks demanded unconditional support, including the use of military force, for the Russian minorities in Moldova and Estonia, and pressed for a "more even-handed approach" to Serbian aggression in Bosnia. In the course of a heated and lively public debate that splashed over the pages of leading Russian newspapers, Kozyrev called his opponents "neopatriots," "neo-Bolsheviks," and a "party of war." He accused them of flirting with the "red-browns" (communists and fascists) and of pursuing a "megaphone diplomacy." Russia could not, Kozyrev declared, "send a military helicopter for every Russian-speaking boy or girl in Moldova."

The derzhavniks, meanwhile, labeled Russian foreign policy as "weak and belated" and insisted that "no one could exclude force from the arsenal of state policy." The Supreme Soviet voted to recognize the Dniester Republic and to disavow Russia's UN Security Council vote on Serbia.[4] Despite Kozyrev's pleas for the president's support, Yeltsin, sphinxlike, was silent, unwilling to commit himself publicly to Kozyrev yet keeping him as his foreign minister and allowing him to pursue, as if by default, policies of his choice.

Given the temperature of the debate and the width of the seemingly unbridgeable chasm between the two positions, no one in Moscow at the time could predict that, a year later, Russia would have a foreign policy doctrine acceptable to most of the responsible politicians.

That such a doctrine became possible was due to certain international and domestic developments that, in the 12 months after March 1992, led both sides to moderate their positions. When Russian foreign policy was born in early 1992, the liberal-internationalists, who at the time were unchallenged in charting the foreign policy of Russia, brimmed with as much enthusiasm about the "new world order" as the Bush White House. Fresh from the burial of Soviet totalitarianism, they were infused with a vision of the world in which the old and tired notions of traditional power diplomacy such as "spheres of influence" and "zones of vital interests" would soon be supplanted by a kind of multinational police force led by the United States. In that dream, the "civilized world" would swiftly and decisively intercede for peace, democracy, and human rights every-where—including, of course, the territory of the former Soviet Union. Preoccupied by the deep economic and political crises inside their country, the makers of Russian foreign policy were only too happy to delegate to the world community most, if not all, duties connected with the maintenance of law and order on the post-Soviet territory. According to a very well-informed Russian observer-derzhavnik:

> [T]he Russian leadership decided [in early 1992] that Russia should not project its authority beyond the borders of the Russian Federation and should refrain from becoming involved in the conflicts taking place in the other republics. Instead of asserting Russian interests in the Near Abroad, the Russian leadership has tried to involve international organizations such as the CSCE [Conference on Security and Cooperation in Europe] and the United Nations, as well as neighboring countries.[5]

Then came the Serbian siege of Sarajevo. Although Kozyrev coura-geously ordered Russia's UN vote cast for sanctions against Serbia, the sight of the international community's impotence—its inability to enforce the new world order or to contain, much less settle, a savage ethnic conflict of a type that is Russia's recurrent nightmare—led the internationalists to reexamine their hopes regarding the ability of the United States and its allies to restore a just peace anywhere. Recalling the Soviet-sponsored massive Cuban military assistance to Ethiopia in 1977–78, Zbigniew Brzezinski used to say, famously, that "SALT lay buried in the sands of

Ogaden." As far as Russian internationalists were concerned, the new world order lay buried in the hills around Sarajevo.

This strategic reappraisal in the Kremlin coincided with the flaring up of ethnic and political warfare in Georgia and Tajikistan and between Armenia and Azerbaijan. After Sarajevo, even the internationalists had to agree with a leading derzhavnik theorist that "the world community has been unable to summon the will and create opportunities necessary for international organizations to become efficient actors in the resolution of these conflicts."[6] The internationalists concluded that, far from being obsolete, force, self-reliance, and unilateralism in defense of Russia's vital interests and those of ethnic Russians in the Near Abroad should be part of Russia's foreign policy arsenal for the foreseeable future.

It was partly in response to this newly acquired toughness in the Foreign Ministry's outlook that the derzhavniks began their own drift to compromise. They welcomed the government's attention to their key concerns and the incorporation of some of their key positions into Russian foreign policy: "even-handedness" in Serbia; "toughness" and lack of "unilateral concessions" in relations with Japan; and the elevation of the issue of ethnic Russians' rights in the Baltics to the level of bilateral and multilateral diplomacy.

Furthermore, the shrillness of the derzhavniks' rhetoric gradually lessened as foreign policy no longer served as a proxy battlefield for domestic political battles: beginning in the late fall of 1992, the political confrontation between the parliament and the president spilled into open warfare. At the same time, one after another, the leading derzhavniks inside the Kremlin (Skokov, Rutskoi, Barannikov) gradually lost their influence. The last political obstacle to a Russian foreign policy consensus was removed with the October 4, 1993, defeat of the "irreconcilable opposition"—a narrow but vocal and energetic ultranationalist restorationist fringe that had been exerting pressure on the moderate derzhavniks in the Supreme Soviet.

And so, after moving toward the internationalist extreme in the first months of 1992, the pendulum of Russian foreign policy did not swing to the other extreme of restorationist fantasies, but settled, instead, somewhere in the middle. Forged in a debate unprecedented in Russian history for its openness and intensity, this consensus on the fundamental priorities and concerns represents most of Russia's responsible political spectrum. It is likely to inform Russian foreign policy for years, if not decades, to come.

The Three Parts of the National Consensus on Foreign Policy

Although the Russian political class is far from unanimous on the choice of means, the placement of emphasis, and the procedures and the institutions for the implementation of foreign policy objectives, at least three of these objectives appear to form the basis of a national consensus. These objectives are Russia as the regional superpower, Russia as a nuclear superpower, and Russia as a world great power. At any given moment, the pursuit of these goals constitutes the core content of Russian efforts abroad—"near" or far.

As one examines the official Russian documents, as well as the interviews and statements of the leading players, experts, and journalists, one is struck by the reversal of the Soviet tradition in which a state's importance and prestige in Moscow were usually inversely proportionate to its proximity to the Soviet capital.

The rationale for this sweeping change of priorities becomes clearer when one examines a list of what the Russian leadership regards as national security concerns: virtually all the "threats" to Russia's vital interests are perceived as emanating from the Near Abroad.

Russia's key concerns in the Near Abroad can be grouped into four categories. They are, in order of importance, nuclear "instability" (that is, incomplete Russian control of the nuclear weapons on the former Soviet territory); the future of Soviet conventional weapons and the Russian troops outside Russia (including their legal status, withdrawal, peace-keeping operations, and involvement in local political warfare); the political and human rights of ethnic Russians; and territorial and border disputes with neighboring states.

The political threats begin with claims on Russia's territory by neighboring states. Other threats include "actions directed against integrationist processes" in the Commonwealth of Independent States (CIS); the "weakening" of ties between Russia and the Near Abroad states; and the disintegration of state "structures," violations of human rights, and the outbreak of armed conflicts in the Near Abroad, any of which developments might lead, among other things, to an "uncontrollable" mass emigration to Russia—something that Russia, given the state of its economy and the presence of at least 2 million refugees on its territory, simply cannot afford. Only the very last of the seven threats is located outside the former Soviet territory—namely, "actions aimed at undermining the role of the Russian Federation in solving key international problems and activities of international organizations."[7]

The military threats, as the Russian policymakers see them, are also to be found almost exclusively in the Near Abroad. According to Russian Minister of Defense Pavel Grachev: "In our view the most probable scenario is not a direct armed invasion of Russia but her gradual entanglement in conflicts in neighboring nations and regions. Given the complex interrelation and interdependence of the various states and peoples, any armed conflict may evolve into a large-scale war."[8]

The perceived seriousness of the threat from the Near Abroad is, apparently, great enough to prompt Moscow to engage in a costly and politically risky process of recovering Soviet conventional assets in the Near Abroad and augmenting Russian conventional capabilities along the southern frontier, even if the latter operation may require renegotiation of key arms control agreements inherited from the Soviet Union. In June 1993, Grachev conveyed to U.S. Defense Secretary Les Aspin Moscow's request that the 1990 Conventional Forces in Europe (CFE) Treaty be revised to allow additional tank, artillery, and armored personnel carrier deployments in southern Russia and the Caucasus. Two months later, Russia's intent to expand the deployment limits was implicit in President Yeltsin's message to Turkish President Suleyman Demirel. In November 1993, Moscow resumed efforts to amend the CFE Treaty to allow for additional deployment. Meanwhile, on September 7 and 8, 1993, Russia assumed well over $100 billion of the Armenian, Azerbaijani, and Kazakh share of the former Soviet debt in return for acquiring unspecified Soviet "assets," most likely of military nature, located in these countries.

While Russia is likely to be increasingly self-reliant in addressing each of these concerns, it will undoubtedly continue its efforts to enlist outside political assistance. In fact, such is the importance assigned by Russia to these issues that the overall state of Russia's relations with other nations will be shaped to a very considerable degree by Russia's perception of their role and efficacy in advancing Moscow's agenda in the Near Abroad. For instance, Moscow's relations with "Southern and Western Asia" (Turkey, Iran, Pakistan, and Afghanistan) are explicitly linked to "their direct influence on the situation inside the CIS,"[9] that is, on the formerly Soviet Central Asian republics. (This "influence" is viewed by Russia with suspicion derived from the perception that these nations are "clearly seeking to parlay the disintegration of the Soviet Union into strengthening of their position, and even, in some cases, into the formation of broad alliances [inside the former Central Asian republics] of ethnic or religious nature.")[10]

Similarly, in the strategic review of Russian relations with Western European countries, Denmark, Norway, Sweden, and Finland are described as nations that "have in their possession the levers of influence in the vitally important [for Russia] areas" of Latvia, Lithuania, and Estonia.[11] In its Baltic policy, Russia plans to "use the mechanisms and capabilities of the members of the Council of the Baltic Sea[12] and the Barents Sea Council[13] with the purpose of exerting influence on the [formerly Soviet] Baltic nations."[14]

The Reintegrationist Agenda:
The Key to Russian Policy in the Near Abroad

Much like its erstwhile Cold War foe, the United States, which has revised and expanded its definition of national security to include free trade, Russia has modified its own national security thinking to place a strong emphasis on economic progress and transition to democracy. Neither is deemed possible without a measure of reintegration with the former Soviet republics.

"The vitally important interests of the Russian Federation are connected, first of all, with the development of her relations with the states of the 'Near Abroad,'" declares "The Tenets." "Russia cannot develop normally other than on the basis of new economic and transportation ties, relations in the area of defense and defense of the borders and the settlement of conflicts."[15] Consequently, "overcoming the destabilizing deintegrationist [*dezintegratsionnye*] processes on the territory of the former USSR"[16] is listed as part of the "main content" of Russian foreign policy. The Kozyrev memo envisions a maximum expansion of the web of "various forms of interstate cooperation" and "harmonization" of policies and a "search" for common interests between Russia and the Near Abroad.[17]

Russia's integrationist designs are not limited to these broad and somewhat nebulous objectives. They are quite specific in outlining a kind of post-Soviet Maastricht process with proliferating suprastate bodies and expanding prerogatives: an "Executive Secretariat," a "Collective Security Council," a "Consultative-Coordinating Council," and a joint peacekeeping force.[18]

Among policy initiatives aimed at cementing ties with the Near Abroad, collective security arrangements are among the "priority" (*prioritetnii*) tasks of Russian foreign policy. Russia is to "enter" such arrangements via the "regional structures of security" among the states of the Near Abroad or, at least, through "cooperation" with them.[19]

Unlike the economic or political motives, the security aspect of the reintegrationist agenda is a relatively new addition, one that represents an important evolution of the national consensus on foreign policy. Even after signing the Treaty on Collective Security with Armenia, Kazakhstan, Kyrgyzstan, Uzbekistan, and Tajikistan in May 1992, Russia was wary of security commitment in the Near Abroad. As late as May 1993, the majority of the 400 "public opinion leaders" of Russia were against Russia's taking upon itself the responsibility for "resolving conflicts" in the Near Abroad, and less than 5 percent of those surveyed thought that military "means of influence" were most effective in this enterprise. (By contrast, 87 percent of the people surveyed advocated the use of economic, diplomatic, or political levers.)[20] The Russian Parliament did not ratify the treaty until July 1993, when the reluctant legislators were prodded by attacks by the Afghan-based Tajik opposition on border posts along the Tajik-Afghan frontier. Security integration has since proceeded steadily, with the creation in August 1993 of the Collective Security Council and the permanent headquarters under the CIS Council of Defense Ministers.

The Emergent Grand Compromise in the Near Abroad

The new Russian foreign policy doctrine stresses a "strictly voluntary and mutual" nature of the reintegration, allowing that some states might not be ready for increased cooperation. There are signs, however, that the degree of this readiness is likely to grow markedly. In what might be called a "grand compromise" in the relations between the new states and Moscow, the former are likely to surrender a measure of independence for membership in a Russian-led economic and political union.

This trend is inevitable given the economic and political legacy of the Soviet Union: the rigid and utterly unbalanced distribution of industrial resources, which makes economic self-sufficiency extremely costly, if not impossible, without massive outside assistance; the near-total dependence on Russian raw materials; and the unsorted and suppressed ethnic rivalries, which, like a strong wine, have only acquired additional potency during six decades in the Soviet cellar. The pressures of the twin economic and ethnic crises, combined with the fragility of the statehoods (and even the nationhoods) of most new states, make the political elites of the Near

Abroad (Estonia, Latvia, and Lithuania aside) look increasingly favorably at membership in a Russian-led alliance that holds at least a promise of containing, and perhaps lessening, the twin crises. The spring let loose in Belovezhskaia Pushcha in 1991 (when the Soviet Union was buried and the CIS was born) is beginning to recoil toward Moscow.

This process became visible early in 1993, long before Azerbaijan and Georgia attracted attention to it by applying for admission to the CIS. As early as March 1993, a leading Russian expert predicted that Georgia, for one, had "no other choice but [to] establish special relations with Russia because Georgia [was] practically on the verge of collapse. A large portion of Georgia is populated by . . . explosive ethnic groups and peoples demanding independence and recognition as autonomous states. Without a Russian presence in the region, Georgia . . . [would] not have any chance to survive."[21]

There is a growing realization in most newly independent post-Soviet states that by the sheer weight of its geostrategic assets (unbalanced by those of the West, which has showed little enthusiasm for massive economic assistance and political support—contrary to the early expectations of the new states), Russia is destined to dominate the post-Soviet space like a giant star, whose gravitation pulls other states into its orbit.

Reintegration of Russia and the Near Abroad could occur in two ways. The first, which might be called an American model, envisions leadership based largely (although by no means entirely) on the attraction of a political system, a giant and dynamic economy, and a thriving culture. The other is a Soviet variant in which this dominance is due almost exclusively to military-political coercion. The former version of Russia's relations with the Near Abroad would likely benefit most of the former Soviet republics. The latter would not only be tragic for the new states involved, but also would inevitably lead to the demise of Russian democracy, with which a Russian domestic empire has never been compatible.

From Internationalization to Russification of the Near Abroad Policy: The Russian Monroe Doctrine

In 1993, Russian policy in the Near Abroad underwent a momentous evolution. Previously, the combination of, on the one hand, the post-Afghanistan syndrome and the trauma of the imperial collapse with, on the other, the anticipation of a new world order had resulted in a posture that was wary, ad hoc, and oriented largely at international political organizations. In 1993, Russian policy grew more assertive, systematic, and self-reliant.

In February 1993, President Yeltsin asked for the United Nations' blessing for Russia's "special powers as guarantor of peace and stability in the region." Although this trial balloon was quickly grounded by instant criticism from the West and the Near Abroad, Russian reaction to a putative White House initiative (centered around a draft of "Directive 13," prepared for President Clinton's signature in August 1993) demonstrated that, despite the potential danger of alienating friends and allies, the "internationalization" of the post-Soviet political and military space was gradually supplanted by its "Russification" as a means of protecting Russia's interests.

Living up to the less than hopeful implications of its numerical designation, Directive 13 outlined a more activist role for the United States and the United Nations in peacekeeping operations in the Near Abroad. It also foresaw certain restrictions on the deployment of Russian peace-keepers in the Near Abroad, as well as, reportedly, "U.S.-Russian policy differences over the mandate, scope and advisability" of peacekeeping operations.[22] Directive 13 was unanimously deplored not only by the neopatriots on the left but also by the Russian democratic and foreign policy establishment. The pro-Yeltsin *Moscow News* decried the "American arrogance of power" and "pressure" on Russia. The Russian ambassador to the United States, moderate *derzhavnik* Vladimir Lukin (he prefers to be called an "enlightened patriot"), while far more diplomatic in expression, was just as negative in principle.[23]

In September 1993, sounding the central theme of his subsequent speech at the UN General Assembly, Foreign Minister Kozyrev wrote in *Nezavisimaia gazeta:*

> Naturally, Russia is not going to abandon her neighbors and friends [in the Near Abroad] despite anything. If we do not master the political will and practical means—that is, to be blunt, troops and equipment—to conduct peacekeeping missions in the zone of the former Soviet Union, this vacuum will be filled by other forces, first of all, by the forces of political extremism, which, ultimately, threaten Russia herself.[24]

The geostrategic imperatives have reasserted themselves. Having reached, in the wake of the Soviet Union's collapse, the outer limits of its own "post-Vietnam" syndrome, Russian foreign policy is coming home. The journey started, appropriately, in the Near Abroad.

Claimed to be explicitly modeled on the Monroe Doctrine of the United States by some of its leading explicators,[25] the new Russian policy toward the Near Abroad appears to be based on the following principles:

- "[A]ll of the territory of the former Soviet Union constitutes a vital sphere within which Russia's interests cannot be denied or ignored."[26]
- "Because of the deep historic, political, cultural and other links with the neighboring states, Russia [can] not and [does] not have a moral right to remain deaf to their requests to secure peace."[27]
- The post-Soviet space is a "unique, sui generis geopolitical space, in which no one but Russia could bring peace."[28]
- The "strengthening" of the CIS borders is one of the key objectives.[29]
- Russia will "actively oppose attempts from outside the CIS to increase tension between the former Soviet republics."[30]
- Russia will "oppose any plans to increase armed forces in the states bordering on the territory of the former USSR."[31]
- Russia will "restrain" the "third" states from "attempts to use in their interests the instability" in the Near Abroad.[32]
- Russia will welcome peacemaking by the United Nations and the CSCE, but only on the condition of "nonpresence" (*otkaza ot prisutstviia*) of foreign troops and military bases on the territory of the former Soviet republics.[33]

The final element of the Russian Monroe Doctrine is the nuclear exclusivity of Russia in the post-Soviet geopolitical space. There is hardly any objective on the Russian foreign policy agenda that, in the immediate future, will rival nuclear exclusivity in the adamancy, determination, and energy with which Moscow will enlist allies (first and foremost, the United States) to its cause. "The Concept" lists—under "key directions of the disarmament process" of all places!—"the concentration in the hands of Russia of the total control over the nuclear forces of the former USSR."[34] Later, an official explicator of "The Tenets" placed "securing the status of Russia as the sole nuclear power in the CIS" among Moscow's main tasks in the CIS.[35]

As with other key objectives of its Near Abroad policy, Russia has been increasingly vocal and persistent in mobilizing international support for its agenda. In the case of nuclear exclusivity, the collection of the Soviet nuclear arsenal under the Russian roof has become a dominant issue in Russo-American relations, and Moscow has succeeded in enlisting active

U.S. support for the transfer of nuclear weapons from Belarus, Kazakhstan, and, albeit not as effectively, Ukraine.

Russia as a Nuclear Superpower

The maintenance of nuclear superpower status is the second corner-stone—the first being regional dominance—of the Russian national consensus on foreign policy. For Russia, its status as the world's other nuclear superpower is by far the most important and precious part of the Soviet legacy, as well as the crucial element in strategic continuity and the mainstay of Russia's claim to a place at the head of the world's table.

As far as military strategy is concerned, sharp cutbacks in the military budget and a rapid decline in conventional capabilities necessitate Russia's increased reliance on its nuclear arsenal for deterrence. Leading Russian experts claim that "Russia will have no real strategic offensive capability and will rely more on tactical nuclear weapons to back conventional forces."[36] According to the Defense Minister Grachev: "Both now and in the foreseeable future nuclear weapons will remain the defining element in European and global stability. Therefore, we regard the Strategic Nuclear Force as the most important guarantor of the military security of Russia and its allies."[37]

Russia's commitment to the maintenance of its nuclear superpower-hood has been evidenced by the omission of the "no first use" pledge in the country's first military doctrine. Because of this commitment, the United States should not take too seriously periodic Russian calls for moratoria on nuclear testing.

Russia as a Great Power

While conceding to the United States the status of the world's only superpower,[38] Russia insists on "remaining, despite the current crisis, one of the great powers because of her potential, her influence on world affairs, and the responsibility which such influence engenders."[39] The maintenance of Russia's great power status is listed in "The Tenets" among the overarching objectives of Russian foreign policy.[40]

In practice, for the United States and its allies Russia's self-proclaimed great power status means that the harmonious nature of Russia's relations with the West after the victorious anticommunist revolution of August 1991 has been replaced with still occasional and manageable, but nevertheless quite real differences stemming from Russia's discovery (or recovery) of its geopolitical interests and an increased assertiveness in their pursuit.

By October 1993, even Kozyrev insisted that "partnership" with the West never meant "unity" and that such a partnership ought to be based on "realism and mutual overcoming of difficulties."[41] Ambassador Lukin was more graphic: "Unfortunately, we still have people [in Russia] who suffer from romantic masochism and are frozen tenderly kissing America. I am sure that one can and should cooperate with America but not to the detriment of our own political and economic interests."[42]

Ambassador Lukin did not specify these interests, but they are not hard to gauge. Russia's political interests with which the United States might interfere are those connected with the Near Abroad and Russia's historic "spheres of influence" (for example, Serbia).[43] The presence of Russian troops in Latvia and Estonia, the participation of Russian military units (with or without Moscow's permission) in ethnic and political conflicts in the Near Abroad, or Russian peacekeeping there: these policies could cause—in fact, they already have caused—U.S.-Russian tension. Kozyrev has hinted at as much: "As regards international problems in our interaction with the United States, the foreground is most likely to be occupied by the conflicts along the perimeter of the Russian borders. One cannot exclude attempts by the United States to displace Russia from her traditional spheres of influence under the guise of mediating or peacemaking efforts."[44]

As to the economic interests mentioned by Ambassador Lukin, the potential for a significant U.S.-Russian conflict comes in the area of arms trade. As it was during the Soviet era, the export of military hardware remains one of the four main hard currency earners, its weight enhanced in the last decade by a worldwide slump in the prices of the other three: oil, gas, and gold.

The "impermissibility" (*nedopushchenie*) of undermining Russia's position in the world arms markets is listed by the official explicator of "The Tenets" among the "specially emphasized" tasks of Russian foreign policy.[45] The failure to expand Russian arms exports was reportedly behind the successive dismissals of two ministers of foreign economic relations: Petr Aven in December 1992, and his replacement, Sergei Glaziev, in August 1993. The vital importance of arms exports for Russia is illustrated by the fact that in 1992 its largest buyer, which spent an estimated $1.8 billion, was China—at the time when China was considered by Russian experts to be "the principal threat" to their country!

After the collapse of the rigid division of arms markets, the configurations of which were dictated by Cold War allegiances, the interests of two of the world's largest arms exporters are bound to come into competition, with inevitable, and loud, political overtones. The first, but by no means last, flare-up of this systemic tension came to a head in the spring and summer of 1993 in what Moscow saw as an unfair denial of lucrative markets, and Washington regarded as involving antiterrorism and non-proliferation issues. The proposed sales of Russian submarines to Iran (reportedly worth $600 million) and rocket engines to India (reportedly for $400 million) caused the sharpest post–Cold War controversy to date between Russia and the United States, twice delaying a visit to Washington by Russian Prime Minister Viktor Chernomyrdin.

Continuity and Change in the Foreign Policy of Postcommunist Russia

The emergent Russian foreign policy is a blend of a dramatic and benign change brought about by Yeltsin's departure from the traditional Russian foreign policy paradigm, on the one hand, and by continuity dictated by both a powerful tradition and geostrategic imperatives, on the other. This continuity is exemplified by Russia's claim to regional superpower and nuclear superpower status and its insistence on a great power role in world affairs.

For the foreseeable future, the greatest challenge to U.S. policymakers is likely to stem from this duality in the content and conduct of Russian foreign policy, in which at different times one or the other element— novelty or continuity—will be emphasized. To remain effective, the U.S. strategic posture vis-à-vis Russia must recognize this reality and take into account both formative impulses. This awareness will help prevent costly and, perhaps, dangerous swings between elation and despair, near-alliance and recrimination.

Similarly, recognition of the three irreducible elements of the national consensus—Russia as the regional superpower, Russia as a nuclear superpower, and Russia as a great power—could minimize errors as U.S. policymakers navigate through several clusters of inevitable strategic choices with which the United States will be confronted in its Russian policy: for example, arms control (nuclear and conventional); nonproliferation of sensitive technologies; Russia and the Near Abroad; Russia, Turkey, and Afghanistan; and the Russia-China-Japan triangle.

Calculating, at any given moment, the balance of the formative influences on Russian foreign policy without trying, in vain, to change them from the outside; and employing and encouraging the new, constructive elements in Moscow's policymaking while acknowledging (but not accepting, and, when necessary, resisting) the imperial inertia will make for a U.S. policy that is rich, diverse, flexible, and, therefore, effective. In the long run, only such a policy will benefit America, Russia, and the world.

Notes

1. Andrei Kozyrev, "The Concept of Foreign Policy of the Russian Federation" (Unpublished memorandum, January 25, 1993), pp. 2, 7.

2. See Martin Malia's essay in this collection.

3. Sergei Rogov, ed., *Russian Defense Policy: Changes and Developments*, CNA Occasional Paper (Center for Naval Analysis, February 1993), pp. 30–31.

4. For an account of Russia's foreign policy debate at the time, see Leon Aron, "The Battle for the Soul of Russian Foreign Policy," *The American Enterprise*, November–December 1992, pp. 10–16.

5. From remarks by Andranik Migranian at the United States Institute of Peace–sponsored conference, "The Emerging National Security Doctrine of a New Russia," Washington, D.C., March 17, 1993.

6. Ibid.

7. See "The Key Tenets of the Concept of Foreign Policy of the Russian Federation" (Unpublished document).

8. Pavel Grachev, "The Immediate Problems of Building and Training of the Armed Forces of Russia," *Voennaia mysl'*, no. 6 (1993), pp. 23–31.

9. Kozyrev, "The Concept of Foreign Policy," p. 42.

10. Ibid., p. 15.

11. Ibid., p. 30.

12. The members are Denmark, Finland, Germany, Norway, Poland, Russia, Sweden, Latvia, Lithuania, and Estonia.

13. The members are Denmark, Iceland, Norway, Russia, Sweden, and Finland.

14. Kozyrev, "The Concept of Foreign Policy," p. 34.

15. "The Key Tenets," p. 9.

16. Ibid., p. 2.

17. Kozyrev, "The Concept of Foreign Policy," p. 11.

18. Ibid.

19. "The Key Tenets," p. 7.

20. Sergei Modestov, "A chto dumaet genshtab?" (And what is the General Staff thinking?), *Novoe vremia*, no. 31 (July 1993), pp. 12, 13.

21. Migranian, conference remarks.

22. See R. Jeffrey Smith and Barton Gellman, "U.S. Will Seek to Mediate Ex-Soviet States' Disputes," *The Washington Post,* August 5, 1993.

23. Vladimir Lukin participated, with the author of this article, in the Voice of America's Russian-language show "Dialogue" in August 1993.

24. Andrei Kozyrev, "Rossiia fakticheski v odinochku neset vremia realnogo mirotvorchestva v konfliktakh po perimetry svoikh granits. I nikto zanee eto ne sdelaet" (Russia, in fact, is carrying alone the burden of peacekeeping in the conflicts along her border. And nobody would do this for her), *Nezavisimaia gazeta,* September 22, 1993.

25. Migranian, conference remarks.

26. Ibid.

27. Kozyrev, "Rossiia fakticheski v odinochku . . ."

28. Ibid.

29. For an analysis of the first instance of the implementation of this principle (in Tajikistan), see Leon Aron, "Yeltsin's Vietnam," *The Washington Post*, August 22, 1993.

30. "The Key Tenets," p. 11.

31. Ibid.

32. Ibid.

33. Ibid.

34. Kozyrev, "The Concept of Foreign Policy," p. 17.

35. Vladislav Chernov (deputy chief of the Administration for Strategic Security, Security Council of the Russian Federation), "The National Interests of Russia and Threats to Her Security," *Nezavisimaia gazeta*, April 29, 1993.

36. General Vladimir Dvorkin (head of the Main Institute of the Armed Forces) and Dr. Alexei Arbatov (head of the Center for Geopolitical and Military Forecasting), *CNA Seminar Report* (Center for Naval Analysis), July 1993.

37. Grachev, "The Immediate Problems of Building and Training of the Armed Forces of Russia," p. 26.

38. Such a concession is implicit in Andrei Kozyrev's recommendation that Russia "should be as far as possible from the conflicts between nations where our direct interests are not engaged" (Kozyrev, "The Concept of Foreign Policy," p. 28).

39. "The Key Tenets," p. 4.

40. Ibid., p. 2.

41. Interview with Kozyrev, *Moskovskie novosti,* October 24, 1993.

42. Ibid.

43. In the case of Serbia, Russia stubbornly opposed bombing of the Bosnian Serbs' positions, advocated by the United States in the United Nations.

44. Kozyrev, "The Concept of Foreign Policy," p. 24.

45. Chernov, "The National Interests of Russia."

2

Tradition, Ideology, and Pragmatism in the Formation of Russian Foreign Policy

Martin Malia

*Of the gods we believe, and of men we know, that by a
necessary law of their nature they rule wherever they can*
—Thucydides

*Homo homini lupus
(A man is a wolf to men)*
—Thomas Hobbes

*Remota iustutia quid sunt regna nisi magna latrocinia
(Without justice states are nothing more than great robber bands)*
—St. Augustine

In the West the Russian tradition, whether under the tsars or under the Soviets, has usually evoked a Pavlovian response: "despotism" and "chauvinism" at home leading to "expansionism" and "imperialism" abroad. Equally reflexive is the judgment that these characteristics are eternal and immutable.

It is with such arguments that German Social Democrats, quoting Marx and Engels on the "Mongol-Byzantine" Russian menace to Europe, voted war credits in 1914. It is through the somewhat panicky conflation of such arguments with a justifiable fear of communism that the West resisted and contained the Soviet Union during the Cold War. And it is with the reprise of such arguments that, after the collapse of communism, a part of Western opinion refuses to believe that the Muscovite bear has really changed its skin and hence might soon be back as Russian "fascism." How founded are these enduring suspicions?

To be sure, throughout most of its history—at least since the consolidation of the tsardom of Muscovy at the end of the 15th century—Russia has been ruled by an autocracy. And just as surely, throughout most of the same period the Russian state has constantly expanded at the expense of its neighbors. True, too, the Soviet Union often used the symbols of traditional Russian nationalism to supplement its vocation as the leader of "proletarian internationalism." Thus, it has been possible for some historians to argue that the Soviet Union was simply old Russia in Marxist disguise, and that there was essential continuity "from the white to the red eagle."[1] At a superficial glance, the continuity and immutability of Russian autocratic imperialism is a plausible explanation of what has been an exceptionally sad and servile national history.

The brute facts regarding the basic power configurations in Russia are not in dispute. There exists, however, a very real issue regarding their meaning. First, how exceptional is Russia's internal despotism in the context of Western history overall? Second, how constant and uniform has the drive to expand been throughout Russian history? This essay addresses these two questions as a preliminary to assessing the chances for a new departure in the present, postcommunist juncture.

In gauging the measure of Russian exceptionalism, both internally and internationally, it is first necessary to define what Russia is an exception from: that is, what do we mean by the "West"? The dichotomy "Russia and the West," or "Russia and Europe," has been a constant both in Russia and in the West since Peter the Great first "cut a window through to Europe," but it assumed particular intensity in the early 19th century when Romantic historicism gave it metaphysical underpinnings. From that time on, the difference between Russia and the West was summed up by Hegel and Ranke's assertion that the "history of Romano-Germanic Europe was the history of freedom," a view that left Russia quite out in the cold of its Asiatic steppes. This view of Russia as evolving on a *Sonderweg* (separate historical path) of permanent oriental despotism is akin to the opinion of such diverse Russian Westernizers as Paul

Miliukov, Georgii Plekhanov, and Vladimir Lenin at the turn of the last century.[2]

But the history of the present century should make us more cautious about where the frontier between freedom and despotism lies. For, in the wake of the catastrophe of 1939–45, there has been much debate about an enduring German *Sonderweg* within the West. It is thus wisest not to talk about the West as a uniform bloc wholly distinct from Russia. Rather, Europe is best regarded as a succession of *Sonderwegen*, in which Russia is the farthest out and slowest moving track, but moving all the same—as Peter was the first to demonstrate. In this perspective, Russia is properly understood as proceeding in the same direction as its more Western neighbors, but with a lag of decades and in a much more convulsive fashion.

Moreover, we should not exaggerate the degree to which the West has been what we now call democratic. Until the end of the 18th century, oligarchic constitutionalism, as in Great Britain, the United Provinces of the Netherlands, and Venice constituted the outer limits of political progress. Elsewhere in Europe monarchical absolutism, in combination with varying degrees of a *Rechtstaat* (a Prussian translation of Montesquieu's *état de droit*), was the norm. After Catherine II (a fan of Montesquieu), Russia began moving, however haltingly, towards Montesquieu's legalistic norms.

It was only with the French Revolution that the question of democracy, as the modern world understands it, was posed—but hardly solved. For modern democracy, unlike the class-based polities of the ancient world, has the ambition of including all men—simply by the fact of their humanity—as equal citizens in the body politic, and of combining the sovereignty of "one man, one vote" with the sense of law developed by antecedent aristocratic constitutionalism. The United States was the first to achieve this amalgam in relatively stable and enduring fashion between the Constitution of 1789 and the Jacksonian suffrage reforms of the 1820s. But even in the "exceptional" United States it took a Civil War to refound the republic on the basis of universal manhood suffrage— and at that in law more than in actual practice until the civil rights reforms of the 1960s.

Western Europe went through the same process either in orderly but very slow fashion (as in Britain), or in rapid but bumpy fashion (as in France), or under paternalistic tutelage and only partially (as in Germany-Prussia). Yet, nowhere did an unchallenged universal suffrage order emerge until the end of the last century—or, as in Britain and Italy, until the beginning of this one. Thus, if we look backward at the obstacles to the progress of democracy rather than forward to its eventual victory (as 19th-century history is usually written), the history of the Romano-Germanic world becomes the "history of freedom" only around 1900—which is not all that long ago.

In this perspective, Russia after 1800 emerges as bringing up the rear, but bringing it up regularly nonetheless. Alexander I—even Nicholas I—and their common servant, Mikhail Speranskii, moved the *Rechtstaat* a notable step forward with a *Svod Zakonov* (Code of Laws) that would last until 1917. But it was Alexander II and the enlightened bureaucrats who served him who really brought Russia into the 19th-century mainstream. By what amounted to a revolution from above, they enacted Peasant Emancipation in 1861 (two years before Lincoln's Emancipation Proclamation), and in 1864 they introduced *zemstvo* reforms of local self-government together with an independent judiciary. These Great Reforms thus cut a second window through to Europe, and at approximately the level where the Stein-Hardenberg reforms of 1807–12 (another revolution from above) had put the autocratic and serf-based Prussia of Frederick the Great. At the time, this lag of 50 years seemed like an eternity, both to impatient Russian radicals and to a condescendingly superior West. But in retrospect it appears more like one phase of a slow overcoming of backwardness throughout Central and Eastern Europe. Indeed, we can now clearly see it as a major narrowing of the gap, and the first major blurring of the Russian *Sonderweg* since Peter.

The second great step toward closing the gap occurred with the revolution from below of 1905 and the "granted" constitution of the legislative State Duma in 1906. These events echoed, again 50 years later, the imperfect German revolution of 1848, and the *Scheinkonstitutionalismus*, or "sham constitutionalism," of an *octroierte* Reichstag—a halfway-house between the Old Regime and modern democracy, a regime that existed also in Austria-Hungary after 1867. Thus, by 1914, Europe was divided into three zones: the old constitutional democracies of the Atlantic West; the newer halfway-house constitutionalisms of Central Europe; and the raw recruit to that hybrid status, rear-guard Russia.

Then World War I destroyed what seemed like a constant, if uneven, march of all Europe toward democracy. It precipitated first the weak Russian constitutionalism, and soon thereafter the more advanced Central European constitutionalisms, into totalitarianism. At the same time, the

Great Depression—also largely a product of the war—disoriented and undermined the constitutional democracies of what was now a beleaguered Atlantic Rim. By the late 1930s, it looked as though the future of Europe might well belong to either a Red or a Brown "dictatorship," as the world then called totalitarianism. The West "whose history was the history of freedom" seemed about to have run its course. Numerous of its luminaries—from George Bernard Shaw to Ezra Pound, from Sidney and Beatrice Webb to Henry Wallace, from Romain Rolland to Pablo Picasso, and professional scholars of both Central and Eastern Europe such as E. H. Carr—bet on one or the other of the dictatorships, and sometimes on one first, and on the other later.

But the fortunes of war once again reshuffled the cards. The conflict of 1939–45 destroyed all the totalitarianisms of the right in Central and East Central Europe, but with a mixed outcome: Germany and Italy at last became stable constitutional democracies, while to the east of the new Iron Curtain, totalitarianism of the left moved in. Yet, by 1989, these "popular democracies," too, were gone, and budding constitutional orders existed up to the Russian frontier. And so the antidemocratic trend of 1918–45 was at last reversed over the whole continent. Then, in 1991, the former Soviet Union joined this march back to the aspirations of 1914—again 50 years after the other interwar dictatorships. As of this writing, Russia's adherence to the democratic camp seems to hang in the balance, and the revanche of the holdovers of nomenklatura communism is gaining momentum. Nonetheless, though some nomenklatura structures may well survive privatization by hijacking a part of it, the old system as a whole cannot be restored. The momentum of marketization and the development from below of a new private sector are irreversible. The centralized Party-state, the Plan, Marxism-Leninism, and the old Union— all are damaged beyond repair. Any new authoritarianism that might emerge would still be a far cry from the former totalitarianism. Russia, with whatever convulsions and even temporary backtracking, can only continue that narrowing of the gap with the West which began when the long hiatus of Sovietism was closed in 1991.

For Russia, like all other nations, *does* change. Its "political culture" is not immutable or monolithic. The challenge to despotism from liberal forces of 1855–1914 and then again in the 1980s is as much a part of that culture as is the more dominant autocratic tradition. The contingency of events and, one hopes, the fortunes of peace will decide how well the liberal component of the national tradition develops.

جسج

A similar diversity of trends, against the background of a similar set of conventional misperceptions, may be observed in the historical development of Russian foreign policy. To begin with the misperceptions, two clichés about Russia's international role are dominant. The first we have already seen: namely, that its expansionism is the projection outward of internal despotism. The second is that its exceptional imperial voracity was driven by a messianic urge that was religious under the tsars and ideological under the Soviets.

This line of argument takes its departure from the assertion of the monk Philotheus of Pskov in 1510 that Moscow was "the third Rome," and that, unlike its two predecessors, it would have no successor. Often the parallel was made with the one-time pretensions of Moscow as the seat of the Third International. But Philotheus was speaking only of the Church, not the state; and his declarations meant that, after the Church of Rome had fallen into "heresy" and then the See of Constantinople had capitulated to this heresy at the Union of Florence in 1439 (and as punishment had been captured by the Turks), Moscow remained the sole center of true Christianity.[3]

But the Muscovite state of the 16th and 17th centuries was never guided by Philotheus' maxim in its foreign policies. The matter of his messianism got into the historiography only when the Poles, after the revolution of 1830 (and for quite understandable reasons), used it to explain their oppression at Russia's hands. It was then taken up by the Western Europeans generally to explain Nicholas I's drive to Constantinople and the Straits. And so it was repeated through all the Turkish and Balkan crises down to 1914, and then recycled to account for Stalin.

In fact, however, Russian foreign policy under the old regime was no more ideological than that of any other European powers. Like all other powers, Russia was expansionist, but essentially for geopolitical reasons. Even within this "pragmatic" framework, Russia's imperialism was in no way exceptional or inordinate.

We should not forget that, beginning with a rough contemporary of Philotheus, Christopher Columbus, *all* of Europe was expansionist, a phenomenon that continued until the great partitions of Asia and Africa on the eve of what Lenin, and the European left generally, called the "imperialist war." Indeed, there was probably more ideology in the Western overseas expression of this expansionism than in its Russian, continental, and Eurasian forms: the Spanish and Portuguese expansions were conducted in part as a religious crusade, continuing the impetus of the Iberian *reconquista*; the New England Puritans migrated to build a godly "city on a hill"; later the British had their "white man's burden" and the French their *mission civilisatrice*. It is difficult to see how all this is intrinsically different from pan-Slav concern in Russia during the late 19th and early 20th centuries for Orthodox Christians under the Turks in the Balkans.

In short, Russian foreign policy under the old regime did have an ideological component, but only toward the end. Moreover, until the early 20th century, pan-Slav ideology was much more the property of society than of the government, which succumbed to it only in the immediate buildup to 1914. Before that, if there was ideology in Russian foreign policy, it was the conservative ideology of legitimism and the Holy Alliance under Alexander I and Nicholas I. But this is a mode of thought that leads to defense of the international status quo, not to foreign aggrandizement. Indeed, the most conservative Russian sovereign of the period, Nicholas I, though he severely repressed the Polish revolt of 1830, did not seek to add new territory to his empire. Russia's constant concern with the Straits and the Balkans from Nicholas I to 1914 can be explained by a geopolitical interest as legitimate as the conflicting geopolitical interest of Britain in defending its lifeline to India through the Mediterranean.

A similar pragmatic geopolitical motivation accounts for most of Russia's constant westward expansion from the mid-17th century to Alexander I. On this frontier, the central problem for Russia was to break out of debilitating isolation from the advanced portions of Europe. This isolation was imposed in part by geography: remoteness from the warm seas and a weak economic base due to poor soil and northern location. But until the 18th century, it was imposed also by Polish, Swedish, and Turkish policy, because Russia's three major neighbors had a self-interest in keeping Russia weak.

In the mid-17th century, Moscow, under Tsar Alexis, began to press on Poland by taking over Ukraine up to the Dnieper River. But it was Alexis' son, Peter, who made the great breakthrough by reaching the Baltic Sea and establishing a virtual protectorate over a now weakened Polish-Lithuanian Commonwealth. All of this, obviously, was viewed as disastrous by Russia's neighbors; but it was not different in kind from Louis XIV's policies on the Rhine or in the Low Countries; or the Austrian Hapsburgs' policies along the Danube; or England's constant resolve to fight to keep any major power from controlling the mouth of the Scheldt "pointed like a pistol at the heart" of Britain; or, later, America's assertion of the Monroe Doctrine.

Catherine the Great essentially completed Peter's work by breaking the vise of Turkish power to the south along the Black Sea and finally eliminating Poland—though at the cost of paying off Prussia and Austria with half the Polish booty as compensation for her stunning gains against Turkey. Alexander I, as a result of his ultimately successful contest with Napoleon for hegemony on the continent, rounded off his Western frontier by the acquisition of Finland, Bessarabia, and the "Congress Kingdom" of Poland. On another, and unrelated front, Alexander II added Turkestan, or Central Asia, much as Western powers were expanding in maritime Asia at the same time. Thus the Russian Empire, in the basic form in which it would endure until 1914, was at last constituted.

It was indeed an enormous affair. But it was hardly more extensive, proportionally speaking, than the aggregation of territories put together by little Britain during the 18th and 19th centuries. Nor was it different in kind from the lesser, but still considerable French Empire, or the foreign territories of Holland and Belgium. Empire-building is simply what great powers do, as Thucydides explained 2,500 years ago in analyzing Athens' Aegean "empire": power abhors a vacuum, and if one wolf-like state does not fill it, another will.

As Thucydides also pointed out, all empires, though they have their origin in pragmatic geopolitical interest, eventually develop a momentum and a hubris that leads to fatal overextension. This occurred with the global European imperial system in the quarter century before World War I. The British, notably, undertook the provocative Boer War. The United States gratuitously divested Spain of its remaining colonies in the Caribbean and the Philippines. Russia participated in this last colonial hurrah in Manchuria and Korea, thereby stumbling into another needlessly provocative war with Japan. But again, the only difference from the other European powers is that they operated over seas while Russia operated over land.

So why was the Western reaction so virulent to Russian expansionism around the rim of Asia—from the Straits, to the "Great Game" with Britain over Afghanistan, to the Far East? This was not because Russia's imperialism was more egregious, but because its autocratic order made it seem to the liberal West not just a rival power, but an alien civilization. Yet, the same may be said about the growing apprehension with which Britain and France viewed semiautocratic Germany and Austria-Hungary, a sentiment shared also by the remote United States. Thus, on the eve of 1914, ideology intruded into international affairs by tending to polarize foreign relations in terms of democracy versus despotism, and of left versus right.

Nonetheless, in the buildup to World War I, semiautocratic Russia found itself allied with the constitutionalist Western powers against its Central European cognates. Thus, in the crisis of 1914, pragmatic geo-political considerations overcame the nascent ideologization of politics between right and left. And so the Russian Old Regime exited history as one of those amoral *monstres froids* that had made up the Concert of Europe ever since Peter brought Russia into the West.

It was with the October Revolution that Russia's international role changed fundamentally, at last giving pride of place—if not always priority of power—to a messianic ideology. But this turn of affairs was as new in Russian history as it was rare in European history generally. Broadly speaking, before the 20th century there were two major periods of ideological politics in modern history. The first was the Wars of Religion of the 16th and early 17th centuries, which polarized Germany, France, and the Low Countries internally and molded competing international coalitions either to advance or to roll back the Reformation. The second period was the French Revolutionary and Napoleonic era, which pitted Old Regime against New, first within France itself and then across most of Europe. In the two cases the major powers largely decided their foreign policies in terms first of religious and later of secular ideological criteria. But in neither case was ideology the sole, and at times not even the dominant criterion. For example, Cardinal Richelieu took the Protestant side in the Thirty Years War in order to break Hapsburg encirclement of France; and at the height of the French Revolution, between 1793 and 1795, the three conservative powers of Europe—Prussia, Austria, and Russia—were far more concerned with aggrandizement through the partition of Poland than with combatting the regicide French Republic.

A third great period of ideological politics was inaugurated by Russia's October Revolution. In a sense, this represented a deepening of the incipient prewar polarization of international politics between left and right. But the October Revolution brought this process a great step further;

after 1917, the outer limit of political progress for the left worldwide was no longer just democracy, but "socialism," and in this matter the gold standard was the world's "first workers' state" and the "first socialist society"—Soviet Russia. By the 1930s, this new force received an antithesis in the revolutionary right of fascism and national socialism, and Europe was back to wars of religion. Even after fascism was destroyed in 1945, the Soviet Union moved into an almost equally charged adversarial relationship with "American imperialism."

Yet, in the Soviet half of this polarity, there was nothing specifically Russian about the ideology involved. The messianism of October was the pan-European pseudoreligion, expressed as a pseudoscience, that was Marxist socialism, though now given a geographic base on the ruins of the Russian Empire. Nor did this messianism seek to further any ends that were specifically Russian: it sought rather to foster the power of the Communist Party–state as the vehicle of the march of history leading to its culmination in socialism. And this Party-state did not derive its power from Russian national resources alone: it lived as much off of the magnetic attraction its socialist mission exerted over the rest of the world. Thus, Soviet foreign policy offers a different mix of tradition, ideology, and pragmatism from the conventional power politics of its tsarist predecessor.

It is only in this period that ideology is clearly dominant in Russia over tradition and geopolitical pragmatism. This does not mean that the latter two factors were now negligible. Geography remained what it had been under the Russian Empire, and the Soviet state had concerns similar to those of its predecessors with respect to a Western glacis, the Straits, Iran, and the Far East. Nor was the Soviet state at all adverse to taking international action on the basis of raw considerations of power: Lenin took the pragmatic course at Brest-Litovsk in order to save the Bolshevik regime, and in so doing scandalized the ideological purists of the left communist opposition. Stalin cut a similar pragmatic deal with Hitler, to the even greater scandal of the world ideological left.

Nonetheless, even at its most cynically pragmatic, Soviet policy remained fundamentally ideological, because the very nature of the Soviet state cast it in an adversarial relationship with the rest of the world. From Lenin to the eve of perestroika, the Soviet regime saw itself locked in an international "class struggle" to the death between "socialism" and "capitalism." Even Khrushchev's "peaceful coexistence" and Brezhnev's "détente" were viewed as other, more cautious modes of this struggle. Moreover, much of the Third World, and a fair part of opinion in the First, shared this dichotomous vision. This ideological impetus in fact created real conflicts between the Soviet Union and "imperialism" in Asia, Africa, and Latin America, where no conflict of economic, strategic, or other practical interests existed. Thus, the Soviet Union conducted its diplomacy and tailored its armaments policy with the aim of ultimately tipping the world "correlation of forces" in its favor.

It should be unnecessary to insist that the Russian Imperial regime never had any such ambitions: it saw no further than the Vistula, the Straits, Iran, or the Yalau. Nor did that regime ever have the global reach provided by sponsorship of "wars of national liberation" in Third World colonies or by "popular fronts" and "peace movements" among workers and intellectuals of the First World. All this is so because the Russian old regime had no ideology other than a dynastic conservatism, whereas the new regime, and all its basic institutions, had the wellspring of their being in the worldwide ideology of socialism, however pragmatic that regime's power politics may at times have been.

Now that all this is over, what may we plausibly expect of the new Russia's international behavior and national security doctrine? The answer, surely, must be a return to some form of pragmatism founded on the enduring geopolitical concerns of any state occupying the major part of what was once the Russian Empire and then the Soviet Union. These concerns will not be ideological, but interests of a classical, circumscribed sort. Still, this does not mean that the Russian Federation will simply return to the international preoccupations of the old Russian Empire: too much has changed both in Russia and the world for any such reprise.

First of all, no such entity as the present Russian Federation has ever existed in the vast spaces of Eurasia. From the time Ivan the Terrible conquered the Khanates of Kazan and Astrakhan in the 16th century until 1991, the state ruled from Moscow and St. Petersburg had never been a national state; it was a multinational empire, whose principle of cohesion until 1917 had been dynastic, and thereafter had been the Party. The Soviet collapse of 1991 created a Russian national state for the first time, or at least a state that was 85 percent ethnically Russian, and whose minority nationalities were so situated, either on the borders or surrounded by ethnic Russia, as to furnish a far less disruptive potential than the minorities of the old Union. With understanding on the part of

Moscow and some luck, the Russian Federation could become a viable, and therefore highly regionalized, new polity. But this will require a number of years, and until it has occurred the new Russia will be highly constrained in all its international policies.

An even greater constraint, and a more potent factor of instability, is the continuing imbrication of Russia with the 14 other states that emerged from the old Soviet Union. The most obvious aspect of this is the presence of 25 million Russians in that novel entity, the Near Abroad. Almost as important are the continuing links through the old Union monetary system, infrastructure, and industrial interdependence. Here is an "international" problem with which neither the Russian Empire nor the Party Empire had to contend. It is the priority for Russia in working toward any new national security doctrine. Until it is resolved, the Russian Federation cannot determine its relationship with its near neighbors from the Balkans to Iran to the Far East, nor with the great power blocs of North America, the European Union, China, and Japan.

A final major constraint on developing Russia's new international role is the fact that its internal conversion from "real socialism" to a "normal society," or from totalitarianism to a market democracy, is far from complete. Without buying into alarmist scenarios about "Weimar Russia" or the triumph of a "red-brown" nationalist reaction, one must recognize that the degree to which the new Russia will realize its democratic potential is by no means clear. On the outcome of this transition will depend in large measure Russia's relations both with the Near Abroad and with the international community generally.

Thus, we are in for a fairly long wait—until the Russian Federation has defined itself as a polity and until this entity has given itself a viable internal economic and political order—before we see what kind of international role Russia wants, or is able, to play. But of one thing we may be certain even now: this role will not be merely a regional one. Although no conceivable new Russia could return to the overreaching ideological ambitions of the Soviet Union, any conceivable Russia will be a major power, roughly in the same category as the European Union, the United States, Japan, and, in the foreseeable future, China. Without ideology, this new Russia will have to stake out its interests pragmatically, in concentric circles moving out from a special relationship with the Near Abroad to the other major powers around the rim of Eurasia.

But what of tradition? Might not the new Russia become a nationalistic, authoritarian, and aggressive power? And might it even seek to take back the breakaway republics of the former Soviet Union and so recreate the old Russian Empire? Indeed, there is now much talk among the country's intellectuals of the "Russian Idea," by which is meant a Russian spirit of *Volkgeist* radically distinct from that of other nations, an Idea that is supposed to fill the psychological void created by the collapse of Marxism-Leninism. The great popularity of the writings of Nicholas Berdiaiev is perhaps the most telling sign of this new mood. And there is also talk in some military circles, and around ex–Vice-President Rutskoi, and obviously by Vladimir Zhirinovsky, of reconstituting the old Union.

Henry Kissinger, among others, constantly warns us against the eventual triumph of such forces because, in his view, authoritarian nationalism *is* the Russian tradition. An even more radical view of the eternally negative character of the Russian tradition was expressed by Kissinger's one-time critic during the era of détente, Richard Pipes. One of Pipes' principal arguments was that Russia, unlike all other European nations, never voluntarily gave up any territory it had once acquired[4] (an assertion that would have been equally applicable to Britain before 1945). Well, since 1991 Russia has let go of all the non-Russian conquests of Tsar Alexis, Peter, Catherine, Alexander I, and Alexander II combined. And Pipes, who also once held that Russia's internal order was unchangingly totalitarian, under the Old Regime no less than under the New, now seems to believe that the country has a real chance at democracy.[5] But if Pipes has changed his view, it is because the tectonic changes in Russia since 1991 have pretty much forced him to do so.

For these changes brought to the surface the long-submerged Westernizing tradition dating back to the Great Reforms of the 19th century, and of which Foreign Minister Andrei Kozyrev and President Yeltsin himself, with his evocation of Peter's "window onto Europe," are now the most visible examples. Thus, a hitherto secondary strain of the Russian tradition has become, for the first time, dominant. Nations are not constants; and it is pseudowisdom to deduce future prospects mechanically from past precedents.

The world around Russia, too, has changed mightily since the last time the gap between Russia and its neighbors was narrowing, in 1914. Without idealizing current aspirations to a "new world order," or minimizing the intractable problems both Russia and the West face in the postcommunist situation, we should note that our concepts of political morality have evolved significantly since the beginning of this century. On the eve of 1914, war was regarded by the majority of the European population as bracing and glorious. The experience of two world wars and the existence of nuclear weapons have reversed this judgment in the public mind, if not always in public practice, and made peace the primary value. Similarly, as of 1914, foreign conquest and colonial empire were regarded as the natural prerogatives of every vigorous constitutional democracy of the West; in the years after World War II, colonialism, racism, and every other form of transgression against human equality were increasingly branded as immoral. And overall, this most violent of centuries has paradoxically witnessed a progressive diminution of regard for force and a concomitant growth of respect for the rule of law—again in terms of official standards, if not invariably of actual conduct.

And at the end of this process of political-cultural revolution, there has now emerged a worldwide consensus that civilized nationhood means constitutional democracy, the market, and the rule of law: socialist revolution and, by and large, the mythical "third way" are no longer serious options for serious people. Russia's exit from communism has brought it into this consensus, at least in aspiration, if not yet in irreversible practice. Indeed, it was the collapse of communism in Russia that provoked the crystallization of that consensus.

Should this tendency continue, we can only expect that it will reinforce the pragmatism of Russia's new foreign policy. Thus, it is idle to project a new authoritarian aggressiveness from ghosts of the pan-Slav past or Philotheus of Pskov. How the new Russia shapes up, and how its foreign policy evolves, will depend above all on the contingencies of present circumstances. This means both the success of internal economic liberalization and constitutional stabilization and the further development of international legality. For it is only through the rule of law that the *monstres froids* that compose the Concert of the Powers are tempered with enough justice to hem in man's universally lupine nature and so transform states from St. Augustine's "robber bands" into civilized polities.

Notes

1. Jan Kucharzewski, *The Origins of Modern Russia* (New York: The Polish Institute of Arts and Sciences in America, 1948).

2. Paul Miliukov, *Ocherki po istorii russkoi kul'tury* (St. Petersburg: Mir Bozhii, 1896; reprint, Paris: Sovremennyia zapiski, 1930).

3. N. Ulianov, "Kompoleks Filfeia," *Novyi zhurnal*, no. 45 (June 1956).

4. Richard Pipes, "Détente: Moscow's View," in *Soviet Strategy in Europe* (New York: Crane, Ruzzak & Co., 1976), pp. 3–42.

5. For example, see *The New York Times,* March 14, 1993, p. 17.

The Legacy of Soviet Policymaking in Creating a New Russia

Charles H. Fairbanks, Jr.

The biggest and most obvious change in Russian policymaking since the dissolution of the Soviet Union is the disappearance of the Communist Party as a national organization, and with it the disappearance of the split in administration between state and party organs at every level. This split was a distinctive and extremely important characteristic of the old system, although it had least impact on the armed forces and the security police, because the party was weaker in their management than in any other Soviet institution. While the highest party bodies, the Politburo and the Secretariat of the Central Committee, paid great attention to defense and security policy, the details of policy were elaborated by the relevant bureaucracies, which had no party rivals at the working level. The disappearance of the state-party split makes much more difference to foreign policy because the Foreign Ministry and the International and "Bloc" Departments of the Central Committee divided authority over foreign policy toward each region in a shifting balance. The nature of foreign policy allowed the Politburo to supervise foreign policy in far greater detail than defense policy; it was frequently reported that Politburo meetings normally considered foreign policy before other issues. Moreover, the commissions through which the Politburo did so much of its business were important means for resolving policy conflicts even between state agencies (such as the Foreign Ministry and Defense Ministry). Insofar as arms control had become a very important dimension of defense policy, the Politburo and its commissions became vitally important for its details as well. The disappearance of the Politburo, the master institution of the entire policymaking system, cannot but reduce the coherence of policy-making overall.

But the issue of the disappearance of communism is one that goes beyond specific institutions and their presence or absence. The habits and networks that existed under communism and were shaped by it are not disappearing overnight, just as those of the Tsarist regime did not disappear overnight. Some leaders of non-Russian republics have even called for the creation of a new, noncommunist ideology. Such calls represent a hankering for the form of communism without its content. There is a phenomenon that no one has tried to define carefully that one might call *subcommunism*, that is, communism with many of its most important elements subtracted. Communism without a dominant center and without an ideology is not communism in the same sense, but something important remains from it.

The Legacy of the Soviet Operational Code

With the disappearance of the Communist Party of the Soviet Union, Soviet ideology too disappeared, and no new ideology of any real strength, either democratic or authoritarian, has replaced it. Instead, we have an allergy to ideology. The effect of ideology on Soviet foreign policy and security policy is a complex question that I cannot enter into here. More important than ideology were the effects of the Community Party's "operational code,"[1] that is, a vast repertoire of tactical precepts—most of them codified in doctrines—regarding how one achieves success in foreign policy and how one deals with military problems. These precepts were a very powerful influence on foreign policy; one cannot understand things like the Popular Front or the Hitler-Stalin pact without them. As late as 1989, they were still playing a crucial role in shaping events. In 1989, for example, Mikhail Gorbachev and Eduard Shevardnadze used the old Leninist doctrine about tactical retreats, the doctrine symbolized by Brest-Litovsk, to create consensus behind the policy of giving up Eastern Europe. To underline the meaning of what they were doing, they chose to hold some of the crucial negotiations with Germany at Brest-Litovsk.

What is happening to this operational code today? It appears to be disappearing fairly rapidly. Russian power today is much less than it was in 1989, but Russian foreign policy is not phrased in terms of a tactical retreat. However, the operational code is not altogether gone. One characteristic of the Soviet operational code was the use of threats in foreign policy, as illustrated by Nikita Khrushchev's use of claimed ballistic missile capability to create a fictitious "missile gap" during the Berlin crisis of 1958–61, by the Cuban missile crisis itself, and by the threats to repeat the Cuban crisis in some fashion or to "place the United States in an analogous position" during the struggle over the NATO deployment of intermediate-range nuclear forces in Europe in 1979–83.[2] When the very pro-Western foreign minister of Russia, Andrei Kozyrev, delivered a speech in December 1992 greatly stiffening the Russian foreign policy positions, and then said it was a hoax designed to show what could happen if the reformers were defeated in Russia, he drew on the same tradition.

Threats, as an element of the Soviet operational code, have to be seen in relation to the abandoned Marxist-Leninist tradition. If we assume that foreign policy is intended to act on the policymaking elites of other countries, threats that are given *public* expression might appear counterproductive, because the public character of these threats complicates, by introducing the question of pride, policymakers' motives for yielding. The employment of threats in foreign policy during the Cold War makes more sense if one assumes, first, that the social systems of the two blocs were in deep opposition and, second, that Western public opinion was one target of Soviet foreign policy because the Western public was assumed to be more sympathetic to Soviet designs than were Western rulers. Although these two premises sometimes seduced Soviet leaders into unwise initiatives, neither of them was altogether false. The use of threats in foreign policy, however disagreeable to other states, had a function within the context of a powerful ideological empire trying to make its power fruitful without waging war. These conditions have changed. The limited elements of the Soviet operational code that linger are now divorced from the context in which they made sense. Russian foreign policy needs a reassessment of this heritage, to preserve what may be useful and to discard what is simply obsolete.

The concern with doctrine itself is a survival of the Bolshevik operational code and a useful one. Russia is a weak state today, but it will be a very strong state some day, and there is a need to connect those two phases coherently so that the present weakness does not destroy future strength. Nor should the anticipation of future strength lead Russia into inappropriate policies during a phase of weakness. In some ways, Russia's present situation is a more extreme version of the weakness the United States experienced during the Vietnam War. At that time, the presence of a highly conceptual doctrine in foreign policy (the Nixon-Kissinger ideas) gave a period of weakness the appearance of dynamism.

The Need for a Russian Foreign Policy Doctrine

Russia is surrounded by a dense network of problems, threats, opportunities, things going wrong, places Russia might intervene, and so forth. Russia needs some kind of doctrine to separate important from unimportant foreign policy issues, to reassure citizens as to the limits of Russian concessions, and to reassure neighbors as to the limits of Russian ambitions. Without a foreign policy and national security doctrine, Russia will be in the position that Italy was in between 1860 and World War I, that is, a weak country that nevertheless tries to make a big impact on world politics. Italy tended to hang around international conferences and crises like a vulture seeing what it could carry off, and that did not work out well for Italy. Italy made tremendous sacrifices in World War I, for example, and received little in return because the other great powers were weary of Italian claims and unimpressed by Italian power. The same thing could happen to Russia.

In developing any doctrine, however, Russian policymakers face the problem of the lack of discipline in the Russian state. In September 1993, Foreign Minister Kozyrev gave a major speech at the United Nations setting forth a doctrine of Russian peacekeeping in the "Near Abroad" in order to protect human rights.[3] The terms in which this doctrine was couched would have had considerable international appeal but for the fact that the speech was given just after the rout of the Georgian army by Russian-equipped Abkhaz nationalists, who broke a Russian-mediated truce to capture Sukhumi. These two events show how difficult it now is for Russia to speak with one voice in world politics.

The failure of Russian officialdom to speak and act in a uniform way is the result of a profound change from Soviet policymaking. The territorial disintegration of the Soviet Union is only the most obvious manifestation of a deeper trend—the disintegration of state structures, both territorial structures and vertical hierarchies of bureaucracies, as the August 1991 coup showed. During the coup, many ministries did not obey Gorbachev, their immediate superior, but their own subordinates, such as the commanders of military districts and of KGB units, in turn did not obey the ministries. At a time of rising sentiment for authority and order in the country, new structures are likely to be created. But, like the present structures, they will not find it easy to implant themselves and become strong.

For this reason, I do not attempt here to describe specific institutions or their functioning because I believe those institutions are transitory. Many of the republics that succeeded the Soviet Union are not viable within their present borders, as one can already see. Russia, Tajikistan, Georgia, Moldova, and Azerbaijan lack central administration of part of their territories, and some of the provinces of Russia, such as the Krasnoyarsk Krai, are beginning to break up into cities and regions. There could well be further disintegration, and there could be a return to a partial union of some kind. Institutions are as chaotic as borders. Two years after the independence of Russia, the Russian Supreme Soviet followed Soviet institutions into oblivion. What I can do amid this fluidity is describe the enduring habits or processes according to which various institutions did their work under the communist system, and then describe how these modes of doing official business are changing and not changing.

Aspects of Change and Continuity

The Role of the Legislative Branch

One change from the Soviet system is that the Russian legislative branch has acquired real decision-making authority. The effect of this change on security policy is, and will be for a long time, simply to add confusion. After all, that is largely the impact that the legislative branch has in the United States. Legislatures such as the U.S. Congress or the Russian Parliament are large, diverse bodies and lack a sense of final responsibility for the outcome of their decisions. They have no sense that the buck stops with them. In fact, it stops with the president in the United States and with Yeltsin in Russia. Consequently, there is a tremendous temptation to adopt policies just to position the legislature vis-à-vis the executive branch, not with the expectation that this or that policy will be adopted. This is a great problem for Russia and, sometimes, a significant one for the United States. In Russia's present situation, this divided authority has the potential to yield far more dangerous outcomes than it does in the United States. As Montesquieu said of Carthage: "Of the two factions that ruled in Carthage, one always wanted peace, the other always war, so that there it was impossible to enjoy the former or do well at the latter."[4]

Yeltsin's initiative in 1993 to set up a bicameral legislature in which one chamber represents the governments of the autonomous republics and provinces will not solve this problem. The "federal" chamber will be the source of an enormous amount of unproductive squabbling over the distribution of power between Moscow and the regions, and between the autonomous republics and the provinces. But Yeltsin's initiative will ease the problem of legislative irresponsibility. To the extent that the representatives in the federal chamber are directly chosen by governments holding real power in the provinces, those representatives will be responsive to people who have a sense of ultimate responsibility for what happens in the provinces. This responsiveness will grow as decisions in Moscow become more irrelevant to life in the provinces. This imperfect situation will be an improvement from when the legislature was not responsive to anyone because, in the absence of strong political parties and interest groups, there was no consistent relation between popular moods and votes.

Leadership and Authority

A defining trait of the Soviet system was a pronounced tendency to look to the top to resolve problems at every level, whether in the whole country, in the Foreign Ministry, or in a province. The authority of the top boss at every level was enormous, and most enormous in the person of the general secretary, particularly in foreign policy, as Gorbachev's foreign policy shows. Gorbachev faced, at least from April 1989 on, strong opposition within the Politburo on domestic issues. In spite of the daring character of his new foreign policy direction and the disasters it produced—above all, the loss of Eastern Europe—he faced less strong opposition in foreign policy. It seems to have been understood that the general secretary had a greater right to speak for the Politburo on foreign policy than in other areas.

Such authority would be very useful now because Russia needs strong leadership. But the level of leadership is falling. It was draining away rapidly even under Gorbachev, as the August 1991 coup clearly illustrated. Why this was happening is a question both interesting and important. To stanch the draining away of authority from the central government, one needs to understand the real foundations of authority in the old communist system and what happened to them. The more successful postcommunist politicians, such as Yeltsin and President Levon Ter-Petrosyan in Armenia, have an instinctive feeling for these factors. But

Western political science has not grasped them. This is shown by the West's failure to understand the fragility of the Soviet system and to allow for any possibility of its collapse.[5]

A starting point for understanding the draining away of leadership authority is to note the private character of the bulk of the Russian public and its boredom with and cynicism toward public life—a cynicism that is much greater in Russia than in many of the other post-Soviet republics. Even personal ambition has failed to develop in the swiftly changing situation (the kind of situation that usually fosters would-be Napoleons). Even in a democracy where administration is orderly and law is strong— as it is not in Russia—most of the authority of higher officials over lower officials rests on habit, on a deeply ingrained sense that the highest officials, whether or not we agree with them, possess or at least represent dignity and importance. The radical demystification of the public world enervates the authority of officials at its very source. It will inevitably confuse and slacken Russian policymaking for a long time to come.

Authority is draining away least in the provinces because governmental structures are much simpler there, being based on brute facts of local power and authority that everyone recognizes. So this process is strengthening the periphery as against the center, and that constitutes a considerable problem for the Russian government.

There is, however, a residue of authority even at the center. Yeltsin, who now generates very little enthusiasm, is obeyed more through habit than anything else. There is still an enormous administrative machine accustomed to look to the top for instructions. Much of this apparatus no longer obeys orders that are inconvenient. But it remains easier to obey orders that do not contradict one's interests; mere laziness inclines in this direction. Another striking example of this residual respect is the center's success in carrying out the confiscatory and arbitrary exchange of old rubles for new in the summer of 1993.

How would it be possible for Russian leaders to recreate a sense of authority? One way of answering this question is to think about other leaders who, in rather similar circumstances of discredited authority, recreated it. The first examples to come to mind are leaders such as Konrad Adenauer in Germany, Alcide de Gaspari in Italy, and Charles de Gaulle in France, who nurtured democracy after the collapse of very different forms of legitimacy. But they were assisted by the continuity of a disciplined civil service. Yeltsin and future Russian leaders are hampered not only by the absence of a professional civil service but also by a much wider disintegration of the state. More interesting are cases like Napoleon, who rebuilt monarchic institutions after the disintegration of the ancien régime's governing institutions and the failure of successive revolutionary experiments during the years from 1789 to 1799, or Augustus Caesar, who restored government that seemed legitimate after 146 years of civil wars, dictatorships, and proscriptions. In the history of Russia, leaders might want to look at the achievement of Mikhail Romanov and Patriarch Filaret in restoring the authority of government after the Time of Troubles. But the efforts of individual leaders were supported in most of these cases by wider reverence for monarchy or patriarchy, a reverence that modernity has worn thin. The collapse of communism was a rare historic event in its swiftness and in the thoroughness of the dissolution that followed.[6] The end of the communist state does not leave, as many people still argue, a normal state that is attempting to make a normal transition to democracy, but something closer to the challenge faced by God in creating order out of something that is "without form and void."

Collective Decision Making

Of course, the authority of the boss was not the only reality of the old system. There was "collegial" and "collective" decision making, which was much more important in the Soviet than in the U.S. system. In the Soviet system, all important decisions in the party hierarchy could formally derive only from a meeting of a group, like the Politburo, members of which had a nominally equal say in the outcome. Even in the institutions of the state hierarchy, usually less powerful, where the formal rule was *edinonachaliie* (one-man decision making), collective bodies such as the *collegia* of ministries played a role they do not play in the United States. Although this collective and collegial policymaking is becoming less prominent because of the disappearance of the party, it remains important. The Russian Security Council in its organization, procedures, and spirit is strongly reminiscent of the old Secretariat of the Central Committee and its apparatus. Like the Secretariat, the Security Council is a small group of select officials, holds meetings of a ritualistic or formal character, frequently does its real work through commissions, and has departments corresponding to the subjects it deals with.

Collegial and collective decision making had—and has—a wider influence on politics because it established a distinctive cycle of decision making with important ramifications for the entire system. In the communist system, decision making was a three-stage process. First, different views about policy were debated vigorously—albeit somewhat esoteri- cally, for people did not usually say directly that they disagreed. Second, unanimous agreement was reached in the Politburo. This was something that Western scholarship did not understand. Yegor Ligachev told me that as long as he was connected with the Politburo, attending its meetings first as a secretary and later as a member, there was never a split vote. That is due to the tradition of democratic centralism, or unity of the party against outsiders, which was much stronger even at the end of the Soviet system than Western scholars had understood. The third stage was the implementation of the policy that the Politburo had agreed on. Very often decisions were not obeyed.

This pattern evolved to some extent from the heritage of revolutionary politics, but also from the formality of collective decision making. The chairman of the meeting, usually the general secretary in the case of the Politburo, had enormous resources with which to obtain the outcome he wanted by various bureaucratic shenanigans: by postponing agenda items, by making decisions *oprosom* (by polling), by appointing commis- sions, by exerting the General Department's power over the paperwork or the Secretariat's power to frame issues for the Politburo, and so forth. However, this worked only as long as the general secretary could get temporary assent in principle for his formula from the important members of the Politburo, who often represented important factions or interests.[7] This cycle had two important consequences that are very powerful today in determining what decision making can and cannot achieve. It tended to create a pattern of shifting back and forth, often abruptly, between left and right. That is a very characteristic Soviet pattern. Stalin, for example, had occupied, with Bukharin, the "right" position against Trotsky, but suddenly turned in the late 1920s to the radical "left" policies of rapid industrialization and forced collectivization. In 1956, Nikita Khrushchev abruptly shifted from a Stalinist policy 10 days before the Twentieth Congress to the de-Stalinizing policy (advocated earlier by Mikoyan against him) for which he became famous. This cyclical pattern probably derives from the practice of collective decision making in the Politburo, where it was very important to get a temporary consensus at the meeting that could then be taken further. The leader conciliated people with whom ultimately he did not intend to work or wanted to destroy. This shifting between extremes does not work in democracies. If Senator Jesse Helms suddenly came out for gay rights in the military, he would lose his old constituency without gaining any new constituency. Democratic

politics enforces relatively consistent policy positions because politicians must appeal to constituencies, that is, relatively stable groups of
voters with continuing policy preferences, groups often rooted in class,
sex, or ethnicity.

There is a trend here, as Russia becomes more democratic, that tends
to eat up political leaders. It destroyed Gorbachev. When Gorbachev moved
to the right in 1990, he did not acquire any real friends on the "right," as
we saw in the coup, but he lost his old friends on the "left." Yeltsin has
been doing the same thing, although not to the same extent as Gorbachev.
Yeltsin's movement to the right in 1992 was part of that pattern, and that
damaged him. By bringing in more conservative figures such as Viktor
Chernomyrdin and Yurii Skokov, Yeltsin did not gain supporters as loyal
as the departed Yegor Gaidar; Skokov had to be dismissed after the 1993
referendum, and Chernomyrdin's attitude during crises fluctuated.
Neither did Yeltsin gain conservative support in the Supreme Soviet,
which became increasingly intransigent in its opposition until Yeltsin
decreed its dissolution in September 1993. Yeltsin comes out of the same
experience of communist policymaking as Gorbachev, and that experience did not prepare him well for the conditions of democratic politics.

The Character of Law

Collective decision making after the fashion just described has been
important in establishing the peculiar character of laws and rules in
Russia. Because the most authoritative decisions were those of the Politburo, and because there had to be total agreement in the Politburo,
decisions tended to be vague and to paper over continuing differences.
Prime Minister Chernomyrdin's very temporary decree on price controls
is typical of a Soviet decree or law. The decree was announced in early
January 1993 as having been in force—unbeknown to Russian citizens
or officials—from January 1, but no text was made available. The provisions were gradually revealed, and shortly thereafter the whole policy was
abandoned. More familiar to Western entrepreneurs in Russia is the
difficulty in knowing what law applies to their business or which signed
agreements will actually be binding.

A Soviet law tended to be not a law as American lawyers would
understand it, but an authoritative concept or idea whose content and
application were to be decided later. Many Soviet laws and decrees of the
Central Committee, which were more authoritative than laws, stated
vaguely that the government would "give emphasis to" something. Soviet

laws were not precise, and the line between law and arbitrary administrative orders was blurred. Even in criminal cases there was "telephone law," a standard phrase meaning that the local party boss called up the judge and told him what to decide. That is the opposite of the kind of law that private business wants. Western law was structured by the emergence of private business that wanted a very precise kind of law so that the businessman would know what he could do, what he could not do, and above all, what contracts could be enforced.

Beyond the relationship of law to private property and the market lies a philosophical background. Thinkers such as Hobbes, Locke, Rousseau, and Kant, who were influential in the formation of Western institutions, sought to strengthen the role of law in order to establish neutral ground rules for politics that would limit political conflict, make possible undivided loyalty to the community, and preserve individual freedom within a community. The enormous importance of law, lawyers, litigation, the Constitution, and the Supreme Court in U.S. life derives from this intentional and highly specific project. It is hardly surprising that the nature and role of law in two systems with such different histories as the Russian and the American are very different.

As in many other areas, the academic field of Soviet studies did not adequately inform the West of the differences between the two systems. Many scholars wrote about Soviet law, noting differences from Western practice, but only a few did justice to the most important point: law was far weaker in the Soviet system. Only since the collapse of communism in 1991, as Westerners have tried to "work" the Russian government at all its levels and we have observed the "war of laws" and other aspects of the disintegration of the state, are we beginning to understand the full impact of the differences regarding the role of law. Perhaps there is some connection between the current disintegration of the state and the weakness of law in the communist system.

Shapelessness

The weakness of law in the Soviet system was closely linked to another trait of Soviet policymaking. The Soviet Union was even further away than the United States from Weberian bureaucracy, with its "fixed jurisdictional areas." Immersion in reports about Soviet bureaucratic life brings an awareness that Soviet administration was pervaded by "shapelessness." I use this term, which I owe to Seweryn Bialer,[8] to mean here the division of one task among several persons or agencies without clearly defined responsibilities, and the opposite—one official who does two or more unrelated tasks. Shapelessness of this kind was a pervasive characteristic of Soviet administration, from top to bottom. Now that Russia is taking the path of the market, it is worth noting that such "shapelessness" can exist also in private business.

The biggest manifestation of shapelessness in the Soviet system, and perhaps its most important source, was the split in administration between parallel state and party hierarchies in most areas of the public business, except the military and the security police. In almost every part of government there were both ministries and Central Committee departments. With Gorbachev's isolation of the party structures from state administration, and then the destruction of the Communist Party in 1991, this massive manifestation of shapelessness disappeared. In foreign policy, the International Department of the Central Committee was quite important at various periods. The disappearance of this department has simplified foreign policymaking.

Be this as it may, we have seen, in the context of the disintegration of the old state, both the president and the parliament trying to control foreign policy. This duality, exacerbated by the practice of ruling by decree, brought back some of the shapelessness that began to disappear with the disappearance of the party. The president now has a much larger "apparatus" or staff of his own than the general secretary had. The various institutions attached to Yeltsin are a potent source of shapelessness; their functions frequently overlap with those of the ministries or with one another.

Overall, shapelessness is a distinctive feature of the old system that has actually increased in salience since the demise of the USSR, as old organizations lose power and authority without being abolished, while new organizations are established to serve the objectives of reform or the ambitions of particular leaders. For example, Peter Stavrakis has written about the disorder in foreign economic relations, where the Foreign Ministry shares responsibility with the Ministry of Foreign Economic Relations and the newly created Russian Agency for International Cooperation and Development, set up by Aleksandr Shokhin, and the State Investment Corporation, headed by Yeltsin's former chief of staff, Yurii Petrov. As Stavrakis perceptively notes, "There are no legal or political guarantees that can prevent the outbreak of turf conflict between these three giant bureaucracies . . . there is clearly no mechanism for inter-ministerial coordination."[9]

This shapelessness is enhanced by the activity across sovereign borders of these foreign policy and foreign trade organizations and of the economic ministries. In the Soviet Union, although the party organizations in the Union republics had a high degree of independence on some issues, the most important parts of the economy were more directly supervised by state hierarchies culminating in the Moscow economic ministries. When the USSR fell apart, these ministries suddenly become important agencies of foreign economic policy; today, there is little coordination anywhere.

Although shapelessness was frequently identified (under other names) as one of the bad features of the old system during the years of perestroika and is perceived as not being "modern," it is still seen as desirable by some officials. Yeltsin's advisor Sergei Shakhrai remarked that "Sometimes even duplication of functions is advisable: the most dynamic and competent institution will survive in the competitive struggle."[10] This is a perceptive observation. Shapelessness brings with it a heavy price in terms of efficient rule and the transition to market relations, but it remains useful to officials to have multiple chains of command and multiple reporting channels from lower officials.

Personal Connections

The difference between the power of law and the official division of labor in the West and what obtained in the Soviet system is a reflection of a more general difference. In Western "decision making," decisions tend to affect broad categories of people. Thus, for example, President Clinton's economic program has spurred a new hunt for tax breaks and subsidies that would benefit certain categories of citizens or businesses. This phenomenon shows, in spite of the many ways one can still get real privileges and exemptions as an individual, the genuine power of law in our society. In the West, citizens tend to seek rules that benefit them as members of a category. Therefore, interest groups and political constituencies develop and become powerful.

In the Soviet system, by contrast, the members of the population tended to seek specific favors for themselves as individuals, for their friends or relatives, or for other members of their ethnic group from specific individuals given by the system power over privileges. This is the most fundamental fact accounting for the importance of *sviazy* (connections) and their more developed form, "family circles" and patron-client relationships, in the Soviet system. Accordingly, in Soviet "decision making," more decisions were made about individual people, as becomes

clear if one compares U.S. personnel systems with the Soviet nomenklatura system. More decisions were also made about technical matters. The
Smolensk archive, for example, shows that the first secretary of a large
province, the master of more than a million people, made tens of
thousands of decisions about specific personal requests (requests for
clemency, for example).[11]

The importance of personal connections is probably now greater than
ever in Russia because of the disintegration of the state and planned
economy. It is difficult to get anything done by one's subordinates in
government without using personal relationships, and it is hard to obtain
the necessities of life without personal connections. Eventually, privatization, the market, and possibly voting will work to break down this
state of affairs. The result will be more policymaking by categories and
more citizen action by categories, that is, by interest groups and constituencies. For now, *sviazy,* family circles, and patron-client networks (often
called "mafias") are more dominant than ever before. Yeltsin's Sverdlosk
crowd and the *Afghantsi* (veterans of the Afghan war) in the army are
current examples.

A number of things are worth saying about these personal connections.
They are not to be disdained, as Russian public opinion now does even
while using them. The use of personal connections is regarded as old-
fashioned; Russians, including academics, tend to overrate the "rational-
legal" character of Western government and the extent to which Western
government functions without personal connections. In fact, personal
connections are an important tool of government in the West. When
much of the modern state is breaking down, they are a necessary way of
coordinating the actions of government. Nevertheless, personal connections do operate more powerfully and more successfully in the less
modern sectors of Russian government. They are much more powerful in
provincial government than in Moscow. Thus, the tradition of relying on
personal connections, and the necessity for doing so at the present
moment, is one of the powerful forces strengthening the Russian provinces as against the center.

In these conditions, the disintegration of the formally unified Soviet
Union has a special impact. There were many personal ties between Russian
officials now working in the Russian republic and those of other republics.
To cite one example, Oleg Soskovets, appointed first deputy chairman of
the Russian Council of Ministers in May 1993, had served recently in the
Kazakh government as director of the Karaganda Metallurgical Combine

and as deputy prime minister of (independent) Kazakhstan.[12] The disintegration of the Soviet Union has converted these into powerful nongovernmental ties between subordinate Russian officials and the governments of the now independent republics—ties that could be used to make policy across republican borders in partial independence of these republics' legal heads of state. It is rumored that the fact that Vladislav Ardzinba, the president of the Abkhaz Autonomous Republic in Georgia, attended the Institute of Oriental Studies with Evgenii Primakov, the head of Russia's foreign intelligence service, may explain the commitment of certain Russian military units on the Abkhaz side in the war that has raged there. Personal connections enormously complicate Russian foreign policy toward the other ex-Soviet republics.

The Legacy of the Past

Seventy years ago, the Russian Empire became the site of a vast utopian project of human transformation. Part of that project was effacing the legacy of the past to a degree never before attempted in human history. It was expected that nationalism would be replaced by internationalism, the various religions by atheism, private-property mentality by full devotion to the collective, bureaucracy by some other mode of administration. This project failed. But because the attempt to efface the past was so radical, because it involved coercion, censorship, and the definition of culture by the central government, the legacy of the past was driven underground. It was ever present but could not be acknowledged. For example, it was never admitted that "nationalism" existed in the USSR, only that "bourgeois nationalism"—in other words, a characteristic of the past, by definition vanishing—existed. With so much underground that was unconnected to the new structure being built and even corrosive to it, the vast new project was like something built on quicksand and without foundations. In 1991, it tumbled to the ground, and another attempt to efface the legacy of the past began. Nevertheless, the legacy of the past, including characteristically Soviet patterns of policymaking, continues to operate, as I have argued above, albeit largely unacknowledged.

A number of factors converge to drive the Soviet legacy, at least in government, underground: the estrangement of the Russian people from the old system and their orientation toward private life; the desire of the elites to hide their past roles; and the political taboo against "neo-Bolshevism," that is, any habits or practices reminiscent of the communist past. Thus, there is an odd symmetry between the communist and the postcommunist experiences in their relationship to the legacy of the past. Perhaps there is a similar danger: that the unacknowledged presence of the past beneath the foundations of what is being built will undermine it. To avoid this danger, the Russian future must involve coming to terms with the past (including the Soviet mode of policymaking)—separating the elements of the past that should be seen as shameful from those that are simply obsolete and those that are still suitable as means to a very different aim.

Notes

1. The most complete description of this operational code remains Nathan Leites, *A Study of Bolshevism* (Glencoe, Ill.: Free Press, 1953).

2. The classic description of this element in Soviet foreign policy is Arnold L. Horelick and Myron Rush, *Strategic Power and Soviet Foreign Policy* (Chicago: University of Chicago Press, 1966).

3. See Daniel Williams, "Russia Asserts Role in Ex-Soviet Republics," *The Washington Post*, September 29, 1993, p. A25.

4. Baron Charles de Montesquieu, *Considérations sur les causes de la grandeur des Romains et de leur décadence,* in *Oeuvres complètes*, vol. II, ed. Roger Callois (Paris: Gallimard, Bibliothèque de la Pléiade, 1951), p. 84.

5. See the special issue of the *National Interest* (no. 31, Spring 1993) on the collapse of communism.

6. For the disintegration of the state in the aftermath of communism, see Charles H. Fairbanks, Jr., "After the Moscow Coup," *The Journal of Democracy* 2, no. 4 (Autumn 1991), and Peter Reddaway's articles in *The New York Review of Books* since then.

7. These generalizations on Politburo decision making are drawn from a study now in progress as part of the author's work on Soviet bureaucracy.

8. On shapelessness see Seweryn Bialer, *Stalin's Successors: Leadership, Stability, and Change in the Soviet Union* (Cambridge: Cambridge University Press, 1980), pp. 10, 16ff, 118–119; and Charles H. Fairbanks, Jr., "Jurisdictional Conflict and Coordination in Soviet and American Bureaucracy," *Studies in Comparative Communism* 21, no. 2 (Summer 1988), pp. 153–174.

9. Peter J. Stavrakis, "Government Bureaucracies: Transition or Disintegration," *RFE/RL Research Reports* 2, no. 20 (May 1993), p. 31.

10. Interview with Sergei Shakhrai, "The State-Legal Administration, What It Is," *Izvestiia*, February 7, 1992, p. 2.

11. See Charles H. Fairbanks, Jr., and Susan A. Thornton, "Soviet Decision Making and Bureaucratic Representation: Evidence from the Smolensk Archive and an American Comparison," *Soviet Studies* 42, no. 4 (1990), pp. 639–640.

12. Valery Konovalov, "Oleg Soskovets . . . ," *Izvestiia*, May 13, 1993.

4

Institutional Mechanisms of Russian Foreign Policy

Mikhail E. Bezrukov

G reat uncertainty surrounds the future course of the Russian Federation's foreign policy. What will be the shape of relations between Russia and other nations, and to what degree will those relations determine Russia's future? Will Russia secure foreign support for its economic reforms? To what extent can Russia's diplomacy ease the shocks of the current transitional period? How successful can the Russian Federation be in protecting its interests during these hard times? Answers to these difficult questions will be significantly influenced by the institutional mechanisms that Russia employs to pursue its foreign policy.

Although the birth of the new Russian federal foreign policy mechanism might seem to have been especially painful and arduous, in many ways it has actually been a success story. In a very short period, the Russian Federation has done what normally takes years to accomplish. The vacuum left by the collapse of the Soviet Union has been filled more or less satisfactorily. While Russian foreign policy structures remain very fragile, they are already strong enough to function.

The Russian Federation's foreign policy mechanism copes with a necessary minimum of critically important tasks, and there is no reason, at least as of now, to think that it might fail to do this in the future. Further shaping of governmental structures in the Russian Federation will, one may assume, considerably improve the efficiency of its foreign policy mechanism.

Still, this mechanism suffers from serious deficiencies. What is even more discouraging is that the weak components of Russian foreign policy structures show signs of a serious malady that it will take time to cure—and probably much more time than many experts think. It looks like the West will have to accept the fact that for some time it will have to deal with an inefficient and very contradictory Russian foreign policy structure. Foreign policies usually reflect what is happening inside countries. It would be unreasonable to expect the deep crisis and chaotic developments inside the Russian Federation (let alone Russia's historic legacy) not to influence the republic's foreign policy instruments.

Difficulties Facing the Foreign Ministry

The Russian Federation's Foreign Ministry is the central, and the most visible, component of Russia's foreign policy mechanism. The period since the collapse of the Soviet Union has been difficult and demoralizing for the ministry, which was suddenly transformed from the Soviet Ministry of Foreign Affairs into the Russian Federation Ministry of Foreign Affairs. The Soviet Foreign Ministry was one of the most conservative of Soviet agencies, following procedures and practices established over the course of many decades. For the Soviet Foreign Ministry, the collapse of the Soviet Union heralded not only dramatic changes in the ruling elite of the country, but also the destruction of its very foundations.

In a relatively short period, many top figures in the ministry lost their positions. In terms of the scale of changes in personnel, the ministry had not experienced anything comparable since Stalin's notorious purges in the 1930s. Meanwhile, careers were made almost overnight not only in the ministry itself but also in embassies and other offices abroad. More and more people with biographies and professional credentials that did not correspond to the ministry's traditional preferences started to pour into the diplomatic service, continuing a process that had begun during the rule of Mikhail Gorbachev.

In the Soviet period, a well-developed infrastructure—which included the Moscow State Institute of International Relations and various academic think tanks—provided the foreign policy community with a steady supply of new, qualified people. Today, this inflow of expertise is becoming very meager. Furthermore, the foreign policy community has lost much of its previous attractiveness. Current salaries are hardly tempting for potential entrants to the ministry, especially if they measure those salaries against far more lucrative opportunities in private business. Experts from think tanks, whose salaries are fantastically small, are probably in the worst position; they look more and more like an endangered species. In addition, the ministry is no longer one of the few windows to the outside world, and those who want to work and travel abroad now have many other career opportunities. As the prestige and benefits associated with working in the ministry have declined, its employees have become much more receptive to offers from other offices and companies; it is not by accident that increasing numbers of highly qualified employees of the ministry have moved to the private sector, mostly to all sorts of joint ventures with Western companies.

The rules of the game have changed not only inside the ministry but also in its external relations with other governmental agencies. In fact, trying to determine its place among other Russian Federation governmental structures is no easy task for the ministry.

Troubles start with the fact that President Boris Yeltsin pays no special interest to the work of the ministry. Strange as it may sound, foreign policy issues today are not at the center of the attention of Russian Federation leaders. In the Soviet period, foreign policy considerations took precedence over all others. Now, domestic matters dominate the attention of the Kremlin, and whatever the Russian Federation's leaders do abroad, they constantly measure it against the Russian domestic political context.

Moreover, foreign policy is often formulated and implemented without the participation of the Foreign Ministry. The activities of governmental economic teams, which have as their operational base various ministries, committees, and commissions, often exceed a narrow definition of economics and have far-reaching foreign policy implications. Consequently, the economic realm now constantly encroaches into the domain that Russian professional diplomats have traditionally regarded as their own.

Although relations with other former Soviet republics ("the Near Abroad"), especially their purely political aspects, clearly fall within the purview of the Russian Federation's Foreign Ministry, an enormous part of the business of managing those relations passes through other governmental agencies. Bypassing the Russian Foreign Ministry is simply a continuation of a previous practice, one that not only creates bureaucratic tensions but also slows down the development of appropriate internal structures for the foreign minister.

An integrated approach by the Russian Federation leadership to different policy issues remains, thus far, only a dream. Reality is different: the Russian Federation leadership acts rather like a fire brigade, rushing from one conflagration to another.

In fairness, however, it should be said that the Russian Federation government can hardly be expected to pour substantial financial resources into the foreign policy community. In the midst of a deep economic crisis, the government has other, more immediate concerns. The foreign policy community must, therefore, seek out opportunities to limit the damage it is currently sustaining. One such opportunity lies in mobilizing the potential of the private sector. Nonprofit institutions such as foundations and research centers are rapidly increasing in number. In many instances, the projects they work on are of interest both to their private donors and the foreign policy community. Unfortunately, legislation has not been sufficiently supportive of nonprofit organizations. Too huge a share of the money allocated for these projects disappears into the pocket of the government, never reaching the researchers. Incentives for private business to donate to nonprofit organizations are likewise inadequate.

Competing Institutions in the Foreign Policy Domain

The problems facing the Foreign Ministry are compounded by the existence of a number of other institutions and bodies that compete with the ministry for control of the shape and direction of Russian foreign policy. Three entities have posed the greatest challenge to the ministry's authority: the parliament's Foreign Affairs Committee, the Security Council, and the Presidential Council.

The Foreign Affairs Committee

The Committee on Foreign Affairs and Foreign Economic Relations of the Supreme Soviet of the Russian Federation (1990–93) became an active foreign policy player even earlier than the Russian Federation Foreign Ministry. After the parliamentary elections of 1990, which signaled the dawn of a post-totalitarian Russia, the Foreign Affairs Committee turned into the main foreign policy advisor to the then-chairman of parliament, Boris Yeltsin. In this capacity, Yeltsin participated directly in the revival of the Russian Federation Ministry of Foreign Affairs.

During the confrontation between the leader of the Russian Federation and the Gorbachev team, the Foreign Affairs Committee and the Ministry of Foreign Affairs were close allies, their relations characterized by a high degree of mutual trust and team spirit. This relationship started to change soon after the collapse of the Soviet Union, when, with the disappearance of their common enemy, differences in the approaches and interests of the ministry and the committee began to surface.

Initially, this conflict was marked by rivalry for the attention of President Yeltsin, with the committee and the ministry both striving to become the president's main partner in shaping the foreign policy of the republic. With time, however, this rivalry turned into clashes over basic issues of foreign policy.

Conflicts between the committee and the ministry are often misinterpreted because their disagreements overlap with the "holy war" between parliament and president. In this war, black-and-white perceptions and interpretations often take the place of more realistic assessments. When applied to the sphere of international relations, these starkly contrasting views create the illusion that only two types of foreign policy are possible for the Russian Federation: either a negative, "traditionalist" one (neocommunist, imperialist, and nomenklatura-driven); or a positive, "reformist" one (democratic, liberal, and pro-Western).

If one looks at the conflicts between the committee and the ministry without preconceptions, it is impossible to overlook the fact that the committee has never been a center of opposition to Yeltsin or a stronghold of communist nomenklatura. This fact, in and of itself, should make people more cautious about using simplistic labels to describe tensions between the ministry and the committee. To see, as some do, a traditionalist behind every criticism of the ministry voiced by the committee is an oversimplification of their relations. It amounts to a refusal to participate in a realistic discussion of foreign policy matters. It is an attempt to say that the ministry has a monopoly on truth and that everything it does is always perfect. Such an uncritical approach challenges common sense, especially given the fact that mistakes, miscalculations, and overly reactive behavior by the ministry are hardly a secret.

Frequent verbal attacks on Foreign Minister Andrei Kozyrev have helped him to earn the reputation in the West of a liberal, pro-Western politician who is under permanent attack from Russian traditionalists of all sorts. But such a reputation is no guarantee that Kozyrev always adopts the wisest position or pilots the truest course. To be a successful minister of foreign affairs in Russia one has to be something more than a liberal, pro-Western political figure. Kozyrev, it should be noted, is not always criticized from ideological positions. Discontent is often expressed with the results of the actions or inaction of Russian diplomats.

Inevitably, the role of vigilant guard and merciless critic that the Foreign Affairs Committee assumes greatly complicates the life of the Ministry of Foreign Affairs. The latter has to keep a wary eye on legislators, whose criticisms of Russian diplomats can be emotionally charged and highly intemperate. Indeed, the conflict between the ministry and the committee is frequently on the verge of transgressing the boundaries of civilized public debate. The alternative to the control exercised by legislators may, however, be even worse. The absence of such control would provide the executive branch with additional opportunities to make mistakes, some of which might have very grave consequences. Furthermore, without clashes of ideas, it would be impossible for Russia to choose a line of behavior in the world that will enjoy stable support inside the Russian Federation. It is precisely the aggressive behavior of the committee that has made the discussion of foreign policy a real one. This very aggressiveness helps to define the parameters of the possible and the impossible in the sphere of foreign policy. And without clarity here, no efficient diplomacy can emerge.

In its work, the committee relies on a group of experts that overlaps with, but is not identical to, the one used by the ministry. This has substantially enlarged the circle of participants in foreign policy discussions and may be regarded as a guarantee that the country will never return to the situation when its foreign policy was shaped by a tiny circle of initiated "wizards."

The Security Council

Chartered to deal with issues of foreign and domestic policies bearing on security, sovereignty, and strategic stability, the Security Council of the Russian Federation was created in June 1992, with Yeltsin as its chairman and Yurii Skokov as its secretary. The principal task of the Security Council, at least according to its original design, is to coordinate activities of governmental bodies in the interests of national security. At the same time, this mechanism can also be used to exercise control over the main governmental agencies.

The Security Council consists of interagency commissions and departments. The "internal nucleus" of the Security Council is made up of its five permanent members: the president, the vice-president, the first deputy chairman of the Supreme Soviet, the prime minister, and the secretary of the Security Council. The Ministries of Economics, Finance, Foreign Relations, Justice, Defense, Security, Internal Affairs, and some other governmental agencies also participate in activities of the Security Council when security issues are connected with areas of their ministerial responsibility.

In December 1992, the Interagency Foreign Policy Commission of the Security Council of the Russian Federation was established by presidential decree to exercise control over the Ministry of Foreign Affairs. Before that, this role belonged to Gennadii Burbulis, former state secretary and éminence grise of the executive branch. According to its regulations, the commission is a "functional body of the Security Council." Its tasks comprise "preparation of projects and decisions for the President concerning principal direction of foreign policy in the sphere of ensuring national security." Members of the commission include, among others, the ministers of foreign affairs, interior, defense, security, justice, and external economic relations.

In spring 1993, "The Key Tenets of the Concept of Foreign Policy of the Russian Federation" became the first official foreign policy document to be developed in accordance with the new decision-making mechanism. This document was approved by the Interagency Foreign Policy Commission and confirmed by a session of the Security Council.

It is difficult at this stage to determine how efficient this commission will be. Quite possibly, however, its creation reflects political rather than administrative needs, with its principal mission being to strengthen the powers of President Yeltsin in the foreign policy domain. It is interesting to note that the first version of the document creating this commission was prepared by Burbulis as early as February 1992 (his version spoke about a General Department on Foreign Policy). Ideas formulated in the Burbulis version were incorporated directly into the Interagency Commission regulations.

The Security Council was designed by Yurii Skokov to become a structure with very wide powers. During his work in the Security Council, Skokov was in charge of overseeing the activities of military forces, national security staffs, counter-intelligence, and foreign intelligence. He was also engaged in foreign policy strategic planning. An experienced bureaucrat, he served as first deputy chairman of the Council of Ministers of the Russian Federation in 1990–91, and he stressed the importance of procedures within the system of governmental agencies.

Not without reason, many critics accused Skokov of attempting to create a shadow government. Skokov used his position as secretary of both the Security Council and the Council of Heads of Republics of the

Russian Federation to enlarge and strengthen his influence within governmental structures. In pursuing this goal, he could rely on his personal connections within the Soviet military-industrial complex, out of which he had emerged. The Skokov experience may be exactly what prompts some members of the Yeltsin team to oppose giving wide responsibilities to the secretary of the Security Council. For example, First Deputy Prime Minister Vladimir Shumeiko has insisted that the secretary of the Security Council should be a "purely technical" bureaucrat, a kind of a supreme registering clerk with no personal political base.

Yeltsin's naming of Marshal Evgenii Shaposhnikov—who earlier was commander-in-chief of the CIS Joint Chiefs of Staff—to replace Skokov in May 1993 suggests that the president opted for a middle course between the overly powerful Skokov and the kind of bureaucrat recommended by Shumeiko. Primarily a professional soldier, Shaposhnikov is considerably less of a politician than Skokov.

Shaposhnikov's successor, Oleg Lobov, like Skokov, has close ties to the military-industrial complex. Though he is a longtime friend of Yeltsin's from Sverdlovsk and can be expected on occasion to have the ear of the president, he is often at odds with reformist ideas. Lobov can be expected to emphasize the preferences of the military-industrial community during his tenure as secretary of the Security Council.

As the U.S. experience with its National Security Council shows, the way in which structures like the Security Council work depends partly on the aims and preferences of the person in charge of the executive branch, and partly on the style and degree of influence of the head of the council.

In the Russian case, the Security Council may well lose its raison d'être if, for example, a redistribution of powers within the executive branch elevates the prime minister to the position of a key player. Under this scenario, the coordinating-controlling body within the system of agencies would be subordinated to the prime minister.

The Presidential Council

On February 23, 1993, Yeltsin signed a decree on improvements in the structures supporting the activities of the president. In accordance with the decree, the Presidential Council was established as a consultative body.

The Presidential Council is charged with preparing proposals on strategies for foreign and domestic policies and determining mechanisms to implement strategies of national development. The council is expected to help the president in his dialogue with different political parties, public unions, and organizations. The president appoints all the members of the council, sessions of which take place at least once a month under the chairmanship of the president.

A body comparable to the Presidential Council existed earlier under the name of the Presidential Consultative Council. The Presidential Consultative Council met from time to time, usually on the eve of important political events, to analyze the current situation. Although this council exercised little real power or influence, membership in it reflected high standing within the Russian Federation's political elite.

The Need for Presidential Involvement

In the Soviet period, the Foreign Ministry was part of a system of agencies run by the Central Committee of the Communist Party. From an organizational point of view, this cumbersome system had many deficiencies. Nevertheless, it did have the benefit of established procedures, which are of course indispensable to bureaucratic organizations.

When the Soviet "center" started to fall apart, the Yeltsin team took over various key elements of the Soviet decision-making channels. Among others, it "appropriated" Soviet staffs responsible for the dissemination of information and control over the implementation of decisions. In many cases, these departments and sections—with almost all of their personnel—were simply attached to the Department of Administration of the President of the Russian Federation, headed by Sergei Filatov. This bureaucratic reshuffle can hardly be called very successful. Stories about the inefficiency of the office multiplied. Some cases were so outrageous that they inspired rumors about "communist plotters" operating within the Department of Administration. It is difficult to say to what extent the political and ideological inclinations of departmental personnel play a role, but it is apparent that the bureaucratic apparatus does not function properly.

Although 1992 saw some stabilization of the federation system for disseminating foreign policy information and controlling the implementation of decisions, the chaotic state of affairs that followed the collapse of the Soviet Union is still far from over.

As noted above, the Russian foreign policy mechanism will need time to become efficient, even under the most favorable conditions. Shortcomings in the mechanism will persist for a significant period and will considerably limit what is possible and attainable.

The main flaws in the Russian Federation's foreign policy mechanism are Yeltsin's vague interest in the foreign policy domain and a certain passivity on his part in determining foreign policy. One way to strengthen the position of the ministry is for Yeltsin to become more involved in foreign policy matters. It is extremely difficult for the foreign minister to operate effectively without the consistent support of the president, especially because Kozyrev has many powerful enemies and an unreliable political base in Moscow. The foreign policy mechanism needs a leader of unquestionable authority. Without such a leader, the foreign policy community will remain amorphous, and the distribution of functions among the foreign policy players will continue to be uncertain.

The president is the most logical candidate to play the role of this leader. Until now, however, Yeltsin has not demonstrated a readiness to direct foreign policy. He has addressed the area only occasionally, concentrating his efforts mainly on domestic issues. This may partly explain why foreign policy behavior is so often impulsive and erratic.

The president's reluctance to involve himself in foreign policy matters is perhaps understandable. Yeltsin tried to play a role in establishing direct relations between the Russian Federation and leading countries of the world before the collapse of the Soviet Union, at a time when the federation's leadership was still competing with the Gorbachev team. The final outcome of these efforts by Russia's leaders is well known: an independent Russia, emerging from the ruins of the Soviet empire, received recognition from other nations. As Russian president, Yeltsin has joined the ranks of world leaders, taking the place previously occupied by Gorbachev. In this story, however, only the end has been a happy one for Yeltsin. From the very beginning, the president received at best a rather cold reception from Western leaders, who were openly siding with Yeltsin's chief adversary. The humiliation he experienced will not be soon forgotten by Yeltsin, especially because he thinks of himself not as an ordinary political figure, but rather as the embodiment of the will of the citizens of the Russian Federation, a country with centuries of history behind it. Tensions between the president and Western leaders started to disappear only during the Moscow coup of August 1991. Reaching out to Yeltsin in the name of defending the legitimate Soviet leader— Gorbachev—Western leaders made an important step toward establishing workable relations with the federation, at the same time protecting themselves against possible accusations of double dealing or the betrayal of previous sympathies.

Subsequently, foreign policy issues have occupied a subordinate place on the president's agenda. Among the many reasons for this, the main one is, of course, the existence of a deep economic crisis and growing political tensions within the Russian Federation. However, two other important factors have helped to divert Yeltsin's attention away from foreign policy.

First, the Russian Federation's leadership underestimated the fact that relations with other former Soviet republics required a qualitatively new approach and, all ties inherited from the Soviet period notwithstanding, relations with these republics should develop like relations with other countries of the world. Moscow has tried, and still tries, to solve problems in its relations with other former Soviet republics "in a family manner," as if the Soviet Union had not disappeared from the political map of the world. Meanwhile, the nations of the Near Abroad have become the preeminent foreign policy issue for Russia, demanding the attention of diplomats and leaders alike. Since 1992, Russia has been drifting in its relations with other former Soviet republics, as if hoping that time alone will solve all problems.

Second, the euphoria that followed the failure of the August 1991 coup delayed recognition by the Yeltsin team of the fact that the elimination of the "protracted conflict" between communism and the free world does not mean that competition and egoistic interests have disappeared from relations between nations. Russia has met with not only friendly and cooperative attitudes from its powerful neighbors, but also pressure. Japan, for instance, applied pressure on the issue of the "Northern Territories," leading to the cancellation of an official visit by Yeltsin to Japan in the fall of 1992. In the summer of 1993, the United States opposed the sale of Russian missile engines to India. As in the case of the Near Abroad, it took Russian Federation leaders some time to appreciate the importance of devoting constant attention to the republic's relations with countries beyond the borders of the former Soviet Union. International issues cannot be addressed only on the eve of major political events, when impressive gestures and instant successes are expected.

Whether Yeltsin becomes a pillar of Russian foreign policy depends on the outcome of the battle for power between the president and the parliament. Clearly, a weak president cannot provide the foreign policy structure of the republic with clear goals, nor can he mobilize the support and resources needed to attain them.

PART II

The Near Abroad and Commonwealth of Independent States

5

Russians Outside Russia and Russian Security Policy

Elizabeth Teague

The Soviet Union was often described as the heir of the Russian Empire. One characteristic shared by both states was the widespread dispersal of ethnic Russians throughout their territories. An immediate consequence of the collapse of the USSR in December 1991 was, therefore, that 25.3 million ethnic Russians suddenly found themselves "abroad," that is, living in the territory of the former Soviet Union but outside the borders of the Russian Federation in one of the other 14 Soviet successor states. This essay examines the impact the "Russians abroad" have had or may come to have on the emerging foreign and security policies of the Russian Federation.

No state could ignore the presence of millions of its co-ethnics concentrated, as many of the Russians abroad are, just across its borders. The Russian government would be unable to provide enough housing and jobs if large numbers of ethnic Russians suddenly decided to return to Russia. If for no other reason, therefore, the Russian authorities have a legitimate interest in the fate of co-ethnics outside Russia's borders. Nonetheless, it sounds more a knee-jerk reaction learned during Russia's imperial past than a sober appraisal of present realities when today's Russian leaders assert that the Russian state has a duty to protect, if need be by force, the rights of Russians living outside its territory. Russia's leaders seem to be widely supported in this attitude by Russian public opinion. This suggests that Russian communities living outside Russia might come to wield an influence over the formation of Russian foreign and security policy second only to the influence of developments inside Russia itself.

Sizable numbers of Russians abroad live in compact settlements, many of them clustered on Russia's borders. Their large numbers notwithstanding, the Russians abroad are not a monolithic group. The largest single community lives in Ukraine, on Russia's western frontier, where many Russians have intermarried with Ukrainians; the next largest group is to be found hundreds of miles to the east, in Kazakhstan. Despite reports of Russian Cossacks going to the defense of fellow Russians as far afield as Moldova and Abkhazia, there is little to suggest that the majority of the ethnic Russians outside Russia identify closely with one another or feel that they share a common identity as Russians abroad; so far, they have shown no sign of joining forces in an effort to influence Moscow's policies. (They are not known, for example, to have formed a political party or any other kind of lobby to represent their interests.)

It is misleading, therefore, to speak of "the Russians abroad" as if they were a united force, capable of exerting concerted pressure on policymakers in Moscow. Doing so overestimates their present cohesion and political significance. Nonetheless, the evidence that imperial thinking continues to exercise some influence both in Russian government circles and over public opinion in general suggests that the issue of how Russian minorities are treated in the non-Russian successor states will for some time be a preferred weapon of Russian politicians eager either to attack the policies of their own government or to rally public support at home. If circumstances arise where the treatment of Russian minorities suggests that they are being discriminated against by non-Russian governments, Russian politicians will not be slow to sound the alarm.

An Identity Crisis

Before one can formulate a national security doctrine or a foreign policy one must, according to Andranik Migranian, have a subject (the state in question), borders around that state, and neighbors on those borders. Speaking in March 1993, Migranian, who is a member of Boris Yeltsin's Presidential Council, observed that Russia had none of these.[1]

To put Migranian's statement another way, the fundamental question facing the makers of Russian foreign policy today is an existential one—that of Russia's own national identity. How Russia defines itself geographically and politically will determine the kind of foreign and defense policy the country will pursue. The task of self-definition is not, however, an easy one.

The dissolution of the Soviet Union presented Russia with problems very different from those facing the other former Soviet republics. Russia has, throughout much of its history, been the center of an empire. Even the Russian Federation was an artificial creation established by the Bolsheviks as a means of legitimizing the continuation of the Russian Empire.[2] Its artificiality was reflected in the fact that the borders of the Russian Federation were not coextensive with the territory occupied by those considering themselves ethnic Russians: many Russians lived outside the federation while many non-Russians lived inside.

The collapse of the USSR in 1991 stripped Russia of much of its empire and thrust it behind borders that had neither historical precedent nor national logic. As Dominique Moisi puts it, traditionally expansionist Russia entered a period of contraction for the first time since the reign of Peter the Great. Moisi compares Russia's situation with that of the Ottoman Empire which, after failing to conquer Vienna in 1683, embarked on a protracted process of decay.[3] Russians fear their country may now have entered a similar decline. The borders of the Russian Federation are still not coterminous with the space occupied by ethnic Russians. The 25.3 million ethnic Russians who found themselves living abroad when the Soviet Union collapsed represented 18.5 percent of the 145,155,489 ethnic Russians who were living in the USSR in 1989, when the last all-Union census was taken.[4] At the same time, 27 million non-Russians live inside the Russian Federation and many of the Russian Federation's constituent republics and regions are demarcated in at least nominal conformity with non-Russian ethnic groups. As the demands of Russia's regions for economic autonomy grow increasingly vociferous, commentators are asking whether the multiethnic Russian Federation may soon, like the USSR before it, be torn apart by centrifugal forces.

This situation reflects a remarkable history of territorial expansion. "Russia's history is the history of a country colonizing itself," wrote the historian V. O. Kliuchevskii.[5] Russia was a land empire whose territorial expansion averaged 50 square miles a day over four centuries.[6] In the words of John Lloyd, "the Russians pushed out, further and further, the borders of the Russian empire in order to find more land, more resources with which to support a population which in the eighteenth and nineteenth centuries grew more rapidly than any other in Europe and whose poor soil, short growing season and low-productivity serf-labour dictated the need for ever greater acquisitions."[7] Ethnic Russians were accordingly

Table 1. Russians Outside Russia (Percentage of those of indigenous and of Russian nationality in the 15 constituent republics of the USSR, according to the censuses of 1959, 1979, and 1989.)

Union Republic	Indigenous Nationality			Russians		
	1959	1979	1989	1959	1979	1989
Armenia	88.0	89.7	93.3	3.2	2.3	1.6
Azerbaijan	67.5	78.1	82.7	13.6	7.9	5.6
Belarus	81.1	79.4	77.9	8.2	11.9	13.2
Estonia	74.6	64.7	61.5	20.1	27.9	30.3
Georgia	64.3	74.4	70.1	10.1	7.4	6.3
Kazakhstan	30.0	36.0	39.7	42.7	40.8	37.8
Kyrgyzstan	40.5	47.9	52.4	30.2	25.9	21.5
Latvia	62.0	53.7	52.0	26.6	32.8	34.0
Lithuania	79.3	80.1	79.6	8.5	8.9	9.4
Moldova	65.4	63.9	64.5	10.2	12.8	13.0
RSFSR	83.3	82.6	81.5	83.3	82.6	81.5
Tajikistan	53.1	58.8	62.3	13.3	10.4	7.6
Turkmenistan	60.9	68.4	72.0	17.3	12.6	9.5
Ukraine	76.8	73.5	72.7	16.9	21.1	22.1
Uzbekistan	62.1	68.7	71.4	13.5	10.8	8.3

Sources: Data from the 1959 and 1979 censuses are taken from *Sotsiologicheskie issle-dovaniia*, no. 4 (1982), pp. 27–43; 1989 census data are taken from the microfiche edition of the census published in 1992–93 by East View Publications, Minneapolis, and from a report on the 1989 census prepared by Ann Sheehy of the RFE/RL Research Institute, Munich, in June 1990.

found throughout the Russian Empire and, as table 1, demonstrates, throughout the USSR as well.

Russia's empire was contiguous with its heartland, not far away across an ocean like the British and French colonies, and the sudden loss of much of its former empire in 1991 presented a psychological challenge quite different from that which faced Britain or France. Finding a new role was not easy for these two countries but, in Moisi's words, "Even without an empire, France was still French and Britain still British." Russia's case was somewhat different. The majority of Russians identified with their impe-rial possessions to such an extent that they rarely thought of them as alien. The reason, Paul Goble asserts, was that Russia began to build its empire "long before the Russian people had consolidated as a nation." As a result, "the boundaries of both the people and the state were never clear. . . . Instead of a clearly defined metropole and colonies, they consisted of a nebulous center and a periphery."[8] When they went to live in Estonia or Kazakhstan, today's Russians abroad did not generally think of themselves as being abroad at all. As Soviet citizens they were encouraged to see themselves as people whose address, in the words of the popular song, was "not a house, and not a street [but] the Soviet Union."[9] One manifestation of this common attitude was the fact that the majority of ethnic Russians in most of the Soviet Union's non-Russian republics did not speak the language of the titular nationality. It is an indication of how difficult it is for many Russians to recognize the newly minted independence of states such as Belarus and Tajikistan, Georgia and Moldova that Russians have now come up with a special term to describe the other 14 states of the former USSR. Russians call them the "Near Abroad" (*blizhnee zarubezh'e*), a usage that became current early in 1992.

Where Are the Russians Abroad?

The 1989 population census, which was the last taken before the Soviet Union collapsed, showed that the majority (17.5 million) of the 25.3 million Russians living in the territory of the USSR but outside the borders of the Russian Federation were in either Ukraine or Kazakhstan.

Ukraine

Just under one-half of the Russians in the Near Abroad live in Ukraine. In 1989, they numbered 11.3 million (22.1 percent of Ukraine's total 1989 population of 51,471,000, of which Ukrainians constituted 72.7 percent). Ukraine's Russians are concentrated in the country's highly industrialized eastern and southern regions, close to the Russian border. Crimea is the only region of Ukraine in which Russians make up an absolute majority (67 percent in 1989), but significant Russian communities are to be found in the regions of Luhansk (where, in 1989, 44.8 percent of the population of the region were Russians); Donetsk (43.6 percent); Kharkiv (33.2 percent); Zaporizhzhya (32.0 percent); Odessa (27.4 percent); Dnipropetrovsk (24.2 percent); and in the Ukrainian capital, Kiev (20.9 percent).

Given Crimea's history (it was annexed from the Tatars and the Ottoman Empire by Catherine the Great of Russia in 1783 and transferred from the Russian Federation to Ukraine by Nikita Khrushchev as recently as 1954), and the heavy concentration of Russians who now live there, it is not surprising that the peninsula has already been the cause of sharp polemics between Russia and Ukraine. Nor is Crimea the only potential bone of contention between these two countries. However, Ukraine's leaders seem to have been at pains to keep ethnic relations within their multinational republic on an even keel. Along with the Central Asian states, Kazakhstan, Lithuania, and Russia, Ukraine guaranteed citizenship to all those who found themselves resident in the republic when the USSR disintegrated—a move applauded by Russia's government, which itself offered to bestow Russian citizenship on any citizen of the former Soviet Union who wanted it.

The refusal of certain other states with large Russian minorities to confer citizenship automatically is a source of considerable Russian resentment. Estonia, for example, adopted a law in 1992 that bestowed automatic citizenship only on those who had lived in the country prior to 1940 or their descendants, thus calling into question the status of some 600,000 ethnic Russians who moved to Estonia following the Soviet annexation of the country. Latvia adopted a citizenship law that is broadly similar to the Estonian one. The treatment of ethnic Russians in Latvia and Estonia is straining Russia's relations with both Baltic countries.

Kazakhstan

While in Ukraine one in five members of the population is Russian, in Kazakhstan the figure is two in five. Kazakhstan was settled by Russians and other ethnic groups under Stalin, who used the republic as a place of exile, and under Khrushchev and Brezhnev, who pursued an intense campaign to develop an agricultural base in the region. As a result, the 1989 census found 6.2 million Russians in Kazakhstan (37.8 percent of the population of 16,464,000). Together, Russians and Ukrainians made up 55 percent of the country's 1989 population, while Kazakhs were 39.7 percent of the population.[10]

Russians are concentrated in Kazakhstan's northern regions, and researchers from the Moscow-based USSR Institute of Geography warned in 1991 of the possibility that, in view of significant border adjustments made in the 1920s, ethnic and territorial disputes might occur in regions of Kazakhstan that border on Russia and have high Russian populations. The areas singled out by the Institute researchers were North Kazakhstan, Kokshetau, Aqmola (formerly Tselinograd), Qostanay, and East Kazakhstan regions; parts of Pavlodar and Semey regions; and the northern parts of West Kazakhstan (formerly Uralsk) and Aqtöbe regions.[11] Some parts of Kazakhstan have already seen disputes between Kazakh authorities and local Cossack communities. However, Kazakhstan's leaders seem, like Ukraine's, aware of the dangers of ethnic tension; Kazakhstan is, moreover, keen to keep its Slav population, because Russians and Ukrainians are the backbone of the republic's skilled industrial workforce.

Moldova

In 1989, only 64.5 percent of Moldova's 4,335,000 population were Moldovan, while 13.0 percent were Russians and 13.8 percent were Ukrainians. Taken together, Russians and Ukrainians made up over one-quarter of Moldova's population. About 25 percent of Moldova's ethnic Russians live in the Denser region—a narrow strip of land sandwiched between the River Dniester and the Ukrainian border, which is the only part of present-day Moldova that never belonged to Romania. Alarmed by proposals for Moldovan-Romanian unification and fearful that Moldova's language law would threaten their economic status by making them ineligible to hold certain jobs, the region's Russian-speaking population in 1990 proclaimed the independent "Dniester Republic." What began as a small-scale conflict between an ethnic Russian minority and the Moldovan authorities has since escalated out of control and caused widespread bloodshed and disruption.

Belarus

Numbering 1.3 million in 1989, Russians made up 13.2 percent of the country's overall population of 10,152,000, while Belarussians constituted 77.9 percent. Belarus' Russian minority is significant, but the fact that the borders between Belarus and Russia are not disputed removes one major potential cause of conflict between the two countries. According to researchers at the Institute of Geography, only three of the inter-republican borders between the Soviet republics are *not* contested, and Belarus is the only neighboring Soviet successor-state with which Russia has no border dispute.[12]

The Baltic States

Following the Soviet annexation of the three Baltic states during World War II, thousands of Balts were deported to Siberia and Russians settled in the homes thereby vacated. The Baltic nations, whose birthrates are low in any case, began to feel threatened with extinction. Lithuania was the best off in this regard: Lithuanians made up 79.6 percent of the population of 3,675,000 in 1989 and Russians constituted only 9.4 percent. In Latvia, however, the situation was very different. Russians and other non-Latvian minorities made up about 44 percent of the population of 2,667,000 in 1989—the highest percentage in the Baltic states. Latvians themselves in 1989 made up only 52.0 percent of the population of their country, while 34.0 percent were Russians, and the population of the Latvian capital, Riga, was close to 70 percent Russian. As for Estonia, 30.3 percent of the country's 1989 population of 1,464,000 were Russians, while 61.5 percent were Estonians.[13] Prior to Estonia's incorporation into the Soviet Union in 1940, Estonians had accounted for almost all the population; thereafter, massive immigration turned Russians into Estonia's largest ethnic minority. Moreover, Russians were heavily concentrated in the Estonian capital, Tallinn, and in heavily industrialized northeastern Estonia, where they formed a majority of the population. In Latvia and Estonia, Russians formed the majority of the workforce in the manufacturing sector, while the indigenous population was concentrated in agriculture and services. This was the result of Soviet-era industrial development based predominantly on imported labor.

As noted above, the Russian government welcomed Lithuania's decision to offer citizenship to all those who were resident in the republic when the USSR disintegrated. However, the adoption by Estonia and Latvia of more restrictive legislation provoked a sharp reaction from the Russian government, which accused the authorities in both countries of infringing the human rights of the Russians living on their territory. The charges were rejected by Latvian and Estonian officials, who argued that human rights should not be confused with civil rights. Human rights, said the Balts, include rights that are universal, such as those to life and free speech, whereas civil rights denote a range of rights, such as the right to vote or hold public office, that are conferred by citizenship in a specific state and are by definition not universal. Though investigators from the Council of Europe and the Conference on Security and Cooperation in Europe (CSCE) have declared that Estonia's and Latvia's citizenship legislation is in conformity with West European norms, the status of the Russian minorities has strained Russia's relations with the two Baltic countries.[14]

Central Asia

During the postwar period, many Russians were keen to move to the Baltic states, which, by virtue of their relatively high standards of living, were viewed as "the Soviet West." They seemed less enthusiastic about moving to Soviet Central Asia. Although Russians are to be found in each of the Central Asian republics, they are concentrated in the towns and in skilled industrial professions. Moreover, as table 1 shows, the share of Russians in the population has been dropping steadily over the past 30 years, partly because of higher birth rates among the indigenous peoples, but increasingly as a result of outmigration by Slavs. Although all the Central Asian states have adopted liberal citizenship laws, Russians have, it seems, been responding to an atmosphere in which they and other Slavs feel increasingly unwelcome. Russians are complaining of a sharp rise in ethnically inspired hostility shown to them by members of the indigenous population. The human rights group Helsinki Watch recorded "numerous attacks," including physical violence, made on ethnic grounds against Russians in Uzbekistan and Tajikistan in 1992.[15]

The population of Kyrgyzstan at the time of the 1989 census was 4,258,000, of whom 52.4 percent were Kyrgyz; 21.5 percent (917,000) were Russians; 12.9 percent were Uzbeks; 3 percent were Ukrainians; 2 percent were Germans; and 2 percent were Tatars. Even in Kyrgyzstan, considered to be the most liberal of the new states in the former Soviet Central Asia, Russians have complained about "more and more new laws discriminating against the non-Kyrgyz population." For example, legislation has been introduced that cuts back on the number of non-Kyrgyz accepted for higher education while increasing the numbers of ethnic Kyrgyz accepted.[16] The republic's parliament recently rejected calls from non-Kyrgyz residents for recognition of dual citizenship and for Russian to be designated the official language of interethnic communication in the republic.[17] As a result, Russians have begun to leave Kyrgyzstan in significant numbers. Between 1989 and 1992, 185,000 Russians were reported to have left the republic. Partly as a result of this, the Kyrgyz have increased their share of the population from a plurality to a majority in the past 30 years.[18]

The population of Turkmenistan at the time of the 1989 census was 3,523,000, of whom 72.0 percent were Turkmen; 9.5 percent (334,000) were Russians; 9.0 percent were Uzbeks; 2.5 percent were Kazakhs; and 1 percent were Ukrainians. Turkmenistan also saw considerable Russian outmigration in the 1980s; this has continued in the 1990s. (As a result, Ann Sheehy has argued, Uzbeks have probably replaced Russians as the second largest ethnic group in Turkmenistan since the 1989 census was taken.)[19]

The population of Uzbekistan at the time of the 1989 census was 19,905,156 people, of whom 71.4 percent were Uzbeks; 8.3 percent (1,653,000) were Russians; 5 percent were Tajiks; 4 percent were Kazakhs; 2 percent were Tatars; and 2 percent were Karakalpaks. Between 1985 and 1992, however, 800,000 Slavs—mostly Russians—are said to have left the republic.

The population of Tajikistan at the time of the 1989 census numbered 5,093,000, of whom 62.3 percent were Tajiks; 23.5 percent were Uzbeks; 7.6 percent (388,000) were Russians; 1 percent were Tatars; 1 percent were Kyrgyz; and 1 percent were Ukrainians. Again, outmigration by Russians and other Slavs from Tajikistan has been accelerating in recent years. In April 1993, it was reported that some 300,000 "Russian-speakers" (probably including Ukrainians and Belarussians as well as Russians) had left Tajikistan "since anti-Russian sentiment began rising in early 1990." It was estimated that only about 200,000 Russian speakers still remained.[20] Many of those were described as "sick, elderly or poor people without money or relatives in Russia that would enable them to move there."[21] So worried are the Tajik authorities about losing the country's skilled industrial workers and medical and scientific specialists that there has been talk of revising the state language law to give Russian equal status with Tajik and perhaps even introducing the right to dual citizenship.[22]

The Transcaucasus

The lowest concentrations of Russians occur in Transcaucasia. For example, the population of Georgia at the 1989 census was 5,401,000, of whom 70.1 percent were Georgians; 8.1 percent were Armenians; 6.3 percent (341,000) were Russians; 5.7 percent were Azerbaijanis; 3.2 percent were Ossetians; and 1.7 percent were Abkhazians. The population of Azerbaijan in 1989 was 7,029,000, of whom 82.7 percent were Azerbaijanis; 5.6 percent were Armenians; and 5.6 percent (392,000) were Russians. In Armenia in 1989 the population numbered 3,305,000, of whom 93.3 percent were Armenians; 2.6 percent were Azerbaijanis; 1.7 percent were Kurds; and only 1.6 percent (52,000) were Russians.

The Evolution of Russian Policy on the Issue

The collapse of the Soviet Union in 1991 caught everyone unaware. Prior to the August putsch, the only people paying serious attention to the status of Russians outside the Russian Federation were the members of the hardline Soiuz (Union) group of USSR parliamentary deputies, set up in 1990 to counter Baltic separatism and to campaign for the preservation of the territorial integrity of the USSR. Soiuz warned of the dreadful fate that would befall Russians if the Union republics gained their independence. In the immediate aftermath of the coup, Mikhail Gorbachev took up the refrain with baleful predictions about what would happen if the USSR were dissolved. The Yeltsin leadership, slow to appreciate the political significance of the issue, brushed these warnings aside and apparently placed its faith in the new Commonwealth of Independent States (CIS) as a forum for the resolution of interstate disputes. Russian Foreign Minister Andrei Kozyrev argued that the best way for Russia to defend the interests of Russian minorities was to persuade the countries where they lived to sign bilateral agreements guaranteeing their human rights.

Disillusion with the CIS soon set in. A war of words erupted between Russia and Ukraine over such explosive issues as control of the Black Sea Fleet, the dismantling of Ukraine's nuclear arsenal, and Russia's historic claim to Crimea. Opposition to Yeltsin's leadership grew within Russia, too, as the Russian government freed consumer prices and launched an ambitious privatization program. Russian policy toward the outside world in general, and toward the other states of the former Soviet Union in particular, became a battleground in the struggle for power between Yeltsin and his hardline opponents. Critics seized on the government's failure to articulate a coherent foreign policy and used it as a stick with which to beat Yeltsin.[23] The refusal of Estonia and Latvia to grant automatic citizenship to Russians living in their territory rallied Yeltsin's opponents, who accused his leadership of being dangerously pro-Western and of ignoring human rights abuses perpetrated in the countries of the Near Abroad against Russian minorities.

In spring 1992, Yeltsin's political advisor Sergei Stankevich published an article asserting that Russia did not have the moral right to remain a passive observer when neighboring states such as Estonia and Latvia practiced "apartheid" against the Russian populations within their borders. Protection of Russian nationals in the Near Abroad must be Russia's first priority, Stankevich wrote, adding that "it is clearly time for Russia to adopt a tougher tone on this issue."[24] The fact that the former Soviet republics in question were now sovereign states was immaterial, Stankevich informed the military newspaper *Krasnaia zvezda*, because "the independence of states does not at all mean that other states cannot place them within the sphere of their vital interests."[25]

Critics of Kozyrev's conciliatory stance called for responsibility for Russia's relations with the Near Abroad to be transferred from the foreign ministry to a new committee to be set up under Stankevich. No such committee was in fact created, and responsibility for Russia's relations with the other members of the CIS remained with the Ministry of Foreign Affairs, but the summer and fall of 1992 saw a steady stream of statements by high-ranking officials affirming Russia's preparedness to come to the defense of its nationals, wherever they might be.[26] The cause was championed not only by the extremist "national-patriotic" wing of the Russian political spectrum, but also by leaders of the centrist Civic Union. This bloc of *gosudarstvenniki* (statists), of which Stankevich and Russian Vice-President Aleksandr Rutskoi were leading members, advocated both the preservation of Russian territorial integrity and a major role for the state in the management of the economy.

By the fall of 1992, the issue had become a major preoccupation of the Yeltsin government and both Yeltsin and Kozyrev felt obliged to issue tough-sounding statements on it. Kozyrev criticized Estonia at the United Nations General Assembly in September 1992 for allegedly violating the human rights of its ethnic Russian minority, and subsequently assured the Committee on International Affairs and External Economic Relations of the Supreme Soviet that closer integration with the other CIS states and the protection of Russian nationals living in those states were the two top priorities of Russian foreign policy.[27] Yeltsin adopted an uncompromising tone on October 27 in an address to the collegium of the Russian Foreign Ministry.[28] In that speech, the Russian president was highly critical of the Foreign Ministry's performance under Kozyrev's leadership. Regarding Russia's relations with the Near Abroad, Yeltsin accused the ministry of reacting to events instead of anticipating them. He complained that the ministry had not been active enough in protecting the interests of Russians outside Russia and instructed it to adopt more assertive policies toward the Baltic states in connection with the "persecution" of the Russian-speaking populations there. On December 1, 1992, in an address to the Seventh Congress of People's Deputies of the Russian Federation, Yeltsin ordered the Ministries of Justice and Foreign Affairs to conclude legal-aid treaties with the other CIS states to protect the rights of Russians living there, and urged the signing of such treaties with Georgia, Latvia, and Estonia, which were not members of the CIS.[29]

If this was what Yeltsin meant when he called for more assertive policies, the countries of the Near Abroad had little cause for concern.

That was the interpretation placed on Yeltsin's pronouncements by Andrei Kortunov, a scholar at the Moscow-based Institute of the USA and Canada. Interviewed in January 1993, Kortunov said there was increasing opposition in Russian society at large, and in the Russian Parliament in particular, to what was seen as Kozyrev's excessively pro-Western foreign policy. This explained, Kortunov said, why Yeltsin and his foreign minister had felt obliged to issue menacing-sounding statements. "They are trying to maintain the lead in foreign policy," Kortunov said. "By moving from the left to center they seek to maintain the initiative, while marginalizing and isolating the extreme critics."[30]

The critics of the pro-Western slant of Kozyrev's policy were not appeased. Alarm bells rang not only in Kiev and Tallinn but also in Western capitals when, at the end of 1992, such prominent Russians as Sergei Karaganov (deputy director of the Moscow-based Institute of Europe), Andranik Migranian, and Evgenii Ambartsumov (chairman of the Committee on International Affairs and External Economic Relations of the Supreme Soviet) began to speak with approval of "a Monroe Doctrine for Russia."[31] Ambartsumov's committee declared that "Russian foreign policy should be based on a doctrine that proclaims the entire geopolitical space of the former [Soviet] Union a sphere of its vital interests. . . . Russia must secure . . . the role of political and military guarantor of stability on all the territory of the former USSR."[32] Migranian summed this up as meaning that "Russia and Russia alone will decide" what happens in "the post-Soviet space."[33] In the judgment of *The Economist*, "This goes far beyond the perfectly proper concern of the Russian government for Russian minorities abroad."[34]

Yeltsin's switch to a more aggressive approach caught the attention of the world when, in a speech to the Civic Union on February 28, 1993, the Russian president issued what seemed to be a call to the international community to allow Russia a free hand to intervene to keep the peace throughout the states of the former Soviet Union. Yeltsin's speech provoked a storm of protest from the countries in question, notably Ukraine.[35] The impression that the Russian government wanted to be seen to be getting tough was backed up a month later when, on March 29, Russian Defense Minister Pavel Grachev announced that his country was suspending the withdrawal of former Soviet troops from the three Baltic states.[36] In March 1993, Yeltsin unveiled proposals to strengthen the CIS, including suggestions for stronger collective security agreements to bring the former Soviet republics under a single defense umbrella. The Russian president also proposed the creation of a joint peacekeeping force to manage regional conflicts.[37]

In early April 1993, Yeltsin explicitly linked the rights of the Russians in the Near Abroad to the stationing of ex-Soviet troops in the Baltic states. During a visit to Vancouver, Yeltsin spoke with approval of the situation of Russian speakers in Lithuania. Emphasizing that Russia was adhering to the agreed schedule on troop withdrawals from Lithuania, Yeltsin went on to say that the treatment of Russian speakers in Estonia and Latvia would determine the pace and scope of withdrawal of Russian troops from those countries.[38] Latvian and Estonian leaders reacted angrily to Yeltsin's remarks. Estonian Prime Minister Mart Laar said he considered Russian policy on the issue "an attempt to reassert control over the Baltic states,"[39] while Latvian officials described Yeltsin's statement as an attempt to force Latvia to change its citizenship policy prior to the adoption of a law on the subject.[40]

The State of Play

Since the USSR dissolved, the Russians abroad have become the focus of an impassioned and acrimonious debate both inside Russia and between Russia and the other former Soviet republics. Inside Russia, the issue has achieved so high a priority on the domestic agenda that it would now be tantamount to political suicide for any Russian leader to question its significance. Russia's neighbors see things in a different light. Russia's assertion of its moral obligation toward ethnic Russians outside its territory has been met with suspicion and distrust by states only recently liberated from Russian rule. They say they are concerned about the possibility that a nationalist government might come to power in Moscow and try to reassert Russian control over the former empire. Those who warn of such a danger see their fears borne out by the support given to Russian separatists in Moldova's Dniester Republic by Russia's 14th Army and bands of free-booting Cossacks from Russia's Don region; by statements questioning Crimea's status within Ukraine issued by the Russian Parliament and by Russian Vice-President Rutskoi; and by Russian foot-dragging over the withdrawal of ex-Soviet troops from the Baltic states. Baltic leaders assert that the Russian army still has the ability, should it wish to use it, to launch a coup d'état in their countries. Like Moldova's leaders, they accuse the Russian leadership of deliberately delaying troop withdrawals in order to maintain a military presence in strategic outposts of the former empire.[41] Georgia's leaders, too, have repeatedly accused Russian forces based in Georgia of backing separatists in the breakaway region of Abkhazia on Georgia's northwestern seacoast; Russian officials deny that their troops have taken sides in the conflict.[42]

Certainly, there are influential groups in Russia today who have not yet come to terms with the collapse of the USSR and who hanker for a return to the Russian-dominated, state-controlled institutions of the past. It was not too long ago, after all, that mainstream Soviet journals were routinely running headlines such as, "There are 285,761,976 of Us, and We All Live in One Country."[43] It has been particularly hard for Russians to adjust to the idea of an independent Ukraine. Some Russian politicians, conscious of the issue's emotional impact, have tried to manipulate public opinion in order to pursue power in the domestic arena. The influence of such people, who are well represented in the Russian Parliament, military, and defense sector, as well as in the media and academia, grew in 1992, as did opposition to the market reforms launched by the Yeltsin leadership. The fact that Yeltsin's statements on this and other foreign policy issues became tougher as domestic opposition to his economic policies increased suggests that the president's switch to a sterner stance may have been a tactical maneuver intended either to appease this group or to steal some of their thunder while allowing his economic reforms to proceed.

Yeltsin's critics were not placated. Moreover, Russian officials, conscious of the strategic importance of the Near Abroad, seemed to find a new use for the issue of the Russian minorities in 1992. During the summer of 1992, Russian officials negotiating the withdrawal of ex-USSR troops stationed in the Baltic states began to link the status of ethnic Russians in those states with the pace of troop withdrawals from them and, Baltic negotiators alleged, started to use the presence of Russians abroad as a bargaining chip.[44] (As noted above, Yeltsin himself did not make this linkage until April 1993.) As Baltic officials perceived it, the real issue for the Russian negotiators was less the civil rights of ethnic Russians than the very considerable property at stake. The Latvian government, for example, has ambitious plans to develop the country's capital, Riga, into a major commercial and trading center—"Europe's window on Russia and the East." Latvian leaders are therefore determined to assume full control of Latvia's three seaports (two on the Baltic coast, one on the Gulf of Riga) as well as of other Soviet-built facilities on Latvian territory. The military port in Liepaja, several defense plants, a military airport, and a submarine-repair plant near Riga are still, however, under the control of the Russian army.[45] Russian negotiators argue that, for the time being, the factories are essential to the Russian economy because they produce items not made elsewhere, and that Russia must, in the interest of self-defense, maintain a number of strategic installations in Latvia, including the radar station at Skrunda and the communications facilities at Ventspils.[46]

Anecdotal evidence suggests that many Russian army leaders may now be keen to leave the Baltic states, where they are conscious of having become an unwelcome presence and where routine operations and maintenance of military facilities are in disarray. It therefore seems likely that the impetus behind attempts to exploit the issue of Russian minorities is coming not from the Russian military but from Russia's civilian negotiators. This conclusion is supported by the state of total dereliction in which some military facilities in Lithuania were found after the departure of the Russian troops; the way the facilities had been run down suggested that there had been a virtual collapse of the Russian military order in at least some parts of the Baltic region.

Scenarios for the Future

In what circumstances might the conditions arise for outright conflict over the Russians in the Near Abroad?

As far as Russia is concerned, the greatest danger would seem to be the possibility that the modernizing Yeltsin leadership might be replaced by a "traditionalist" ("statist" or "national-patriotic") leadership. This would likely mean the introduction of a more active and aggressive foreign policy in Moscow. Whereas the Yeltsin leadership has tried to advance the cause of Russians in the Near Abroad through negotiations, including talks with individual states, as well as within the framework of the United Nations, Council of Europe, CSCE, and regional forums, a traditionalist government would be more likely to threaten the use of force. Such an attitude is conveyed by Stankevich's assertion that, while force may be only "the four hundredth policy instrument" available to Russia to protect the interests of ethnic Russians outside its borders, "even so it should still be present in the arsenal."[47]

A traditionalist Russian leadership would also be more likely to act unilaterally, without seeking international sanction. Even in his controversial speech of February 1993, when Yeltsin seemed to call for Russia to be allowed a free hand to intervene throughout the former USSR, the

Russian president did not abandon his preference for negotiation but appealed to the international community for its support. The danger that a more conservative leadership might prefer to act alone became evident when such influential foreign policy specialists as Ambartsumov and Migranian began to speak with approval of "a Monroe Doctrine for Russia." Karaganov, for his part, continued to insist that it was essential that Russia engage in peacekeeping only under the aegis of an international organization such as the United Nations or CSCE. Saying he believed instability on Russia's borders was inevitable for some years to come and that, to protect itself from spillover, Russia might be forced to engage in a number of "low-intensity conflicts" in the Near Abroad, Karaganov insisted that international cooperation was essential if Russia was to be prevented from "plunging into an unlimited rough-and-tumble."[48] However, Karaganov said, the West's inability to decide whether to intervene in the Bosnian crisis had alarmed him by raising the possibility that Russian leaders might find themselves with little option other than to act alone.[49]

If Karaganov is right, it is possible that, at some point in the near future, Russian leaders may resort to unilateral action to defend the rights of an ethnic Russian minority somewhere in the Near Abroad. The ability of the Russian government to resort to force will depend to a considerable extent on the speed with which ex-Soviet troops are withdrawn from the Baltic states and other countries. The more rapid and complete the withdrawal of these troops from the non-Russian successor states, the less likely it is that disputes over the status of Russian minorities will lead to violence and the more likely it is that conflicts will be resolved peacefully. Conversely, if troop withdrawals are further delayed, Moscow's capacity to use force and the nervousness of neighboring governments will both be increased.

Several situations that might trigger such an intervention spring to mind. One might arise as a result of the social tensions that would ensue if Russians in a non-Russian successor state found themselves suffering a sharp drop in living standards relative to the indigenous population. Another such situation would involve ethnically motivated physical violence inflicted on ethnic Russians by members of the indigenous population. Either situation could be exacerbated if it were accompanied by the rise to power of an aggressively nationalistic government in the non-Russian successor state in question.

Increased hostility toward Russians has already been reported from Tajikistan and Uzbekistan and violence against Russian speakers seems likely to grow in several of the non-Russian successor states. Much has been said about Russia's identity crisis, but the new countries on Russia's borders are also engaged in a complex process of state- and nation-building. While some of them had qualified as full-fledged nations prior to the breakup of the Soviet Union,[50] others, particularly those in Central Asia, had never previously enjoyed independent statehood and have had independence thrust upon them. The chances seem small that the process of nation-building in all these new states will be entirely free from social instability and manifestations of militant nationalism; civil strife has broken out in Tajikistan and Georgia and, as mentioned above, Russian speakers are leaving the Central Asian republics in growing numbers. Meanwhile, Russia has a strong interest in protecting the rights of its co-ethnics abroad, if only to prevent a flood of refugees into Russia at a time when the country is already having difficulty providing jobs and housing for its existing population. If Germany, with its population of 80 million, is anxious to ward off the return of 2 million ethnic Germans from the former Soviet Union, how much more alarmed must Russia be by the prospect of an influx of 25.3 million ethnic Russians? In the words of The Economist, "Russia can no more turn a blind eye to the way they are treated than Germany could if 13 million Germans—a proportionate number—lived in countries surrounding Germany."[51]

There will be further alarm in Moscow, for much the same reason, if Russians in the non-Russian successor states find themselves suffering conspicuously higher rates of unemployment than the indigenous populations and a sharp decline in living standards relative to the rest of society. This situation is quite likely to occur. Economic restructuring will inevitably entail the closure of factories in the defense sector and other branches of heavy industry. In the non-Russian republics of the USSR, much of such production was concentrated in Russian enclaves, which are now facing the threat of unemployment. Because Russian workers in the Near Abroad were on average better off than the indigenous population, they stand to lose more than the local population as a result of economic restructuring, and the likelihood of unrest along ethnic lines is therefore further increased. This problem is already emerging in northeastern Estonia, where heavy industry is manned by ethnic Russians and concentrated in a Russian enclave centered on the town of Narva.[52] However, the threat of high unemployment for Russian workers is not confined to the Baltic states: northern Kazakhstan is another potential trouble-spot, as is eastern Ukraine.

It may be hypothesized that the risk of conflict between Russia and one of its neighbors will be greatest when high Russian unemployment occurs in an ethnic Russian enclave located close to the Russian border and when there is, in addition, friction between the enclave and the national government over issues such as voting rights and language requirements for certain jobs. Ukraine and Kazakhstan appear to be aware of this danger and to have taken steps to avert it, but Estonia's citizenship law and the draft law on citizenship being considered by Latvia, both of which make it difficult for those who moved to the country after its inclusion in the USSR to become citizens, seem likely to exacerbate ethnic tensions. While Estonians and Latvians understandably fear that granting citizenship to the large numbers of Slavs who settled in the Baltic states during the Soviet period could swamp the national identity of the newly independent countries, not all such settlers are necessarily members of a pro-Russian, pro-imperial fifth column. Efforts to find a role for them in the new societies now taking shape appear to offer more hope of future stability than deliberately excluding them from the political process. At present, it is true, public opinion polls suggest that members of Russian minorities in these two Baltic states are far more concerned about the threat of unemployment than about whether or not they will lose the right to vote in national elections.[53] Russian minorities in the Baltic states are, however, extremely alarmed that they may be excluded from certain jobs if they are unable to display competence in the state language. As the law stands, ethnic Russian physicians run the risk of losing the right to practice medicine if they cannot speak Estonian, even though they may live in those parts of Estonia that are settled by Russians and where all their patients are Russian speakers. As Philip Hanson has noted, "Unemployment and poverty are easily linked with the issue of national identity."[54]

Getting trade between Russia and its neighbors back onto a healthy basis could help improve the economic situation in all the former successor states and thereby ease tensions all around. In general, active and well-functioning international trade encourages good relations in other spheres, but production and living standards in all the Soviet successor states have suffered short-term damage from the contraction of what used to be interrepublic deliveries, either through reduced availabilities at established terms of trade or through terms of trade changes that have reduced one partner's ability to import from the other (as when, in 1992, Russia adjusted energy prices to some of its partners in the Near Abroad to world levels). The longer that trading relationships between Russia and its neighbors are bedeviled by price distortions, currency inconvertibility, and other, more deliberately constructed impediments such as embargoes and export controls, the more likely it is that relations will deteriorate. Interdependence among the successor states is likely to remain high for the foreseeable future. If trade is impeded, all parties will suffer and interstate friction may arise that could have unpleasant repercussions for ethnic Russian minorities in the Near Abroad. That, in turn, could provoke a further escalation of tension between Russia and its neighbors.

Conclusions

If Russia is to live at peace with its neighbors and with itself, it and they will have to agree where Russia's boundaries begin and where they end.[55] Russia has border disputes of varying intensity with many of its neighbors, including a long-standing territorial quarrel with Japan, but the situation seems most sensitive where Russia's boundaries with the other Soviet successor states are concerned. It is no coincidence that these borders are fuzziest in places where large numbers of ethnic Russians live on either side of the frontier. The most inflammable "hot spots" are the Crimean peninsula, the northern Caucasus, and Russia's borders with the Baltic states.

Russia, while no longer a superpower, remains a major regional power and as such has legitimate interests outside its borders. Russia's concern for the 25.3 million ethnic Russians in the Near Abroad is one such interest. As a major exporter of raw materials and importer of grain, Russia requires access to world markets through ports that are free of ice in winter; above all, it needs peace and stability on its borders as it struggles to reform its economy and restructure its political system. Instability in the countries on Russia's periphery not only would reverberate within Russia's multiethnic population, but also would threaten the country with a flood of refugees with which it would be unable to cope. Tensions between Russia and its neighbors would, moreover, have harmful effects not only on Russia but also on the non-Russian successor states whose efforts to build stable economic and political systems would be undermined.

While Russia does indeed have a legitimate interest in what happens on its periphery, "the question," to quote *The Economist* again, "is how Russia deals with this legitimate interest."[56] Russian leaders may choose means conducive to compromise and international harmony, or they may opt for confrontation and the threat or use of force. It is necessary only to recall how the impact of unemployment on the 3.5 million Germans in the Sudetenland was exploited by Nazi leaders in the years preceding World War II[57] to realize the opportunity for mischief making that was offered to unscrupulous politicians when, with the collapse of the Soviet Union in 1991, 25.3 ethnic Russians suddenly found themselves living abroad. Until Russia and its neighbors agree what kind of country Russia is, where its new borders lie, and what role can usefully be played by the Russians abroad, Russia's foreign and security policies will remain inchoate, and conflict between the successor states of the Soviet Union will continue to be a serious possibility.

Notes

The author is grateful to Philip Hanson, Vladimir Ivanov, and Natalia Melnyczuk for comments on an earlier draft of this paper. The views expressed here are, of course, those of the author.

1. Andranik Migranian spoke at the conference on "The Emerging National Security Doctrine of a New Russia" held in Washington, D.C., on March 17–19, 1993, under the auspices of the United States Institute of Peace. Migranian is a prominent Russian scholar and journalist who also serves as an advisor to Evgenii Ambartsumov, chairman of the Committee on International Affairs and External Economic Relations of the Supreme Soviet.

2. Vera Tolz and Elizabeth Teague, "Russian Intellectuals Adjust to Loss of Empire," *RFE/RL Research Report* (February 21, 1992). For further discussion of the debate on Russia's postimperial role, see Vera Tolz, "Westernizers Continue to Challenge National Patriots," *RFE/RL Research Report* (December 11, 1992).

3. Dominique Moisi, "Nation Searching Its Soul for True Sense of Identity," *The European*, March 19–25, 1992.

4. For census data on the population of the USSR broken down by nationality, see *Soiuz*, no. 44, 1990, pp. 15–16. For analysis, see Ann Sheehy, "The Ethnographic Dimension," in Alastair McAuley, ed., *Soviet Federalism, Nationalism and Economic Decentralisation* (Leicester: Leicester University Press, 1991), pp. 56–88.

5. Quoted in Archie Brown et al., eds., *The Cambridge Encyclopedia of Russia and the Soviet Union* (Cambridge: Cambridge University Press, 1982), p. 57.

6. Richard Pipes, *The Formation of the USSR: Communism and Nationalism 1917–1923* (Cambridge, Mass.: Harvard University Press, 1964), pp. 1–2.

7. *The Financial Times*, August 31, 1991.

8. Paul A. Goble, "Russia and Its Neighbors," *Foreign Policy* 77, no. 2 (Spring 1993), p. 80.

9. "Moi adres ne dom i ne ulitsa, moi adres Sovetskii Soiuz."

10. As Ann Sheehy has pointed out, at the time of the 1979 census Kazakhs were a minority in their own republic. By 1989, their numbers had increased sufficiently for this no longer to be the case. (See the report on the 1989 census findings prepared by Ann Sheehy of the RFE/RL Research Institute in June 1990.) The latest available data, moreover, show that the number of Kazakhs in Kazakhstan increased so sharply in 1992 that, at the beginning of 1993, Kazakhs outnumbered the combined totals of Russians and Ukrainians for the first time in recent history. (See *RFE/RL Daily Report* [June 25, 1993]).

11. Olga Glezer, Vladimir Kolosov, Nikolai Petrov, Vladimir Streletskii, and Andrei Treivish, "Samaia politicheskaia karta SSSR" (The most political map of the USSR), *Moskovskie novosti*, no. 11, March 17, 1991, p. 8.

12. Ibid. The only other uncontested borders were said to be those between Belarus and Latvia and between Lithuania and Latvia.

13. Some 36,000 Russians reportedly left Estonia in 1991–92, but most of Estonia's Russian population feel they have nowhere else to go and total outmigration is not expected to exceed 40,000. Philip Hanson, "Estonia's Narva Problems, Narva's Estonian Problem," *RFE/RL Research Report* (April 1993).

14. For details, see Dzintra Bungs, Saulius Girnius, and Riina Kionka, "Citizenship Legislation in the Baltic States," *RFE/RL Research Report* (December 18, 1992), pp. 38–40.

15. Human Rights Watch, *Human Rights World Report 1993* (New York: Human Rights Watch, 1992), pp. 236–237. Helsinki Watch is part of Human Rights Watch.

16. Gennadii Pavlyuk, "Russkii vopros v Kyrgyzstane: chto vperedi?" (The Russian question in Kyrgyzstan: What lies ahead?), *Molodezhnaia gazeta* (Kyrgyzstan), October 30, 1991.

17. *RFE/RL Daily Report*, April 15, 1993, contribution by Bess Brown.

18. Report on the 1989 census prepared by Ann Sheehy of the RFE/RL Research Institute in June 1990.

19. Ibid.

20. *Interfax*, April 3, 1993.

21. *AFP*, April 28, 1993.

22. *ITAR-TASS*, April 15, 1993, cited by Bess Brown in the *RFE/RL Daily Report*, April 16, 1993.

23. For details of the many attacks leveled against Kozyrev, see Suzanne Crow, "Competing Blueprints for Russian Foreign Policy," *RFE/RL Research Report* (December 18, 1992); and John Lough, "The Place of the 'Near Abroad' in Russian Foreign Policy," *RFE/RL Research Report* (March 12, 1993).

24. Sergei Stankevich, "Derzhava v poiskakh sebia" (A great power in search of itself), *Nezavisimaia gazeta*, March 28, 1992. An English version appeared in *The National Interest*, no. 28 (Summer 1992), pp. 47–51, accompanied by comments from Western specialists. Leon Aron and Francis Fukuyama both wrote that the most significant aspect of Stankevich's article was the stress it put on the need for Russia to defend the rights of Russians in the other Soviet successor states.

25. *Krasnaia zvezda*, October 10, 1992.

26. For details, see Suzanne Crow, "Russia Prepares to Take a Hard Line on 'Near Abroad,' " *RFE/RL Research Report* (August 14, 1992); and Anatole Shub, *New Phase in Russian Politics,* USIA Research Memorandum (Washington, D.C.: USIA, December 31, 1992).

27. See Alexander Rahr, "Russia: The Struggle for Power Continues," *RFE/RL Research Report* (February 5, 1993), p. 3.

28. For details, see John W. R. Lepingwell, "Yeltsin Calls for Tougher Foreign Policy," *RFE/RL Research Report* (November 6, 1992), p. 17.

29. *ITAR-TASS*, December 1, 1992. Russia had already concluded such a treaty with Lithuania.

30. *The Christian Science Monitor*, January 28, 1993.

31. Rowland Evans and Robert Novak, "Russia's 'Monroe Doctrine,'" *The Washington Post*, February 26, 1993. Enunciated by President James Monroe in 1823, the doctrine stated that the United States regarded the Western Hemisphere as within its exclusive sphere of interests and that any attempt by a European power to control any nation in the Western Hemisphere would be regarded as a hostile act against the United States itself. As the United States grew more powerful, interpretation of the doctrine widened; the Roosevelt Corollary of 1904 asserted that the United States reserved the right to intervene in Latin American countries guilty of sustained wrongdoing. The classic study of the doctrine is Dexter Perkins, *A History of the Monroe Doctrine* (Boston: Little, Brown & Co., 1963).

32. Quoted in *The Economist*, November 13, 1992.

33. Migranian, speaking at the conference referred to in note 1.

34. "Imperfect Peace," *The Economist*, November 13, 1992.

35. Suzanne Crow, "Russia Seeks Leadership in Regional Peacekeeping," *RFE/RL Research Report* (April 9, 1993), pp. 28–32.

36. John Lepingwell, "Another Halt to Russian Withdrawal from the Baltic States?" RFE/RL Research Institute program brief, March 30, 1993.

37. *New Times*, nos. 12–13, March 1993.

38. *Reuters*, April 4, 1993.

39. *Reuters*, April 5, 1993.

40. Ibid.

41. Vladimir Socor has argued that the presence of the Russian-speaking minority in Moldova is being used by chauvinist and military circles in Moscow to whip up tensions in the republic and thereby create a pretext for Russia to keep troops in the country. Russia's overriding interest, Socor argues, is not to protect the Russian minority, since they are not at real risk, but "to retain a strategic outpost in the rear of Ukraine and on the threshold of the Balkans."

Vladimir Socor, "Russian Forces in Moldova," *RFE/RL Research Report* (August 28, 1992), pp. 38–43.

42. *AFP, ITAR-TASS, Reuters*, April 6, 1993.

43. That is how *Izvestiia*'s weekly supplement, *Soiuz* (no. 32, August 1990, p. 12), headlined its report on the all-Union population census of 1989.

44. Dzintra Bungs, "Soviet Troops in Latvia," *RFE/RL Research Report* (August 28, 1992), p. 24; and Riina Kionka, "Armed Incidents Aggravate Russian-Estonian Relations," in the same issue of *RFE/RL Research Report,* p. 35. See also the following articles in that issue: Stephen Foye, "Russian Troops Abroad: Vestiges of Empire," pp. 15–17; Saulius Girnius, "Progress in Withdrawal of Troops from Lithuania?" pp. 29–33; and Vladimir Socor, "Russian Forces in Moldova," pp. 38–43.

45. Talk given by Ojars Kalnins, the Latvian ambassador to the United States, at the Heritage Foundation in Washington, D.C., on April 13, 1993.

46. Bungs, "Soviet Troops in Latvia," pp. 18–28; and Jan Arvids Trapans, ed., "Conference in Salzburg," *RFE/RL Research Report*, no. 49 (1992), p. 21.

47. *Krasnaia zvezda*, October 10, 1992.

48. Sergei Karaganov, "Russia Needs a Foreign Policy Consensus," *Moscow News*, no. 11, March 12, 1993.

49. Karaganov spoke at the Institute for Defense Analyses (IDA) in Alexandria, Virginia, on March 30, 1993; for a report of his talk, see the IDA Seminar Series, "Changes in the Former Soviet Union," April 1993.

50. Roman Szporluk, "The National Question," in Timothy J. Colton and Robert Legvold, eds., *After the Soviet Union: From Empire to Nations* (New York: W. W. Norton & Co., 1992), p. 87.

51. "Russia as Bully," *The Economist*, April 3, 1993.

52. Hanson, "Estonia's Narva Problem, Narva's Estonian Problem."

53. This was the conclusion of an opinion poll conducted for the Council of Europe in Estonia in 1992. See also Hanson, "Estonia's Narva Problem, Narva's Estonian Problem."

54. Hanson, "Estonia's Narva Problem, Narva's Estonian Problem."

55. This point is also stressed by Michael McFaul, *Democratic Prospects in Russia and Eastern Europe* (Washington, D.C.: Center for Strategic and International Studies, 1993), p. 44.

56. *The Economist*, April 3, 1993.

57. The Sudetenland describes sections of northern Bohemia and Moravia that were incorporated into Czechoslovakia in 1919, after the disintegration of the Austro-Hungarian Empire. The Sudetenland lay on Czechoslovakia's border with Germany and its population was predominantly German speaking. With the coming of the Great Depression in the early 1930s, the highly industrialized Sudetenland was far more severely hit by unemployment than were Czechoslovakia's mainly agricultural lowlands. Unemployment prepared the ground for militant nationalism, and the resentment of German-speaking workers was further fueled by local Nazi leaders, who accused the Czech authorities of discriminating against the German minority. Interethnic relations became so tense that, at the 1938 Munich Conference, Adolf Hitler persuaded European leaders to allow Germany to annex the Sudetenland. See *The New Encyclopaedia Britannica*, 15th edition (Chicago: Encyclopaedia Britannica, Inc., 1992).

6

Russian Statehood, the CIS, and the Problem of Security

Igor' Kliamkin

The novelty of the security problem for Russia today is not just that we are not talking—and, in fact, can no longer talk—about defending, much less disseminating throughout the world, this or that state ideology. Nor is this novelty confined to changes in military doctrine: the very delay in the development of a new doctrine points not so much to the sluggishness of the military brass as to the fact that the prerequisites for such a doctrine have yet to emerge.

The fact of the matter is that a military doctrine touches first and foremost upon the relations of a given state with other states, relations based on a well-defined concept of national interests. In today's Russia, however, a concept of national interests cannot be formulated with any degree of clarity because the new Russian state is itself still under construction. (It could be said that successful state-building, which could provide political cover for economic modernization, is, in fact, Russia's main national interest.)

In these circumstances, the problem of Russian national security is, above all, an internal problem: its content is defined not so much by its relations with the "far abroad" in general, and the West in particular, but by the situation in Russia itself and in the former Soviet republics that surround it. Accordingly, the threat to Russia's security today is not, given

---

This essay has been translated from the Russian by Leon Aron.

its nuclear status, that of an invasion, but of the disintegration of the Russian state even before it has had a chance to form and strengthen. The threat to security is found not in the military sphere, but in the catastrophic state of the Russian economy and in the fragility of the political system, which is inadequate to the task of carrying out economic reform. It is in this sense that the word "security" is used ever more frequently by the representatives of very different political groups.

This is not to say that the traditional notion of security as a prevention against military threat from abroad no longer exists. For Russia, the problem of slowing the arms race in qualitative, and not just quantitative, terms—a problem that has been left largely untouched in the recent arms control negotiations with the United States is extremely important. But this question, too, is inseparably linked to Russia's economic viability and political stability. We have only to remember that one of the catalysts for Mikhail Gorbachev's perestroika was Ronald Reagan's Strategic Defense Initiative, which propelled the arms race to an economically unreachable level for the Soviet Union.

If we accept the premise that the main problem for Russia is the threat of the disintegration of its state, then present and future conflicts with the former Soviet republics become the paramount issue. Militarily, these states pose no danger to Russia. The danger is that territorial conflicts, unresolved politically, may turn into ethnic conflicts, which in turn are dangerous because they are capable of spreading and inflaming similar conflicts inside Russia. It is here that the threat to Russian statehood and, consequently, to Russian national security is the greatest.

Another peculiarity of this problem is that it is common to all the members of the Commonwealth of Independent States (CIS), especially the key ones, Ukraine and Kazakhstan, which are very diverse in their ethnic composition (a quarter of the Ukrainian population is Russian, and less than half of the citizens of Kazakhstan are ethnic Kazakhs). This common danger alone calls for the creation of a system of collective security for the CIS states. In a more general sense, this means that the strengthening of the CIS is one of the key factors in strengthening the statehood of each of the constituent states.

The common character of this problem is somewhat obscured by the fact that the creation of joint structures to maintain security is impeded by the unwillingness of CIS member states to become involved in "hot spots" far from their borders. Partly for this reason, Ukraine refused in May 1992 to sign a CIS collective security treaty. At the same time, one should point out that this treaty is hardly functional today because of a wariness on the part of the Russian Parliament, which is reluctant to ratify the treaty because of the perceived danger of becoming entangled in conflicts between CIS members and nonmember states.

A solution to this problem might lie in separating issues regarding intra-CIS relations from issues involving CIS members' relations with nonmember states. These are two distinct areas of national security, but the former seems the more critical today. It is critical, first of all, from the point of view of preventing the disintegration of the core of the CIS by deflecting potential conflicts among its four largest member states (Russia, Ukraine, Belarus, and Kazakhstan), conflicts that would jeopardize global as well as regional security.

The disintegration of the CIS could result in the interruption of the democratic cycle in Russia's development and permit the assumption of power by nationalist forces favoring an ethnic-imperial statehood (as opposed to the erstwhile communist-imperial one). If the CIS core breaks apart, the resultant conflicts would inevitably infuse the problems of security with the already wounded national pride of Russia. Such conflicts might then grow into armed clashes, after which the problem of security would be tied to the question of military victory and the results of such a victory. Given current trends in Russian public opinion (discussed below), these results clearly would not be favorable to democracy.

Thus, today, the danger of the restoration of the Russian Empire is not to be found where many observers and experts are looking for it. The danger lies not in the strengthening of the CIS—not in the creation, for that purpose, of various coordinating, interstate structures—but in the disintegration of the CIS and, especially, of its historic core. Today, the strengthening of the CIS is not a movement toward an empire, but perhaps the only opportunity to avoid the overall disintegration of statehood for the larger part of the former USSR. Subsequent attempts to consolidate statehood on the basis of ethnic ideology would, in the case of Russia, inevitably take on an imperial character and lead to Russian expansion into the territories of former Union republics inhabited by ethnic Russians. In other words, the fortification of the CIS today is the most important guarantee not only of security but also of democracy in the nations of the commonwealth.

The truth is that the CIS, which sprang up in the place of the USSR, is not simply a product of tradition. It is the recognition, willing or unwilling, of the fact that the new states are too weak and too closely tied to one another by centuries of common history and by the Soviet militarized and centralized economy to navigate political waters alone. It is a recognition, willing or unwilling, that the new states can avoid instability and establish firm foundations only if they preserve over their heads a common roof, even if no more than a symbolic one initially. Preservation and, if possible, strengthening of the commonwealth is the only civilized way of constructing each of the constituent states.

It is true that, in their disintegration, two other communist federations (Yugoslavia and Czechoslovakia) have not created commonwealth-like structures. But it is also true that both of those federations emerged only in the 20th century and their constituent parts were not as closely bound by history as were the former Soviet republics. Furthermore, for a number of Yugoslav republics, disintegration has resulted in tragedy. As for those states (such as Slovenia) that have avoided tragedy and maintained their security, they possess advantages that most former Soviet republics do not have: a homogeneous ethnic composition and a preparedness for participation in Western markets within the foreseeable future. These advantages are precisely what the Czech Republic is counting on as, together with Hungary and Poland, it tries to push its way into the Western "zone of influence."

None of the CIS states can count on rapid progress in penetrating Western markets. They must, therefore, preserve their "common market," which, taking into consideration the dominant role that the state sector still plays in their economies, will be impossible without creating at least some coordinating suprastate structures. This is the main argument of the Kazakh president, Nursultan Nazarbayev, who has advanced it for a long time, albeit without success so far.

The main reason for this failure to fashion coordinating suprastate structures is the special position of Ukraine, without an examination of which any speculations about the future of the CIS would be pointless—as would be any speculations about the maintenance of security on the territory of the former USSR.

Ukraine's policies are explained not by the personal ambitions of President Leonid Kravchuk, nor of any other Ukrainian politician, but by very special conditions. Of the four largest CIS states, Ukraine is the only one in which a more or less influential national movement—"Rukh"—had been active prior to the republic's independence. The democratic movement in Russia (embodied by "Democratic Russia") was not national but anticommunist (and, to that extent, anti-imperial), while neither Kazakhstan nor Belarus had any organized mass movements. It was Ukraine's position that played the decisive role in the liquidation of the USSR in December 1991: at the time, not a single political party in Ukraine was ready to sign a new Union Treaty and agree to the preservation—even in a much weakened state—of Mikhail Gorbachev's "center."

This special position is interesting in another respect as well. Ukraine's situation is perhaps the most complicated one of all the CIS member states. It is a kind of a political and psychological trap. The Ukrainian political elites, irrespective of their political hues, cannot give up the idea of distancing their country from Russia for, in the memory of the Ukrainians, Russia and the imperial center are one and the same. For this same reason, they cannot feel comfortable in the CIS, where Russia, not without grounds, claims the dominant role.

But the greater the political distance Ukraine seeks from Russia, the deeper the crisis in Ukraine's economy becomes—and that crisis is inseparable from the issue of Ukrainian statehood. At the same time, attempts to endow Ukrainian statehood with the weight and authority of a nuclear power (this goal, although not declared openly, is firmly in the minds of most Ukrainian political activists) threaten to lead Ukraine into total isolation.

First, Ukraine would be isolated from the world community, which not only will not condone nuclear proliferation, but also will not forgive the unwarranted delay in carrying out agreements already signed. Yet, without the support of the world community, Ukraine will not survive. Second, Ukraine's position as a nuclear power would lead to its further isolation from Russia and to the growth there of imperial sentiments. Such sentiments are already widespread, because the trauma inflicted upon the collective Russian psyche by the liquidation of the USSR is a very deep one and is healing with great difficulty—or, to be more precise, is not healing at all.

Beginning February 1992, I conducted, for the Moscow-based Public Opinion Foundation, regular surveys of Russians and Ukrainians (except in western Ukraine) on key economic, political, and ideological issues. The sample in each survey, undertaken once every three months, included 2,500 to 4,000 people from key social segments: managers of state enterprises and collective farms, workers, private entrepreneurs, farmers, military officers, and so forth.

The results of the surveys have been unambiguous: the citizens of Russia cannot accept Ukraine as an independent state, no longer a part of Russia, politically *equal* to Russia. For example, 70 percent of the Russians surveyed supported the creation of a Russian armed force, but only 20 percent were favorably disposed to the formation of an independent Ukrainian army. If people are happy that they may live as they wish but, at the same time, are upset that their neighbor chooses to do the same, this is hardly a sign of satisfaction with the newly acquired independence. Rather, this is a response of the traumatized imperial mind-set to the challenge posed by Ukraine and other republics of the former USSR.

Moreover, most citizens of Russia were not unfavorably predisposed toward the possibility of the disintegration of Ukraine: one out of two Russians polled was happy about the prospect of the Crimea's secession from Ukraine, while only one out of five was unhappy at the idea. There is little democratic feeling in these numbers but a great deal of wounded imperial feeling: Since you have chosen to leave us, may you find yourself in the worst of all possible situations.

Such sentiments are just as dangerous for the future of Russian statehood as they are for that of Ukrainian statehood—at least as far as the Russian and Ukrainian democracies are concerned. They are an indicator of a psychological, if not yet political, climate ripe for national-patriots and neocommunists offering dreams of a restoration of the Soviet empire. The more Ukraine distances itself from Russia, the more this climate will grow—and not just in Russia, which has already begun to put economic pressure on its neighbor (especially where energy supplies are concerned), but also within Ukraine, were 11 million ethnic Russians are anxious about being isolated from their historical motherland.

It is especially important to bear in mind that imperial sentiments are widespread in the Russian armed forces. One example of this was the February 1993 All-Army Officer Assembly, which had gathered against the wishes of the military leadership. During sessions of the assembly, slogans calling for the re-creation of the USSR and the punishment of those held responsible for its liquidation were much in evidence. Although the assembly may not have been very representative of the Russian armed forces as a whole, the tenor of the gathering was certainly symptomatic of a growing sentiment within the military.

The data I obtained in the course of my sociological surveys also point in the same direction. Although a comparatively small segment of the Russian officer corps is supportive of an outright restoration of the Soviet Union, the great power (*derzhavnyi*) attitude is widespread. For instance, a full one-half of the Russian officers polled were against the Yeltsin-Kravchuk agreement on the joint ownership of the Black Sea Fleet, and almost a third were "absolutely" against it. Such strong opposition has not been found in any other socio-professional group. Given such sentiments, it seems highly likely that, should the core of the CIS fall apart and armed conflicts break out among the constituent states, the armed forces would become the key political base of parties with an imperial orientation.

A final danger of Ukraine choosing to distance itself from Russia is that it is likely to lead to the isolation of the Ukrainian political elites from their own population. When, on December 1, 1991, Ukrainians voted for independence they did so almost unanimously, and they took calmly the liquidation of the Soviet Union. Even the mood of the ethnic Russians in Ukraine was not so very different from that of the Ukrainians. The idea of independence was perceived by the majority not as ethnic, not even as political, but as economic. At the end of 1991, the standard of living in Ukraine was higher than in Russia, and state independence and the movement away from Russia were thought to hold the key to future prosperity. Once these hopes were not realized, the mood began to change rapidly, and visible differences began to appear between the "top" and "bottom" of Ukrainian society on the issue of relations with Russia.

According to my data, it was the ethnic Russians in Ukraine who first began to worry. Already by the summer of 1992, their attitude toward everything connected with the liquidation of the USSR and Ukraine's distancing itself from Russia (for example, the plans to introduce a Ukrainian currency and Ukraine's exit from the CIS) was different from that of ethnic Ukrainians by a margin of 20 to 25 percent. By the end of that year, however, the positions of the Russians and the Ukrainians began to converge—not because the Russians had changed their minds, but because the Ukrainians began to think similarly. This turned out to be the sentiment of Ukraine as a whole. In March 1992, 35 percent of its citizens condemned the liquidation of the USSR, and by November, 60 percent did—almost as large a percentage as in Russia.

Overall, Ukrainian statehood, which, unlike Russia's, grew out of a national movement, is, just like the Russian one, in a state of deep crisis even before it has had a chance to form and consolidate. In these circumstances, any concept of national security is, at best, a symbolic one. In such a crisis, the key starting point of the national security agenda must be consolidation and strengthening of statehood.

But what might serve as a foundation on which to undertake such a process of consolidation? The experience of Russia since the dissolution of the Soviet Union shows that common territory, if unsupported by the existence of a national idea, is too weak a foundation for the purpose. At the same time, the experience of Ukraine demonstrates that a national idea, when cast exclusively in political terms as an idea of national independence, without touching the ethnic core of national conscious- ness, is likewise incapable of consolidating a society undergoing a deep economic crisis.

Yet, the peculiarity of the situation in both Russia and Ukraine lies in the fact that the ethnic idea is not popular. In both nations, no more than 10 percent of the population regard the interests of their ethnic group as paramount. This represents a considerable safety margin and a moral foundation on which to build a new statehood gradually and safely, without courting disaster. But to seize this historic opportunity means to try to combine two phenomena that in Western Europe, for example, were separated by decades, even centuries: the formation of nation-states and their integration into broader international structures.

Thus, the relative painlessness of nation-building in the former Soviet republics would be directly proportionate to the rapidity with which the actors realize the necessity of forming coordinating suprastate structures of a confederative nature. Since the purely political idea of a nation—a "political nation," so to speak—is highly problematic, especially given a severe economic crisis, the choice is between two bases of nation-building: ethnic, the appeal of which will grow if economic and political crises continue; and confederative.

The arguments against the latter often point to the weak and dysfunc- tional nature of most confederations. In the case of the post-Soviet states, however, this argument does not apply, for the nature of the Soviet Union and the manner of its deconstruction are unique. The fabric connecting the constituent parts of the former Russian Empire is of a special strength, woven out of the centuries, and the sudden rending of that fabric has created colossal dangers that can only be overcome if some form of continuity with the past can be sewn together.

The weakness of another argument against a confederation—that it would be a road back toward the empire and the "center"—has already been discussed. If anything, it is precisely this sudden tear in the historical fabric that is most likely to lead to the resurrection of the imperial structures. Only in this case might the trauma inflicted on the imperial, state, and political consciousness translate itself into a crisis of a national and ethnic character.

Should this happen, should the "Russian idea" enter the mass consciousness, this would indeed mean a spiritual and psychological revolution— with all the natural consequences that attend revolutions. Despite all the appeals of its proponents to tradition, to the "roots," to the "soil," the truth of the matter is that the "Russian idea" goes against tradition. It is radical, not conservative. Russia has never been a nation-state of the Russians, and the national idea did not play the role it played in Western Europe at the time of Russia's transition from a traditional society to a modern one. It is worth remembering that when Russia began that transition, it did so on the basis not of a national idea but of social ideals: the Russian revolution of 1917 was the first upheaval that tried to attack the problems of national modernization under internationalist, social slogans.

If today the communists and neocommunists ally themselves with the national-patriots in a single political bloc this means that the mobilizing power of the social idea in nation-building has already been undermined, while the ethnic idea has not yet developed. This conclusion is supported by the polls conducted by the Public Opinion Foundation and other research centers that reveal support for communist and national-patriotic parties in all layers of Russian society to be no higher than 5 percent.

The current political struggle in Russia is essentially about the best way to restore Russian statehood. Gradually, leaders in all the former Soviet republics are coming to understand that the danger of the restoration of the Russian empire comes not from the current Russian leadership, which supports the strengthening of the CIS, but from other forces that are opposed to the commonwealth. This understanding was evident in a number of statements made by President Kravchuk from February 1993 onwards. Kravchuk suggested that the coming to power in Russia of the national-patriots and the communists would mean the collapse of hope for the peaceful development of nations on the entire territory of the former USSR, and would start a slide toward wars more devastating than those in the former Yugoslavia. Unfortunately, there is less appreciation of the fact that the alternative to this route is not weakening the CIS, but strengthening it. Russian imperial forces could come to power only if the CIS were to begin to disintegrate.

Over half of the Russian population sees the problem of national security as one stemming from the disintegration of the former state, and sees that problem's solution in an authoritarian, strong-arm regime. This sentiment is especially prevalent among officers of the Russian armed forces, managers of state enterprises, and the urban working class. To be sure, this authoritarian idea is nebulous and coexists—remarkably enough—with an almost unanimous refusal to sacrifice the liberties acquired in the last few years, especially the freedom of press. It is less an endorsement of dictatorship than a desire for some sort of order. Still, if the crises in the economy and, especially, in the process of state-building deepen, the predilection for order may translate into a predilection for dictatorship.

Yet, to consider a dictatorship a guarantee of Russia's security is like considering secure the current situation in the former Yugoslavia. Despite a significant segment of the population leaning toward the strong-arm approach, an authoritarian regime could be established in Moscow only by force—at the very least because it would be rejected by the former autonomous republics within Russia. Their resistance would inevitably lead to ethnic coloration of the ensuing political conflicts. And that would mean that an authoritarian regime, should it manage to survive, would have to exploit Russian national and ethnic ideology. This, in turn, would abruptly destabilize the situation on the entire territory of the former USSR and create a precondition for the coming to power of the local nationalists, who would attempt to establish their own authoritarian regimes. Such regimes undoubtedly would be resisted by the local ethnic Russians, who would be supported by Russia. And so the program of the restoration of Russia in "its historic borders" advocated today by the Russian communists and national-patriots would begin to be implemented.

In short, the establishment of an authoritarian regime would be unlikely to achieve anything but the repetition of the Yugoslav experience, namely, an accelerated disintegration achieved through great bloodshed. But the final outcome is not at issue here. It is very doubtful that those Russians who today support the strong-arm solution are eager to experience its consequences. They are just looking for a way out of the crisis of the Russian statehood, a way to eliminate the dangers that resulted from the destruction of the entire security system. For them, authoritarianism represents one of the variants of Russian state-building—the imperial-ethnic variant.

Authoritarianism, however, is not going to bring about a civilized solution. The problem of Russian security cannot be solved that way. The only democratic, civilized answer lies in strengthening the CIS and forming such supranational structures as are necessary to permit and effect the joint transformation of the common communist economy, which still endures. Only in this way will new states acquire strong reformist regimes capable of guaranteeing the security of their citizens and preventing violence, regimes that would have no need to exploit nationalism or inflame ethnic hatreds.

If one adopts this view of the problem of security that confronts the Russian Federation and other states of the former Soviet Union, the first order of importance must be assigned not to relations with nations beyond the borders of the former Soviet Union but to relations with states within the CIS, particularly relations with Ukraine, Belarus, and Kazakhstan. The solution to problems of intra-CIS relations will define the nature of the statehood Russia achieves, and that in turn will determine Russia's national security concept.

The future course of relations among the CIS member states will have a bearing on global and European security as well. Many European politicians perceive the internal instability of the CIS nations as a serious threat to European security, reasoning that as long as instability prevails, Russia will be unlikely actually to implement whatever concept of security it declares.

The West's perception of the situation plays a major role in the entire equation. Unfortunately, however, that perception is often inaccurate. Many Western politicians and experts deduce imperial tendencies in the CIS precisely from those factors that, in fact, constitute a counterbalance to neoimperialism. These Western observers contend that strengthening the CIS would lead to the fortification of Russia's position in the former Soviet republics and to its political and economic domination of the "Near Abroad."

At least three reasons can be found for this point of view. First, for a long time, the West insisted on the preservation of the Soviet Union because it much preferred to deal with one state headed by a predictable leader instead of with a slew of new states led by unknown politicians. Once the Soviet Union fell apart, it became very difficult, psychologically as well as politically, for the West to continue to adopt a position that might be misconstrued as smacking of support for the alleged imperial designs of Moscow.

Second, a fairly widely held view in the West assigns at least some of the blame for the Yugoslav tragedy to the cautious initial position of the West and its delay in recognizing the new states there. Therefore, everything that might be interpreted as a potential danger to sovereignty of new states is a priori rejected. Yet, as has been argued, it is the disintegration of the core of the CIS, rather than its enhancement, that would pose a threat to the independence of the new states. Of course, such strengthening would mean Russian domination, but such domination is inevitable and can be prevented only by a total disintegration of Russia. The real issue is not whether Russia will be dominant, but whether it will become a center of a regenerated imperial policy or, by stark contrast, a guarantor of democratic development and stability in the entire post-Soviet space.

Third, an opinion exists within some Western political circles that it would be better to deal with a weak Russia surrounded by still weaker new states, than with a Russia enhanced by the integration processes on the territory of the former USSR. This attitude appears to neglect the fact that a further weakening of the CIS is likely to lead to the disintegration of the largest of its member states, including Russia, and thus improve the political prospects of those who seek to resurrect the Soviet empire.

So far, a concept of national security for a postcommunist Russia does not exist because Russian statehood has not yet formed. The nature of this statehood will determine the nature of the national security concept that is eventually adopted. And the nature of Russian statehood will be determined to a decisive degree by the nature of relations among the key members of the CIS. If the West supports tendencies toward integration—rather than separation—among these states, it will aid the formation of democratic relations among them and, as a result, help create a democratic, and not imperial, concept of national security of a new Russia.

7

Russia in a Peacekeeping Role

Susan L. Clark

A mong the many challenges facing the Russian leadership today is the need to define the country's national interests and its role in Europe, Asia, and the world as a whole. Russia must elaborate these definitions in the context of an increasingly unstable environment as it confronts several security dilemmas, including preventing the Russian Federation's own disintegration, protecting the Russian diaspora, coping with instability on and within its own borders and in the "Near Abroad," and trying to counter fears that others in the former Soviet Union are trying to isolate Russia from the rest of the international community. Peacekeeping is one of the key vehicles that Russia is likely to use to address these concerns.

As of the time of this writing (March 1993), one can identify four different levels or types of peacekeeping in which Russia has participated: under the auspices of international organizations such as the United Nations and the Council for Security and Cooperation in Europe (CSCE); under arrangements by the Commonwealth of Independent States (CIS), such as in Tajikistan; within the Russian Federation itself, as in North Ossetia; and on a bilateral basis outside the framework of the CIS, as in Georgia's South Ossetia. Thus, in some cases, Russia has undertaken peacekeeping with the international community, at other times with CIS peacekeeping structures, and sometimes Russia has acted on its own.

Following a brief discussion of Russia's role in UN peacekeeping efforts in the former Yugoslavia, this essay will focus on Russia's involvement in peacekeeping within the CIS.[1] It will provide a chronology of CIS agreements (from the time of the commonwealth's inception to March 1993) related to peacekeeping as well as analyses of the use of peacekeeping forces in Moldova and Tajikistan. These descriptions offer the basis for contrasting peacekeeping *plans* with the *reality* of what has happened. Finally, this essay will suggest some of the motivations behind Russian interest in the peacekeeping mission and assess possible implications of this role.

The importance of, and ambiguities surrounding, the idea of peace-keeping are underscored by statements by President Boris Yeltsin himself. In a speech on February 28, 1993, to the political council of Russia's Civic Union, he advocated that "responsible international institutions, including the United Nations, should grant Russia special powers as guarantor of peace and stability in the region of the former [Soviet] Union."[2] The reaction of the world community and, especially, the other states of the former Soviet Union (FSU) to such a proposal are discussed below. Simply stated, such assertions have raised concerns that Russia may seek to exploit the peacekeeping mission in the pursuit of impe-rialist ambitions.

The International Context

In today's changed political and military environment, the threat of local and regional instability has brought the peacekeeping mission to the forefront. Frequently combined with humanitarian assistance efforts, peacekeeping under the auspices of the United Nations or some other multilateral institution (such as the CSCE) appears to be viewed through-out the world as the main means for resolving current and future localized conflicts. The most obvious example today is in the former Yugoslavia, where Russian (and Ukrainian) forces have joined those of other countries under the UN peacekeeping umbrella.[3]

Russia began in early 1992 to form its first battalion of peacekeeping forces, consisting of 900 volunteer paratroopers serving on a contract basis; their dispatch to the former Yugoslavia was approved by the Russian Parliament on March 6, 1992.[4] However, this effort has not been without its controversies, most notably the question of the Russians' allegiance to their Serb brothers. Russian officials in the Foreign Ministry, parliament, and the military have all been reluctant to expand the UN mandate to include the use of military force, and they argue that any strengthening of sanctions should be applied not only to the Serbs.[5] In addition, there have been allegations of Russian peacekeepers providing Serbs with access to confiscated weapons, which highlights the difficulties of peacekeeping at the international level, let alone Russia's efforts to enforce peace within the borders of its former empire.

The debate about participating in international peacekeeping naturally includes discussions of the benefits and problems associated with such participation. On the positive side, peacekeeping is viewed as an important vehicle for improving Russia's prestige in the international community and for contributing to its integration into Europe. This argument was supported during the January 1993 visit to Moscow by Supreme Allied Commander in Europe General John Shalikashvili, when he discussed with Russian Defense Minister Pavel Grachev ways to cooperate in peacekeeping and noted that it is "quite probable" that NATO and Russian peacekeeping forces will train together in the near future.[6] A July 1992 *New Times* article also noted the "prestige" argument and related it to Yeltsin's domestic agenda: "By boosting his [Yeltsin's] international prestige, he seeks on the one hand to compensate for his declining rating at home, and on the other, to point out to possible rivals that they are second-rate provincials."[7]

President Yeltsin has additionally contended that participation in international peacekeeping missions can offer Russian military forces unique and valuable experience, which could then be applied to inter-ethnic conflicts closer to home. From the military's perspective, international peacekeeping provides the armed forces with a legitimate mission at a time when their purpose is being debated. Finally, in what is probably an attempt to diffuse critics who question how—and why—Russia should be paying for peacekeeping activities when so many of its own citizens are now living at or below the poverty level, it has been pointed out that each participant in the UN effort is paid by the United Nations, which also pays the countries providing these troops. These payments can, in turn, help defray Russia's dues to the United Nations, which must be paid in hard currency.[8]

Among the arguments voiced against Russia's participation in the former Yugoslavia, many parliamentary deputies have expressed doubt about the political advisability of sending troops there. In part, it is reasoned, the Serbs are Russia's brothers; in part, there is a concern that Russia not be dragged into a civil war. Above all, there is a feeling (mirrored by much of the Russian public) that Russia has enough troubles of its own at home. More generally, some question the utility of Russia's involvement in areas that are perceived to be far from Russia's national interests (however they might be defined). Finally, as long-time *Krasnaia zvezda* reporter Aleksandr Golts asserted in July 1992: "There are no guarantees that the parties involved in the conflicts will not regard international forces as aggressors. And the possibility is in no way ruled out that the deployment of UN peacekeeping forces will result not in pacification but in a further escalation of force."[9]

CIS Efforts to Create Peacekeeping Forces

Chronology of Events

In the context of the creation of peacekeeping forces in the CIS, it is perhaps surprising to some—particularly those who believe Russia is interested in peacekeeping as a way of regaining some of its "lost" territory—that Russia has not always been at the forefront of these efforts.[10] Indeed, it was Kazakhstan's President Nursultan Nazarbayev who proposed in early March 1992 that it was necessary to begin developing special peacekeeping forces to serve in CIS regions, having in mind especially the continuing unrest in Nagorno-Karabakh.[11] On March 20, 1992, during the CIS summit held in Kiev, an agreement covering collective efforts to quell national conflicts, monitor cease-fire agreements, and provide military observers and forces for these activities was signed by Armenia, Belarus, Kazakhstan, Kyrgyzstan, Moldova, Russia, Tajikistan, and Uzbekistan. Azerbaijan and Ukraine signed conditionally, noting that participation was contingent upon their parliaments' approval. This agreement further stipulated that the CIS would use troops from member states not involved in the particular conflict, that these forces would be manned on a contractual basis only by volunteers, and that they would be placed under joint command. Their use would be approved only by the CIS Council of Heads of State, following requests for such assistance by at least one CIS state and with the agreement of the belligerent parties.

Little progress was made in implementing this agreement by the time of the CIS meeting in Tashkent in mid-May 1992. At that time, two protocols on the formation of peacekeeping forces were signed covering material-technical support and their financing. At a meeting on July 6, heads of state reached an agreement in principle on the creation of joint peacekeeping forces; according to Russian Foreign Minister Andrei Kozyrev, these forces would consist of 2,000 to 10,000 troops and could be deployed by the end of July.[12] At another CIS meeting, in Tashkent on July 16, 1992, participants worked out a protocol on temporary procedures for establishing and deploying a CIS peacekeeping force, based on documents prepared in advance by the CIS military command. Yeltsin signed this protocol on July 21, 1992; reportedly, an envoy dispatched from Moscow succeeded in obtaining seven signatures from the other states by August 12, 1992.[13]

The protocol calls for each signatory to form and train special military units and groups of observers. The size of each state's contribution is to be determined by the overall size of its armed forces. Thus, those with small militaries would probably provide a battalion, while larger armies would supply several regiments or a division.[14] Under the protocol, the peacekeeping forces are granted limited rights of the use of force: for self-defense or for separating belligerents (which could then raise the question of differentiating between peacekeepers and peacemakers, discussed below). As with previous discussions, the protocol stipulates that only volunteers are to be members of this force; it also explains that the peacekeeping units are to be organized on a permanent basis. More generally, the protocol explains that the peacekeepers' "main mission is to establish the primary conditions for strengthening peace and understanding achieved by the parties in a conflict, to protect the civilian population and to help establish closer ties between the opposing sides."[15]

For its part, Russia began the formation of peacekeeping forces in early 1992, in connection with the decision to send a battalion to participate under UN auspices in the former Yugoslavia. Colonel General Viktor Dubynin of the General Staff noted in an interview in September 1992 that, in accordance with the CIS agreement, a motorized rifle division was undergoing training in the Volga Military District. It was armed only with light small arms and was deployed in armored personnel carriers and trucks.[16] At that time, Russia had a 900-man airborne assault battalion in the former Yugoslavia, a 950-man reinforced airborne assault regiment in South Ossetia, Georgia, and a 2,750-man force (consisting of one assault regiment and three motorized rifle battalions) in Dniester, Moldova.[17] By January 5, 1993, *ITAR-TASS* reported that more than 13,200 Russian servicemen were taking part in various peacekeeping activities.[18]

In terms of the types of forces used and being developed, Defense Minister Grachev and other military leaders have underscored the importance of a more mobile force for the Russian military's various new functions, including international and CIS peacekeeping. Within this context, the airborne troops are seen to provide the backbone for the mobile forces.[19] The heavy reliance on airborne troops to perform peacekeeping functions has not been warmly embraced by all their leaders. For example, in an interview on October 9, 1992, Colonel General Evgenii Podkolzin, the commander of the airborne troops, presented his view: "The politicians are now using the airborne troops as a police force. That is not our task . . . but what do you do if there is no other real force capable of intervening in local wars and stopping them? Only we, the airborne troops, are currently capable of halting conflicts in 'nearby foreign parts.'" He further stressed that the first of Russia's mobile forces (from which peacekeeping forces would be drawn) were being trained in the same manner as the airborne forces, and that they would replace the latter in conflict zones.[20]

The problem remains that an actual CIS peacekeeping force has yet to be created. Colonel General V. Samsonov, chief of CIS Joint Armed Forces Main Staff, in an interview with *Krasnaia zvezda* on February 17, 1993, commented that individual countries in the CIS have begun to make some efforts in this direction (citing Kazakhstan's willingness to send some of its troops to conflicts on CIS external borders, as well as the decision by Russia, Kazakhstan, Kyrgyzstan, and Uzbekistan to send troops to the Tajikistan-Afghanistan border), and that he remains convinced that a specialized CIS peacekeeping force will be established. He recognized, however, that some important obstacles remain, such as the fact that although the heads of state have approved in principle the mechanism for sending in peacekeeping forces, there is still no legislative mechanism to do so.[21]

Differing Attitudes toward the Peacekeeping Mission

Not surprisingly, there have been disputes among various Russian institutions and personalities about the peacekeeping mission. For example, the Foreign Ministry has been largely supportive of such a CIS force— arguing that it would meet Russia's national interests[22]—although in July 1992 Foreign Minister Kozyrev cautioned that Russia will not act as a gendarme in CIS peacekeeping activities.[23] He has since adopted a more resolute stance (probably as a way of trying to diffuse some of the pressure from the nationalists), noting that Russia's real security challenges lie in regional conflicts; it must, therefore, focus its "efforts, attention, and resources" on preparing rapid deployment forces for use in regional conflicts and peacekeeping.[24] Similarly, as the lone high-ranking civilian in the Ministry of Defense, Andrei Kokoshin has cited peacekeeping "successes" in Moldova and South Ossetia, as well as participation in the former Yugoslavia, as demonstrating that "Europe feels that the Armed

Forces of Russia are becoming a weighty factor in Russia's international positions and an important element in ensuring stability and security in Europe as a whole."[25]

The military leadership has its own perspective. Defense Minister Grachev has made clear his determination to protect the Russian diaspora at all costs, averring on June 5, 1992, that he "would answer any infringement 'upon the honor and dignity of the Russian population in any part of the CIS' with the 'most resolute measures,' right up to the dispatch of armed units."[26] This position is reflected in Moscow's draft military doctrine released in May 1992, which asserts Moscow's right to protect Russian-speaking minorities anywhere in the FSU, using military force if necessary, although this document does add that such intervention can occur only after a consensus is obtained from all CIS member states.[27] There are also legitimate concerns that peacekeepers can become caught in the middle between the belligerents; an *International Affairs* article raised the possibility that if troops found themselves cut off from food, energy, and other supplies, could the belligerents not use these supplies as barter for buying peacekeepers' weapons?[28] Perhaps most significant, the participation of Russian troops in peacekeeping efforts leads others to question whether Russia is trying to pursue imperial policies.[29]

There is some room for sympathy for the Russian leadership trying to work out its role in peacekeeping activities. In many respects, Russia's leaders are caught between the proverbial rock and a hard place. On the one hand, countless areas of instability (either already evident or brewing just below the surface) exist throughout the FSU. Most (if not all) of the FSU states believe that these conflicts must somehow be controlled; otherwise the threat of spreading instability becomes too great. At the same time, Russia is sometimes the only state willing to send peacekeeping forces.[30] This reluctance has been evident in the efforts aimed at developing a collective security policy in general and in the formation of peacekeeping forces more specifically. For example, Turkmenistan's President Saparmurad Niyazov explained his country's refusal to sign the Tashkent collective security agreement on the grounds that "adherence to it could have embroiled Turkmenistan in disputes between member states that were none of Turkmenistan's direct concern."[31]

Marshal Evgenii Shaposhnikov articulated this dilemma in a *Nezavisimaia gazeta* article in January 1993:

> At present only Russian troops are acting as peacekeepers. Some people have tried to use that to insinuate that Russia is taking "imperial" steps.

That is totally incorrect and unjust. However, it is very important to ensure joint participation in peacekeeping actions in practice. The "hot spots" represent a problem for us all. And we must overcome them together.

He further pointed out that Russian peacekeepers are operating under bilateral agreements with the "host" nation.[32]

Perhaps a way to discredit the imperial argument, if the Russian leadership is serious, is to insist more forcefully and immediately on the creation of a genuine structure for a CIS force rather than relying on bilateral arrangements to send in peacekeepers. Even *Pravda* recognizes the potential for being ostracized by the world community if Russia pushes too hard on its own (as has happened with the Serbs in Yugoslavia): "If one day Russia stands up in earnest for a Russian-speaking population somewhere in the CIS, they [the international community] will punish us too," like the Serbs.[33] The question becomes how strong are the hard-line nationalist forces in Russia that regard protection of the Russian diaspora to be far more important than alienation from the international democratic community?[34]

Some analysts, such as Sergei Karaganov, deputy director of the Institute of Europe in Moscow, have sought to develop a line of thinking that can straddle these two worlds. The gist of his argument is that Russia must play an "enlightened post-imperial role" throughout the FSU, which would include the protection of all human and minority rights, not just those of Russian speakers. More precisely, he has argued:

A decisive component of Russia's new mission in the world is to ensure with help from the world community that the ex-Soviet area does not become a geostrategic hole radiating instability and war and ultimately endangering the very existence of humanity.

One can talk as much as one likes about the need for Russia to set itself apart from Central Asia, pull out of the Transcaucasus and desist from sending its troops to impose peace or prevent war. But there is no getting away from our destiny, history and geography. Unless we curb and settle conflicts due to the disintegration of the Union and its social system, they are bound to spread to further regions, raising waves of migration, terrorism, [and] violence on Russian soil as well. . . .

Our recent policy of ignoring violations of minority rights in the Baltic republics was amoral and shortsighted. But what some people say now about being ready to defend "Russian-speaking people" and none but them anywhere and at all times is just as impracticable and dangerous. This approach is open to question also from the moral point of view. . . . To suppress the rights of some is to trigger an inevitable chain reaction.[35]

Even this attempt to put peacekeeping and the protection of civilians into a broader context, however, is subject to considerable skepticism, above all because Russia is not viewed as a neutral power in any of these conflicts (current or future) within the former USSR.

One way to alleviate some of this skepticism would be to involve the international community (that is, non-CIS states) in these efforts. However, there is also a debate among various Russian officials on the appropriateness of involving non-CIS members in peacekeeping within the FSU. On the one hand, Deputy Foreign Minister Sergei Lavrov in mid-1992 noted that he favored *collective* peacekeeping forces to settle FSU disputes: these forces would comprise European troops, including ones from CIS states; only if these efforts fail should a regional solution be rejected in favor of the United Nations.[36] Thus, Lavrov does not oppose the involvement of non-CIS states; he only wishes to keep external involvement limited to regional organizations, at least initially. In April 1992, a former people's deputy took a more forceful stance for UN assistance and against CIS involvement. According to Yurii Shchekochikhin:

> There is not and there cannot be any profit from the use of Commonwealth troops from Russia, from Ukraine, or from any of our new states, if they try to stand between Georgians and Ossetians, between Azerbaijanis and Armenians, or between Moldovans and Russians in the Trans-Dniester: the mistrust is too strong in people wearing our traditional military uniform. . . . *Only calling in UN troops can stop the blood today.*[37]

On the other side of the debate, Shaposhnikov has forcefully rejected the idea of troops being brought into conflict regions such as Dniester and Nagorno-Karabakh:

> The CIS is quite capable of dealing with all the issues that arise within the CIS, and that includes these military conflicts, etc. Otherwise, are we to agree that peacemakers will arrive from somewhere to make peace between us? . . . I am not, of course, against some commissions being set up with peacekeeping purposes or the United Nations taking part in the work of those commissions; I say yes to this, but no to the troops.[38]

The other factor in this equation is whether non-CIS states would be willing to play a peacekeeping role, even if asked to do so.

The Practice of Peacekeeping in the Former Soviet Union

It is clear that peacekeeping efforts within the FSU have not taken shape in accordance with a carefully prescribed plan. To understand better the reasons for Russian involvement and the process that has been followed so far, this section examines two case studies of peacekeeping in the FSU: in the Moldovan-Dniester conflict, and in the civil war in Tajikistan.

Moldova

In September 1990, the Russian-speaking community on the left bank of the Dniester River declared its own republic, the Dniester Soviet Socialist Republic, independent from Moldova.[39] Many people among the Dniester population were strongly supportive of the USSR and, following its disintegration, proclaimed their interest in becoming part of a new USSR or perhaps of Russia. As Vladimir Socor of Radio Liberty explains, the conflict between Dniester and Moldova is not so much an ethnic one as a geopolitical and ideological dispute.[40] Headquartered in Dniester's capital of Tiraspol is the former Soviet 14th Army, which Yeltsin unilaterally placed under Russian jurisdiction on April 1, 1992.[41] It is the role of the 10,000-man 14th Army in the Moldovan-Dniester dispute that has fueled much of the controversy among the parties involved.

It is generally agreed that the Dniester insurgency would not have been possible without assistance from the 14th Army.[42] Dniester first began setting up its own forces in fall 1991, and the widely reported involvement of then-leader of the 14th Army, Lieutenant General Gennadii Yakovlev, in supplying weapons and military equipment played a vital role in their creation. Indeed, Yakovlev's excessive involvement ultimately led to his removal from that post, but his actions raised serious questions about whether Moscow was in control of this force (and therefore was condoning this behavior) or whether the force was effectively operating on its own. Neither interpretation painted an encouraging picture.[43]

Until their introduction in late July 1992, the debate about peace-keeping forces in Moldova-Dniester largely centered on who would contribute such forces and what role (if any) the Russian 14th Army would play. The Russian position was that the 14th Army could, indeed, perform a peacekeeping function and maintain neutrality in the process. This view was propounded by a wide variety of officials, including the 14th Army's commander Yurii Netkachev, who indicated in April 1992 that his force was ready to act as a peacekeeper, but he would not be willing to do so until a political decision had been taken by the CIS heads of state.[44] President Yeltsin was reported to adhere to much the same line.[45] Netkachev's successor, Lieutenant General Aleksandr Lebed, has not demonstrated particular concern about having the backing of political decisions, asserting instead that while the 14th Army would maintain neutrality, "the neutrality will be of a different quality. It will be armed neutrality."[46] Marshal Shaposhnikov and Generals Boris Gromov, Nikolai Stolyarov, and Boris Piankov also supported the idea of the 14th Army's involvement, although Piankov suggested that this should be in collaboration with CSCE observers.[47] During their trip to Dniester in April 1992, both Vice-President Aleksandr Rutskoi and Sergei Stankevich indicated that the 14th Army had this right and the capability, with Stankevich adding that although the CIS had agreed to create a peacekeeping force, "until this force is formed, we must sanction the 14th Army, which is already in the conflict zone and is being attacked from all sides, to take a position that would separate conflicting sides."[48] Foreign Minister Kozyrev presented the idea of the 14th Army participating in peacekeeping in the region as part of his proposal at the April 1992 meeting of the foreign ministers of Moldova, Romania, Ukraine, and Russia aimed at resolving the Moldovan-Dniester dispute.[49] Not surprisingly, the Dniester separatists have been fully supportive of the 14th Army's role, frequently arguing that it is only this force that represents a guarantee for peace and stability.[50] They would also like the 14th Army to become part of their own military force.[51]

The reaction by other states to the 14th Army's potential role has been quite negative. At the April 1992 foreign ministers' meeting, for example, both Ukrainian Foreign Minister Anatoly Zlenko and his Romanian counterpart, Adrian Nastase, questioned the 14th Army's ability to perform a peacekeeping function. The Moldovan side flatly opposed such an idea.[52] Their basic argument against the 14th Army was that it appeared "excessively politicized and not suitable for a peacekeeping role."[53] Moreover, one should not assume that all elements of the 14th Army support such a role. According to Major General V. Kozhevnikov in April 1992, "Can we be certain that the military will not for the umpteenth time end up guilty of something and will not be scapegoats . . . in a political confrontation?"[54]

Other solutions were sought that would exclude the 14th Army's participation, including a proposal in early July 1992 for the involvement of peacekeepers from Ukraine, Belarus, Bulgaria, Romania, Russia, and Moldova.[55] However, the Belarussian leadership quickly decided that it could not send such forces because that would violate the country's policy of neutrality (it would only be willing to assist in political solutions).[56] Bulgaria and Romania also decided not to send such a force. A discussion by a Russian General Staff officer mentioned, in addition to Ukraine and

Bulgaria, the possibility of Poland and Finland participating in a peace-keeping force; Moldova did not agree because it would have to pay non-FSU states in hard currency.[57] With the collapse of other options, by mid-July Moldova appeared to feel that neither the international commu-nity nor the CIS would be able (or willing) to assist in the resolution of the conflict with Dniester.

On July 21, 1992, Presidents Boris Yeltsin and Mircear Snegur reached an agreement—on a bilateral basis—that provided for the introduction of a tripartite peacekeeping force (from Russia, Moldova, and Dniester); Russian recognition of Dniester as a part of Moldova with special status; the right of Dniester to self-determination should Moldova change its status—In other words, opt for unification with Romania (Snegur's leadership has steadfastly opposed the idea of unification with Romania); and the gradual withdrawal of the 14th Army. Throughout the process, Snegur was very careful to differentiate between Russia's "democratic forces," led by Yeltsin, and its "conservative revanchist circles."[58]

On July 29, 1992, the first peacekeepers arrived; according to Agence France-Presse (AFP), they comprised 3,800 Russians, 1,200 Moldovans, and 1,200 Dniester national guards.[59] All told, the force consisted of some five to six Russian, two to three Moldovan, and two to three Dniester battalions.[60] The Russian forces included airborne troops from the Tula Airborne Division, as well as three battalions of ground forces. All forces were under the command of the Unified Control Commission, headquartered in Bendery, including Russian Generals Vladimir Zhurbenko and Eduard Vorobev and Moldova's represen-tative, Nicolae Chirtoaca.[61]

By late August, Zhurbenko stated that the belligerents had been disengaged and, although the peacekeepers have sporadically come under fire since their introduction, by and large, the peace has held. Still, the 14th Army remains a significant bone of contention between Moldova and Dniester and between Moldova and Russia. By January 1993, it appeared that the openly pro-Dniester head of the 14th Army, General Lebed, was focusing his support away from the current Dniester leader-ship (accusing them of incompetence and corruption) and toward a minority Dniester faction; he nevertheless remained committed to sup-porting the Dniester region itself in its efforts to separate from Moldova.[62] Given Lebed's orientation, it is not surprising that Moldovan authorities still see the 14th Army as a destabilizing element, but Yeltsin has contin-ued to refuse to discuss any specific schedule for its withdrawal and to insist on linking any future withdrawal to the determination of the political status of the Dniester region.

Tajikistan

During 1992, Tajikistan found itself embroiled in a civil war, with between 20,000 and 70,000 people killed between May and December.[63] By the beginning of 1993, control of the border between Tajikistan and Afghanistan presented a serious security concern for the region. It is this latter mission that peacekeepers from CIS states were sent to fulfill in March 1993. In the case of Tajikistan, the Central Asian republics, at least initially, took as active a role in trying to resolve this conflict as did Russia. Before turning to the process of peacekeeping efforts in Tajikistan, however, a brief summary of the general domestic conflict is necessary.

The fighting in Tajikistan began in late May 1992 after President Rakhmon Nabiev, a former communist, agreed to turn over one-third of his government's ministerial posts to a coalition of democratic, nationalist, and Islamic groups. Nabiev's supporters in the south did not approve of this compromise and began actions to bring his government down. Risking oversimplification, the two opposing sides can be broken down as follows. On the one side, there are anticommunist, prodemocratic, and pro-Islamic supporters; they include the Democratic Party of Tajikistan, the Tajik nationalist movement Rastokhez, the Islamic Renaissance Party, and another nationalist movement, Lali Badakhshan. On the other side are procommunist forces, many of which are united into a Popular Front of Tajikistan that opposes fundamentalism and the democratic opposition.[64]

In September 1992, President Nabiev was forced to resign, at least in part because of a planned bilateral military agreement with Russia and Yeltsin's decree in August that placed CIS border troops in Tajikistan under Russian jurisdiction, raising the opposition's concerns that Russia was seeking to reestablish control over Tajikistan.[65] As a result of Nabiev's resignation, the opposition (prodemocratic, pro-Islamic) forces gained greater control. In October 1992, the procommunists, who were in the process of taking parts of the capital of Dushanbe, were temporarily thwarted in their efforts partly due to the actions of the Russian 201st Motorized Rifle Division, protecting what it then regarded as Tajikistan's legal government.[66] Nevertheless, by November, the procommunists controlled most of southern Tajikistan, and the coalition government resigned on November 10. By the end of 1992, the procommunist elements were back in "control," although it cannot be said that they controlled all of Tajikistan; the country remained badly fractured.

In terms of external assistance and the role of Russia's 201st division in Tajikistan, the Russian government appeared to be mainly concerned about protecting Tajikistan's border with Afghanistan and protecting state installations. For example, in mid-July 1992, Yeltsin promised to strengthen troops on this border,[67] while the 201st guarded state installations. On the likelihood of sending peacekeepers to the area, Colonel General Vorobev contended in early October that such a step was premature because there was no cease-fire in place, and that if the Tajik government could not maintain peace, CIS military forces (as opposed to peacekeepers) would more likely be dispatched.[68] The Russian government does not appear to have been encouraging the Tajiks to accept the 201st in a peacekeeping role (as was the case of the 14th Army in Moldova), but rather agreed to this only after the Tajik government had requested it (see below for details). Still, there is evidence that the 201st has not remained neutral, and that its proclivities lie with the procommunist government, which in turn supports the continued presence of the 201st (including in a peacekeeping role).

For their part, the Central Asians have been interested in resolving Tajikistan's unrest largely because they fear the possible spread of instability to their own states. Bess Brown further explains their motivations and fears, reasoning that Uzbekistan's government constantly raises the specter of Muslim fundamentalism, Kazakhstan and Kyrgyzstan are concerned about social and ethnic unrest, and Turkmenistan is to some extent worried about Afghanistan's influence.[69]

As head of the CIS military forces, Marshal Shaposhnikov visited Tajikistan in late August 1992 and reportedly reached a preliminary agreement with Nabiev on the deployment of peacekeepers should a cease-fire be effected; however, a month later (after Nabiev's resignation) Shaposhnikov noted that "military experts did not succeed in convincing the republic's leadership of the need to deploy peacekeeping forces."[70] During the same time, military observers from Russia, Kazakhstan, and Kyrgyzstan traveled to Tajikistan to assess the likely effectiveness of a CIS peacekeeping force.

The reaction among procommunist political forces in Tajikistan to the possible introduction of CIS peacekeepers was largely favorable, whereas the opposition did not embrace the idea. In September and October 1992, the procommunists frequently stated that such a force represented the only means capable of stopping the civil war and stabilizing the situation. Among the supporters of this idea were the chairman of the Kulyab Oblispolkom, the leader of the National Movement of the Lukyab region, the chairman of the Committee for National Security, the deputy chairman of the Tajik Supreme Soviet, and the executive of the Leninabad Regional Council of People's Deputies.[71] In contrast, Deputy Prime Minister Davlat Ismonov (once again an "opposition" figure) complained in early October that interference by Russia and other CIS states had given support to the procommunists, and he called for the Russian army's immediate withdrawal from hot spots.[72]

Kyrgyzstan, particularly Vice-President Feliks Kulov, was very involved in early October 1992 in trying to broker an arrangement for peacekeepers; the Tajik government appealed to the CIS on October 8, based on an agreement by both belligerent sides, to send in joint CIS units from Kyrgyzstan and Kazakhstan. Kulov advocated the use of a 350- to 400-man Kyrgyz peacekeeping force (which could also include Kazakhs), but only after a cease-fire and only to carry out police functions. Its main task would be "not to disarm the warring groupings but to give an opportunity to the republic's leadership to strengthen the state power structure, law enforcement bodies, and to stabilize the economic situation."[73] But while other Kyrgyz officials asserted that Russian and Uzbek forces could not be used in a peacekeeping effort in Tajikistan, the Kyrgyz Parliament proved unwilling to allow the dispatch of its own forces, partly out of fear of being dragged into the civil war and having no guarantees for its force's safety, and partly because of its principle of noninterference in the internal affairs of others.[74]

With the failure of the Kyrgyz effort, on October 21, 1992, acting President Akbarsho Iskandrov turned to Russia, asking for the use of the 201st as peacekeeping forces. Two days later, the Tajik government appealed to the United Nations to send a peacekeeping mission and humanitarian assistance as soon as possible. General Vorobev is reported to have responded that it was likely the request for the use of the 201st would be met, but he expressed "fear that certain circles would accuse the Russian army of interference in Tajikistan's internal affairs" and that the 201st would be drawn into the conflict.[75] In early November, Foreign Minister Kozyrev stated that Russian troops in Tajikistan "probably will become the nucleus of peacekeeping force and act as a disengaging and stabilizing factor," but that they would not become involved in the republic's internal politics.[76] Clearly, leading Russian officials became increasingly sensitive to how Russia's involvement in peace-keeping might be perceived and were trying to diffuse political criticisms in advance. The reality, however, frequently contradicted these more altruistic statements.

On November 30, 1992, foreign and military representatives from Uzbekistan, Kazakhstan, Kyrgyzstan, and Russia meeting in Termez reached an agreement on the need to introduce peacekeeping forces, but stipulated that a cease-fire first had to be secured. According to Shaposh-nikov, they had "worked out a mechanism for introducing these forces. . . . It is now up to the parliaments," which must give their approval to the sending of these troops.[77] Herein lay the next obstacle: by the end of the year, only Uzbekistan (on December 9) had approved the sending of its forces; it was not clear if Kyrgyzstan would reverse its previous decision; and Russia and Kazakhstan had yet to discuss the issue in their parliaments (Kazakhstan postponed the discussion until late January 1993). The plan apparently called for roughly one battalion each from the participating countries, while reports differed on the possible participation of the Russian 201st.[78] During the Termez talks, Defense Minister Grachev stressed that "the peacemaking forces must be manned on an interstate basis. The 201st Motorized Rifle Division can provide the technical facilities for this," but he objected to the use of the 201st in its present form as the basis for a peacekeeping force.[79] The kidnapping and murder of several Russian soldiers in December by the Islamic Renaissance Party only heightened concerns about the lack of safety guarantees and rein-forced a proclivity for Russians to oppose the pro-Islamic faction, now again in opposition.[80] Moreover, the Tajik government in late January 1993 appointed an ethnic Russian as its new defense minister, further reinforcing a close relationship between Russia (and its 201st Division) and the Tajik government.

The new year brought new discussions of what to do in Tajikistan. At the CIS summit meeting in late January 1993, the plan to send peace-keeping forces and humanitarian assistance was reaffirmed. According to an Azerbaijani official attending the meeting, each CIS republic was to send a battalion to Tajikistan, but Belarus, Ukraine, and Moldova all indicated they would not do so.[81] A Russian report in early February stated that five battalions, composed of Russians, Kazakhs, Kyrgyz, and Uzbeks, would be sent "soon" to Tajikistan. The proposal submitted to the Russian Supreme Soviet was for sending a 500-man contingent.[82] These battalions were to be deployed along the Tajikistan-Afghanistan border. In addition, the Russian government placed the 201st at Tajikistan's disposal (albeit still under Russian control) for border reinforcement.

In short, a multinational CIS peacekeeping contingent began to be deployed to Tajikistan in early March 1993. Its primary mission, however, was meant to be different from that which was discussed in fall 1992. Namely, instead of acting as a separating force between warring Tajik factions (which were clearly engaged in an internal dispute, albeit one fueled by external assistance), the *main* focus was to be on strengthening security on an external CIS border (in this case, the border between Tajikistan and Afghanistan). Moreover, a six-person UN mission, in Tajikistan at least until April 20, 1993, sought to guarantee the impartiality of the CIS peacekeeping forces, as well as to help stop hostilities and guarantee human rights.[83] Such international participation should be encouraged by all FSU states and willingly embraced by the Western community to help ensure that peacekeeping missions are not used for alternative motives. Unfortunately, this was not the case: the international community paid little attention to the Tajik conflict; atrocities were committed by various belligerents; and "peacekeepers" were involved not only in border protection but also in the internal Tajik conflict.

Intentions versus Reality

As the case studies illustrate, the actual use of peacekeeping forces in the FSU has differed from CIS plans for these efforts. At the same time, there have been some consistencies in implementation.

It is important first to underscore that, as of March 1993, the mechanisms for an actual CIS peacekeeping force were still not in place and that there was hardly universal support among the CIS states for such a force. Plans indicated that a CIS peacekeeping force would comprise troops from the following countries: Russia, Kazakhstan, Armenia, Uzbekistan, Kyrgyzstan, and Tajikistan. In November 1992, the Committee of Chiefs of Staff of the CIS Armed Forces agreed to designate some elements of the participating nations' armies as peacekeeping forces; these forces will make up three echelons.[84] Altogether, this plan called for the peacekeeping force to be equivalent to some 24 divisions, with Russia supplying about one-half of these forces.

The first echelon would consist of mobile forces, ready to be deployed in three to five days, with one motorized rifle division from Russia, motorized rifle regiments from Kazakhstan and Uzbekistan, and battalions from Kyrgyzstan, Tajikistan, and Armenia. The second echelon would consist of about eight division equivalents and be ready for deployment in 10 to 15 days. The third echelon would consist of reinforcement forces equal to some 14 divisions and be ready for deployment in 30 days. If this plan is implemented, as Sergei Rogov and others point out, the problem is that "almost the entire Commonwealth force will be provided by Russia with some additions by Kazakhstan, while others' participation will be insignificant." Also, they caution, "the legal base for those peacekeeping forces is highly questionable, and most probably the plan will simply not work except to provide Russian military involvement the image of a multilateral action."[85] In any event, the January 1993 decision at the CIS meeting in Minsk to dispatch peacekeeping forces to Tajikistan was the first such collective CIS decision, but even this remained distant from the idea of creating a truly multilateral CIS peacekeeping force.

In Russia's peacekeeping efforts to March 1993, there were two points at which plans coincided with reality.[86] Specifically, the enlisted troops that were sent to the regions for peacekeeping duty were volunteers, and they were serving on a contract basis. Beyond this, what quickly becomes clear is that no two cases of peacekeeping efforts were identical.

In contrast to CIS plans, Russian peacekeeping efforts primarily relied on bilateral agreements with the affected state rather than on CIS auspices. Thus, in the case of Moldova and South Ossetia, the Russian government worked out an arrangement for Russian participation in peacekeeping. However, in the case of Tajikistan, there were several bilateral efforts, particularly those by Kyrgyz and Uzbek officials as well as Russians, but the ultimate decision to send troops to the region used multilateral forums (for example, the November 30 meeting and the CIS January 1993 meeting), rather than bilateral arrangements.

Another important distinction between CIS plans and the reality of peacekeeping efforts lay in decisions to involve the belligerent parties in these forces. Peacekeepers in Moldova-Dniester consisted of troops from Moldova, Dniester, and Russia, including the 14th Army (which repeatedly was involved in supporting the Dniester separatists). Similarly, in South Ossetia, the peacekeepers came from Georgia, Russia, and Ossetia. Interestingly, even the Russian Ministry of Foreign Affairs supported such arrangements, arguing that the participation of belligerents in the peacekeeping process ensures their cooperation. This solution runs counter to the thinking of the international community, where the United Nations has sought to ensure that nations participating in a given peacekeeping operation are perceived to be neutral.

This raises a related issue: the problem of using Russian military forces already stationed in conflict regions. Serious doubts have been expressed about the neutrality of these forces, most notably in the case of the 14th Army in Moldova, but also in respect of the 201st division in Tajikistan. Indeed, in the case of the former Yugoslavia, there are serious concerns about Russian forces operating under the UN mandate being blatantly supportive of their Serb brothers. The absence of a commitment to neutrality is a major stumbling block to hopes for an appropriate Russian role in peacekeeping efforts, both in the FSU and in the world community.

Finally, another problem in peacekeeping experiences in which Russia has been involved is the need to differentiate between peacekeeping and peacemaking. Although CIS plans call for peacekeepers to be introduced only after a cease-fire is in place and merely to enforce that cease-fire, in fact, the forces have more frequently become peacemakers when the cease-fire fails. Such was the case in South Ossetia and in Tajikistan.

Russian Motivations in Peacekeeping

The central question in examining the reasons behind Russian interest in the peacekeeping mission boils down to whether Russia is using this mission as a means of asserting imperialist ambitions and regaining its empire (or at least preventing the loss of additional territory) or whether there is simply no other country willing or able to perform this mission. The simple answer is that there is no simple answer; both motivations can be seen to be at play.

Some political factions in Russia certainly assert their desire and determination to regain what they consider to be rightful Russian territory. Closely linked with this idea is the argument that the Russian government has the fundamental right and duty to protect the Russian diaspora. This argument has been articulated by Sergei Stankevich and Pavel Grachev, among others. On the other hand, some Russians seek to broaden the peacekeeping mandate to try to avoid some of the accusations of Russian imperialism. Some, such as Sergei Karaganov, argue that Russia must perform a peacekeeping mission in the FSU, but that it must do so to protect human rights in general, not just the rights of the Russian diaspora. From a Western perspective, even this line of thinking seems like an excuse by Russia to try to maintain its influence in what are now independent and sovereign states.

At the same time, while recognizing the validity of the imperial argument, it should be noted that the Russian government also has a legitimate concern about the willingness and ability of other states to perform a peacekeeping mission in the FSU. The willingness of others to participate is brought into question by at least two factors. First, several of the new states have adopted neutrality commitments, which they believe exclude them from participation in a multilateral peacekeeping effort. Thus, Belarus affirmed its willingness to do everything possible on a political level to help resolve the Moldovan-Dniester conflict, but it refused to send troops there, citing its neutrality commitment. Similarly, Turkmenistan refused to become involved in attempting to resolve the Tajik unrest, arguing that it is an internal affair not affecting Turkmenistan. A second important factor is the unwillingness of parliaments to approve the dispatch of national forces in a peacekeeping mission. This is frequently linked to issues of neutrality and refusal to interfere in the internal affairs of others, but it can also be a case of a parliament being influenced by the public at large. For example, in the case of both Kyrgyzstan and Kazakhstan, the parliaments proved extremely reluctant to send troops to Tajikistan, at least partly due to public pressure and demonstrations against this idea.

On another level, evidence points to a general reluctance among the international community to offer an alternative to a Russian-dominated process by becoming involved in such peacekeeping missions. The argument has been made that, even if the international community proved willing to perform such a function, the length of time the process would take would probably be too long. In addition, some Russian officials— such as Marshal Shaposhnikov—steadfastly oppose the introduction of non-CIS forces into former Soviet regions.

Finally, there is a legitimate concern about the ability of the new national armies of the FSU (aside from Russia's) to execute a peacekeeping mission, at least among those states that have indicated a willingness to do so. They generally lack both an indigenous officer corps to provide leadership and the training, expertise, and equipment to perform peacekeeping functions. All these factors combine to make a solution to the peacekeeping problem a difficult one.

In the end, if Russian officials want to dissuade Western nations and former Soviet states from the notion that Russia is seeking a means of asserting imperial ambitions, Russia should assume an even more active role in establishing an actual CIS peacekeeping force, rather than continuing to rely primarily on bilateral solutions. In addition, it should appeal to Western institutions for greater involvement. Such involvement would not necessarily mean the dispatch of Western troops. Instead, it could follow the model used in Tajikistan, where a small team from the United Nations serves for several months to ensure the impartiality of CIS peacekeeping forces being sent to the region. Such observer efforts would require minimal expenditure and could provide an objective external assessment of actions by Russian troops (and others). The West must, in turn, be ready and willing to embrace such efforts.

Implications of Russian Peacekeeping Efforts

The economic factor in the peacekeeping equation cannot be ignored. Whereas participation in international peacekeeping activities can actually provide some financial benefit, the economic drain on Russia from CIS peacekeeping is evident. According to a September 1992 report citing an officer of the General Staff, each peacekeeper was paid between 8,000 and 12,000 rubles in addition to his regular monthly salary. According to this official, every day that peacekeepers were deployed in South Ossetia, Dniester, and Yugoslavia cost 2.2 million rubles and $12,000; this price excluded transport, fuel, food, and combat equipment and property depreciation. As of September 1, 1992, Russia had already spent 190 million rubles and $730,000, while "despite all the accords, no other country in the Commonwealth . . . , including those where the peace-making forces are situated, has paid a penny for this."[87]

Calculating exact costs given Russia's constantly spiraling inflation rate is extremely difficult. However, even if one assumes the minimum payment of 8,000 additional rubles per month (a very conservative estimate, because military salaries were again raised substantially in January 1993), the personnel cost alone for the more than 13,200 men deployed in early 1993 would be more than 105 million rubles each month. This does not even begin to take into account the costs of training personnel to perform peacekeeping functions or the costs of deployment (such as fuel, ammunition, and loss of and damage to weapons and equipment).

From a more general perspective, the political and social implications of Russian peacekeeping apply to both the domestic situation and to

Russia's relations with other countries. Domestically, the debate about peacekeeping can act as yet another source of tension between the various political factions (hard-liners versus reformers, to oversimplify the situation). A key question is whether it will be possible to find a middle ground for peacekeeping participation on which the diverse factions can agree; much will depend on how the actual mission is portrayed.

Even more serious is the potential for conflict, both military and political, that peacekeeping can raise between Russia and other states of the FSU. Indeed, an overly assertive Russian role in peacekeeping risks putting Russia in political conflict with Western countries as well. This potential problem is well illustrated in President Yeltsin's February 1993 call before the Civic Union for Russia to be given the right to undertake, and the responsibility for carrying out, peacekeeping activities in the FSU. He also called on the West to endorse such a role.

Not surprisingly, the reaction among other former Soviet states was negative. Most notably, the Ukrainian foreign ministry asserted that this represented yet another attempt by Russia to establish a dictatorship in the FSU and to infringe on the internal affairs of other states.[88] From the West's perspective, we may have no alternative but to accept such a Russian role; this does not mean, however, that we should offer a blanket endorsement of this idea. The key is to encourage a broader international role, particularly in the form of international observers deployed to ensure the neutrality of peacekeeping efforts in the FSU.

With the host of ethnic, social, and economic tensions in the FSU, the likelihood of new local conflicts is extremely high. A mechanism for dealing with this instability must be found, but it must be done within a context of Russian participation in, not domination of, the process. Otherwise, fears that Russia will use the peacekeeping mission as a pretext for asserting rights over newly sovereign states could prove well founded.

Notes

1. Russia has also been involved in peacekeeping in Georgia, not (in 1993) a CIS state, based on a bilateral agreement reached between Eduard Shevardnadze and Boris Yeltsin. Because this is outside the CIS framework, it is not discussed in detail in this essay, although some elements of this experience are mentioned in the general discussion.

2. As quoted in John Lloyd, "Yeltsin Calls for Peacekeeping Role on Borders," *The Financial Times*, March 1, 1993, p. 1.

3. While Ukraine is participating in the UN peacekeeping efforts in the former Yugoslavia, Russia is dealt with here because it faces the greatest range of possible peacekeeping roles and associated difficulties. Soviet, and now Russian, forces have participated in other UN peacekeeping missions as well: in 1988 in Sinai, in April 1991 in the Persian Gulf, in September 1991 in the Western Sahara, and in January 1992 in Cambodia. In the latter case, while the Russian Foreign Ministry supported Russia's "broadest participation," the Russian military command was not supportive of this idea. See, for example, "Battalion May Join UN Forces in Cambodia," *Interfax,* February 28, 1992, published in Foreign Broadcast Information Service, *Daily Report: Central Eurasia* (hereafter FBIS-SOV) FBIS-SOV-92-042, p. 30.

4. In June 1992, the United Nations asked Russia to send another battalion of 400 men; the parliament approved Yeltsin's request on this score on July 17.

5. See, for example, "Government to Participate in Yugoslavia Talks," Radio Odin, August 10, 1992, translated in FBIS-SOV-92-155, p. 11; "Lukin Says Russia to Back FRY Resolution," *Vesti,* August 12, 1992, translated in FBIS-SOV-92-157, p. 11; "Commentator on Military Intervention in FRY," Moscow World Service, August 11, 1992, published in FBIS-SOV-92-157, p. 12; Sergei Sidorov, "Will a Second Battalion of Russian 'Blue Berets' Be Sent to Sarajevo?" *Krasnaia zvezda,* July 22, 1992, p. 3.; and Michael Dobbs, "Russia Unveils Plan to End Bosnia War," *The Washington Post,* February 25, 1993.

6. As noted in "RFE/RL News Briefs," supplement to *RFE/RL Research Report* (February 12, 1993), p. 1.

7. Vladimir Kulistikov, "Boris Yeltsin Looks Abroad for Army Action to So Avert Misbehavior Back Home," *New Times,* no. 30, July 1992, p. 3. Western analysts have also made this point about peacekeeping distracting attention from Russia's domestic problems; see Suzanne Crow, "Russian Peacekeeping: Defense, Diplomacy, or Imperialism?" *RFE/RL Research Report* (September 18, 1992), p. 40.

8. See, for example, Galina Vinitskaia, "Extra Battalion for UN Forces in FRY Viewed," *ITAR-TASS,* July 17, 1992, translated in FBIS-SOV-92-138, p. 38; *Interfax,* February 28, 1992, published in FBIS-SOV-92-042, p. 30; and "Blue Helmets to be Sent to Yugoslavia," *Interfax,* March 6, 1992, published in FBIS-SOV-92-045, p. 34.

9. Aleksandr Golts, "A World Army for a World Government?" *Krasnaia zvezda,* July 4, 1992, translated in Joint Publications Research Service, *Central Eurasia: Military Affairs* (hereafter, JPRS-UMA), JPRS-UMA-92-026, p. 54.

10. The motivations for Russia's peacekeeping efforts are discussed in detail below, including this idea of preserving an imperial role.

11. "Kazakhstan President's Statement," *Nezavisimaia gazeta,* March 5, 1992, p. 2.

12. Reported in "Military and Security Notes," *RFE/RL Research Report* (July 17, 1992), p. 57.

13. It was signed by Armenia, Kazakhstan, Kyrgyzstan, Moldova, Russia, Tajikistan, and Uzbekistan; it was not signed by Azerbaijan, Belarus, Turkmenistan, or Ukraine.

14. Discussed in Roman Zadunaiskii, "'Draft Documents' Prepared for Tashkent Meeting," *ITAR-TASS*, July 15, 1992, published in FBIS-SOV-92-137, pp. 3–4. For more information on the planned force, see below.

15. Interview with Colonel Vasilii Volkov, "A Unified Army: Arguments of the Military," *Sovetskaia Belorussiia*, August 14, 1992, p. 2, translated in JPRS-UMA-92-036, p. 2.

16. Interview with Colonel General Viktor Dubynin, "Peacemaking Forces Are Costing Us an Arm and a Leg, But Ending Fratricidal Wars Is Worth More than Any Money . . . ," *Izvestiia*, September 2, 1992, translated in FBIS-SOV-92-173, pp. 24–25.

17. Ibid.

18. In addition to the contingent to the former Yugoslavia, it reported more than 600 men in South Ossetia, more than 1,500 in Dniester, 1,000 in Abkhazia, and 5,500 in North Ossetia and Ingushetia. "13,224 Russian Blue Helmets Serving in Hot Spots," *ITAR-TASS*, January 5, 1993, translated in FBIS-SOV-93-002, p. 33.

19. Lieutenant Colonel Oleg Vladykin, "Russia's Mobile Forces," *Krasnaia zvezda*, December 18, 1992, p. 2.

20. Interview with Colonel General Evgenii Podkolzin, *Komosomolkaia pravda*, October 9, 1992, Translated in FBIS-SOV-92-200, p. 19.

21. Interview with Colonel General V. Samsonov, "The Commonwealth and National Security," *Krasnaia zvezda*, February 17, 1993, p. 2, translated in FBIS-SOV-93-031, p. 5; and Andrei Naryshkin, "Chiefs of Staff Meet to Discuss Security Treaty," *ITAR-TASS*, February 18, 1993, published in FBIS-SOV-93-032, p. 1.

22. "CIS Peacekeeping Force Proposed," *Interfax*, February 17, 1992, published in FBIS-SOV-92-032, p. 5.

23. Zadunaiskii, "'Draft Documents' Prepared," in FBIS-SOV-92-137, p. 4.

24. Interview with Andrei Kozyrev on January 6, 1993, as reported in "RFE/RL News Briefs," supplement to *RFE/RL Research Report* (January 15, 1993), p. 7.

25. Interview with Andrei Kokoshin, "Kokoshin Sees Enhancement of Armed Forces' Image," Russian Television Network, January 6, 1993, translated in FBIS-SOV-93-004, p. 27.

26. As quoted in "Weekly Review," *RFE/RL Research Report* (June 19, 1992), p. 68. For statements by other military officers, see, for example, that by Deputy Defense Minister Colonel General Toporov reported in "Military and Security Notes," *RFE/RL Research Report* (October 23, 1992), p. 41.

27. For further discussion, see Stephen Foye, "Post-Soviet Russia: Politics and the New Russian Army," *RFE/RL Research Report* (August 21, 1992), p. 12.

28. Leonid Rodin and Aleksandr Frolov, "Mediation in Ethnic Conflicts," *International Affairs* (Moscow), no. 9 (September 1992), p. 70.

29. See, for example, Dubynin, "Peacemaking Forces Are Costing Us."

30. For example, Kyrgyzstan's parliament refused to approve the dispatch of its own force to Tajikistan in fall 1992. Marshal Evgenii Shaposhnikov referred to this problem in late December 1992, arguing that collective security and peacekeeping were not really working in the CIS. Citing the Tajikistan case, he noted that despite an agreement among Uzbekistan, Kyrgyzstan, Kazakhstan, and Russia on supplying peacekeepers, at that point only Uzbekistan (note, not Russia) had approved the plan. "Shaposhnikov . . . Sees 'Trend toward Upsetting Nuclear Security,'" *Interfax,* December 21, 1992, published in FBIS-SOV-92-245, p. 2.

31. As cited in Bess Brown, "Turkmenistan Asserts Itself," *RFE/RL Research Report* (October 30, 1992), p. 29.

32. Interview with Shaposhnikov, "CIS Joint Armed Forces Commander in Chief Gathers Together 'Nuclear Club,'" *Nezavisimaia gazeta,* January 21, 1993, p. 2. There are, of course, other countries' forces currently serving as peacekeepers in the FSU, contrary to Shaposhnikov's statement. He offered similar comments in another statement broadcast by Radio Moscow World Service on February 10, 1993, published in "Shaposhnikov on Russian Troops in CIS Hot Spots," FBIS-SOV-93-026, p. 5.

33. Suzanne Crow, "Russia's Response to the Yugoslav Crisis," *RFE/RL Research Report* (July 24, 1992), pp. 34–35.

34. Among those supporting the argument of protecting the Russian diaspora (as opposed to the broader notion of protection, articulated by Karaganov, below) were Vice-President Aleksandr Rutskoi, Defense Minister Pavel Grachev, and Sergei Stankevich.

35. Sergei Karaganov and Aleksandr Vladislavlev, "The Idea of Russia," *International Affairs,* no. 12 (December 1992), p. 35. Karaganov's ideas are also discussed in Rowland Evans and Robert Novak, "Russia's 'Monroe Doctrine,'" *The Washington Post,* February 26, 1993.

36. Vladimir Solntsev, "Deputy Foreign Minister Lavrov . . . Suggests Regional Forces," *ITAR-TASS,* June 24, 1992, published in FBIS-SOV-92-123, p. 25.

37. Yurii Shchekochikhin, "Call the UN, and They Will Be Able to Stop the Blood," *Literaturnaia gazeta,* April 22, 1992, p. 9, translated in FBIS-USR-92-050, p. 1; his emphasis.

38. Interview with Shaposhnikov on Moscow Russian television network, July 11, 1992, translated in FBIS-SOV-92-134, p. 20; similar statement in July 1992, as quoted in Foye, "Post-Soviet Russia," p. 12.

39. Although Russians have been most vocal on the left bank, it should be noted that they are actually only the third largest ethnic group: Moldovans represent 40 percent of the population there (although most live in the rural areas), Ukrainians 28 percent, and Russians 26 percent. For more details, see

Vladimir Socor, "Creeping Putsch in Eastern Moldova," *RFE/RL Research Report* (January 17, 1992), pp. 8–13.

40. Vladimir Socor, "Russian Forces in Moldova," *RFE/RL Research Report* (August 28, 1992), pp. 38–43.

41. Aside from the 14th Army, the future of the additional former Soviet forces on Moldovan territory was to be decided later—they would either be transferred to Moldova, or would be disbanded, or would be withdrawn to Russian territory. Interview with Shaposhnikov, *Komsomolskaia pravda*, April 4, 1992, pp. 1, 3, translated in FBIS-SOV-92-067, p. 8.

42. See ibid. and Vladimir Socor, "Russia's Fourteenth Army and the Insurgency in Eastern Moldova," *RFE/RL Research Report* (September 11, 1992), pp. 41–48.

43. The current head of the 14th Army, Lieutenant General Aleksandr Lebed, has also been overtly in favor of the Dniester separatists.

44. "Army Waiting to Act as Peacekeeping Force," *ITAR-TASS,* April 6, 1992, published in FBIS-SOV-92-066, p. 67.

45. As reported by Shaposhnikov, *Komsomolskaia pravda*, April 4, 1992, in FBIS-SOV-92-067, p. 8.

46. A. Khantsevich, "The General Speaks with a Soldier's Frankness," *Komsomolskaia pravda*, July 7, 1992, p. 1, translated in JPRS-UMA-92-026, p. 31.

47. Colonel Mulyar et al., "The 14th Army is Ready to Play the Role of 'Blue Helmets' in the Dniester Region," *Krasnaia zvezda*, April 8, 1992, p. 1; "Military and Security Notes," *RFE/RL Research Report* (April 17, 1992), p. 51; "Weekly Review," *RFE/RL Research Report* (June 12, 1992), p. 57.

48. "Further on Rutskoi's Remarks," *ITAR-TASS,* April 5, 1992, translated in FBIS-SOV-92-066, p. 64; interview with Sergei Stankevich, Moscow Central Television, April 6, 1992, translated in FBIS-SOV-92-069, pp. 26–27.

49. "Kozyrev Proposal on Conflict," Radio Odin, April 6, 1992, translated in FBIS-SOV-92-067, pp. 2–3.

50. For example, in April 1992, the Dniester Supreme Soviet appealed to the CIS to set up a peacekeeping force based on the 14th Army—see "Further on Rutskoi's Remarks," *ITAR-TASS*, April 5, 1992, translated in FBIS-SOV-92-066, p. 64. It also sought the involvement, in addition to Russians, of Ukrainians and Belarussians (while being opposed to the inclusion of Moldovans or Romanians)—see "Dniester Parliament to Appeal for CIS Forces," *ITAR-TASS,* April 14, 1992, published in FBIS-SOV-92-073, p. 49.

51. See, for example, statement by Dniester Minister of Defense Stefan Kitak in Aleksandr Tago, "Moldova: Passions Surrounding the 14th Army Are Not Subsiding," *Nezavisimaia gazeta*, September 18, 1992, p. 1.

52. "Foreign Ministers Discuss Dniester in Chisinau," in FBIS-SOV-92-067, pp. 3–4, 6.

53. Noted in Suzanne Crow, "The Theory and Practice of Peacekeeping in the Former USSR," *RFE/RL Research Report* (September 18, 1992), p. 34.

54. Reported by Colonel N. Mulyar et al., "14th Army Will Fulfill Orders of Russian Government Alone . . . ," *Krasnaia zvezda*, April 11, 1992, translated in FBIS-SOV-92-072, p. 54.

55. On July 7, 1992, the Moldovan Parliament adopted a decision to establish joint forces to disengage the armed belligerents and to appeal to these other states to participate in this effort. Septimiu Roman, "Joint Units for Disengagement of Forces Decision," Bucharest Radio, July 7, 1992, translated in FBIS-SOV-92-133, p. 72.

56. "Plans to Send Troops to Dniester Denied," *ITAR-TASS,* July 7, 1992, translated in FBIS-SOV-92-131, p. 61; and "No Peacekeeping Troops to be Sent to Moldova," *DPA,* July 22, 1992, translated in FBIS-SOV-92-142, p. 47.

57. Dubynin, "Peacemaking Forces Are Costing Us."

58. "Moldova's Snegur Requests Peacekeeping Operation," *ITAR-TASS,* July 10, 1992, published in FBIS-SOV-92-133, p. 3.

59. As reported in Crow, "The Theory and Practice of Peacekeeping," p. 35.

60. There are differing reports on the composition of this force. See ibid.; "Russian 14th Army Enters Bendery 24 July," Novosti newscast, July 24, 1992, translated in FBIS-SOV-92-144, p. 57; and Gabriel Ionescu, "Accord Opens Way for Deploying Peacekeepers," July 29, 1992, Bucharest Radio, translated in FBIS-SOV-92-147, p. 46.

61. Vladimir Luskanov, "Peacekeepers' Role in Dniester Viewed," Novosti newscast, July 26, 1992, translated in FBIS-SOV-92-147, p. 47; Gabriel Ionescu, "States' Military Observers to Begin Activity," Bucharest Radio, August 22, 1992, translated in FBIS-SOV-92-164, p. 45.

62. "RFE/RL News Briefs," supplement to *RFE/RL Research Report* (January 22, 1993), p. 13.

63. Much of the background discussion on this conflict is drawn from Bess Brown, "Tajikistan: The Conservatives Triumph," *RFE/RL Research Report* (February 12, 1993), pp. 9–12.

64. See ibid. and article in *New Times*, no. 2, January 1993, pp. 10–13.

65. Bess Brown, "Tajikistan: The Fall of Nabiev," *RFE/RL Research Report* (September 25, 1992), pp. 14, 17.

66. Brown, "Tajikistan: The Conservatives Triumph," p. 10. This is an ironic twist for those who believe that Russian military forces would automatically support procommunist, and certainly anti-Islamic, forces.

67. Andrei Pershin et al., "Presidential Bulletin," *Interfax,* July 15, 1992, published in FBIS-SOV-92-137, pp. 67–68.

68. "Russian Commander: Peacekeeping Deployment Premature," *Interfax,* October 1, 1992, published in FBIS-SOV-92-192, p. 33.

69. Brown, "Tajikistan: The Conservatives Triumph," pp. 9–12. In November 1992, Turkmenistan's President Niyazov declared that his country would remain neutral and that the Tajik conflict must be resolved at the international level, with Tajik leaders cooperating with the CIS, the United Nations, and the CSCE. Noted in Igor' Zhukov, "Andrei Kozyrev's Two Days," *Nezavisimaia gazeta*, November 7, 1992, p. 3.

70. Brown, "Tajikistan: The Fall of Nabiev," pp. 14, 17; Galina Gridneva, "Shaposhnikov May Send UN Forces to Conflict Area," *ITAR-TASS*, August 28, 1992, translated in FBIS-SOV-92-168, p. 45; and Sergei Ostanin, "Shaposhnikov on Forces in Karabakh, Tajikistan," *ITAR-TASS*, September 25, 1992, translated in FBIS-SOV-92-188, p. 6.

71. Anatolii Ladin, "Kulyab Asks for Aid," *Krasnaia zvezda*, September 19, 1992, p. 1, translated in FBIS-SOV-92-185, p. 48; "National Movement Chief Supports CIS Troop Aid," *Interfax*, September 22, 1992, published in FBIS-SOV-92-185, p. 47; Andrei Pershin et al., "Presidential Bulletin," *Interfax*, October 16, 1992, published in FBIS-SOV-92-202, p. 49; "Russian General Thinks Peacekeeping Forces Premature," *Interfax*, October 21, 1992, published in FBIS-SOV-92-205, p. 52; and "Leninabad Executive Urges Support for Call CIS Peacekeepers Bid [sic]," *ITAR-TASS*, October 20, 1992, published in FBIS-SOV-92-203, p. 45.

72. Interview with Deputy Prime Minister Davlat Ismonov, "Deputy Premier Calls for Withdrawal of Russian Troops," Radio Dushanbe Network, October 3, 1992, translated in FBIS-SOV-92-193, pp. 53–54. Similarly, after the decision in late November by Russia, Kazakhstan, Kyrgyzstan, and Uzbekistan to send peacekeeping forces, the leader of the Tajik Democratic Party said the decision was "belated" and that "as long as Russia's 201st division remains in Dushanbe, there will be no peace in Tajikistan and in Central Asia as a whole." "Democratic Party Leader on Peacekeepers, Russian Ties," *Interfax*, December 6, 1992, published in FBIS-SOV-92-235, p. 20.

73. Andrei Pershin et al., "Presidential Bulletin," *Interfax*, October 12, 1992, published in FBIS-SOV-92-198, p. 34.

74. "Parliamentarian Warns against Troops in Tajikistan," *Interfax*, October 13, 1992, published in FBIS-SOV-92-199, p. 51; and Andrei Pershin et al., "Presidential Bulletin," *Interfax*, October 15, 1992, published in FBIS-SOV-92-201, p. 49.

75. "Russian Commander Comments," *Interfax*, October 20, 1992, published in FBIS-SOV-92-204, p. 43.

76. As noted by Galina Gridneva and Georgii Shemlev, "Kozyrev Says Russian Troops Might Become Peacekeeping Nucleus," *ITAR-TASS*, November 6, 1992, published in FBIS-SOV-92-216, p. 60.

77. L. Levin, "Military Reach Unanimous Opinion in Termez," *Moskovskaia pravda*, December 10, 1992, p. 8, translated in FBIS-SOV-92-243, p. 3.

78. According to a report by Mikhail Shevtsov, "Military Advisers End Peace Mission to Tajikistan," *ITAR-TASS*, December 4, 1992, published in FBIS-SOV-92-235, p. 1, the 201st would only continue to "guard key economic, administrative, and military facilities." This is contradicted by a report in "Weekly Review," *RFE/RL Research Report* (December 11, 1992), p. 71, that the 201st would participate in peacekeeping.

79. Aleksandr Pelts, "Tajikistan Government Proposes Program to Get Republic Out of Crisis," *Krasnaia zvezda*, December 1, 1992, p. 3, translated in FBIS-SOV-92-234, p. 44; and "Weekly Review," *RFE/RL Research Report* (December 11, 1992), p. 71.

80. Brown, "Tajikistan: The Conservatives Triumph," p. 11.

81. "CSCE's Rafaelli's Visit Examined," Radio Baku Network, January 25, 1993, translated in FBIS-SOV-93-015, p. 72.

82. "Tajikistan Peacekeeping Mission Considered," *Interfax,* January 25, 1993, published in FBIS-SOV-93-015, p. 34; and "CIS to Deploy Battalions along Tajik-Afghan Border," Radio Moscow World Service, February 9, 1993, published in FBIS-SOV-93-026, p. 4.

83. "UN Mission Guarantees Impartiality of Peacekeeping Forces," *Interfax,* January 27, 1993, published in FBIS-SOV-93-016, p. 53.

84. The following information is taken from Sergei Rogov, ed., *Russian Defense Policy: Challenges and Developments,* CNA Occasional Paper (Alexandria, Va.: Center for Naval Analyses, February 1993), pp. 53–54.

85. Ibid., pp. 54, 55.

86. Suzanne Crow has written two particularly good articles about the problems of peacekeeping and Russian motivations. See *RFE/RL Research Report* (September 18, 1992), pp. 31–40.

87. Dubynin, "Peacekeeping Forces Are Costing Us."

88. "Government Critical of Yeltsin UN Bid for 'Special Powers,'" *Interfax,* March 1, 1993, published in FBIS-SOV-93-039, p. 47.

PART III

Russia and the Far Abroad

8

Russian-U.S. Relations on the Pacific: Missing Links

Vladimir Ivanov

Since the dissolution of the USSR in December 1991, Russia's position in Northeast Asia has become more promising. The promise lies in the unique opportunity to develop a nonconfrontational security posture, contribute to political cooperation in the North Pacific, and gain access to the markets of the Asia-Pacific region. For the first time in its modern history, Russia enjoys a stable and, for the time being, nonthreatening security environment in Northeast Asia. Siberia and the Far East are the only parts of the country where borders have not been changed by the dissolution of the Soviet Union. There is no longer a conflict of ideologies or a clash of strategic interests with the United States. China is an important economic and political partner. Relations with Japan are better than at any time this century. Diplomatic relations with both Koreas have given Russia the potential— still mostly neglected—to play a constructive political role in Northeast Asia.

Russia, however, also faces an unprecedented difficulty. This difficulty lies in implementing new foreign policy and national security doctrines that will not contradict Russia's primary goals of national, economic, and social renovation. Current political crises and a pervasive sense of economic desperation make it no easier to fulfill this promise or overcome this difficulty. Russia inherited major weaknesses in its Asia-Pacific posture, as well as distorted domestic priorities. Objectively speaking, Russia is a relatively small, isolated, and vulnerable part of Northeast Asia, a country whose main concerns were for a long time focused on security needs and defense-related issues, not economic development.

During the Soviet era, the Russian Far East was regarded more as a bastion than a gateway. The influence of the military and the domination of the communist bureaucracy in local affairs were felt much more strongly in Irkutsk, Khabarovsk, and Vladivostok than in Moscow. Now, instead of external factors, domestic problems such as the weakness of the private sector and the persistence of political chaos prevent the central government from paying adequate attention to the development of the Far Eastern region, the future of which continues to be dependent on decisions taken in Moscow. The economy of the region is based almost entirely on natural wealth. Raw materials extracted and produced in the Russian Far East are transported elsewhere to be processed. The services that the region once provided to the armed forces and its role in defense production and procurement have been downsized. A lack of infrastructure and the fact that extraction industries and defense-related enterprises are poorly suited for privatization severely impedes the development of the region's economy. The collapse of existing economic links, both within Russia and with other former Soviet republics, presents a new set of difficulties for the Russian Far East.

Russia's economic situation constrains its diplomacy and stifles even modest hopes for its closer association with the Asia-Pacific region. A fundamental question needs to be addressed in this context: What kind of relations should Russia develop with the United States on the Pacific? Put in more general terms: Should Moscow prepare itself for cooperation and long-term reconciliation or for a new round of uncertainty and insecurity? The answer is neither clear, nor easy, nor dependent on the actions of Russia alone.

Most U.S. analysts agree that as far as the United States is concerned, the most important part of Asia is Northeast Asia. Not surprisingly, this is also the case as far as postcommunist Russia is concerned. Since 1992, the Russian bureaucracy has regarded the prospects for partnership with Washington in the Asia-Pacific region with interest and optimism. In a number of statements made by Foreign Minister Andrei Kozyrev during 1992 and 1993, the United States was described as the most important country for Russia in all areas of its foreign policy, including the Asia-Pacific region.[1] Close cooperation in the region with the United States has been anticipated on the basis of shared democratic values and a common interest in regional stability. Writing in 1992, Vladimir Lukin declared that Russia must view the bonds between the United States and countries of the Asia-Pacific region "not as a threat to [Russian] strategic interests but as an integral part of a pattern of regional relations that has proven its stability and effectiveness."[2]

Indeed, if Moscow accepts the notion that economic recovery based on market reforms and modernization is the best way for Russia to integrate itself into regional economic relations and political processes, Moscow should also be aware that the United States and Japan are the leading sources of such key elements of modernization as direct foreign investments and technology transfers. Those same two countries are also the leading players in the G-7 group of nations. Clearly, therefore, Russia's economic involvement in the region is likely to remain limited unless there is a marked improvement in Russo-Japanese relations, as well as positive changes in relations between Japan and the United States, on the one hand, and Russia, on the other. However, with all prevailing regional patterns and formations demonstrating the strong nexus between economic and security relations, normal economic cooperation within this triangle will be impossible without a comprehensive security accommodation. Ironically, Moscow's new values, economic interests, and security aspirations conflict with the residual influence of its Cold War military deployments and the nuclear strategic standoff.[3] How much will the security and political interests of the United States and Russia converge, overlap, or collide in Northeast Asia in the second half of the 1990s? Currently, there is virtually no discussion of such questions. Indeed, at present the main problem Russia faces is the lack of any real dialogue with the United States on the prospects for bilateral and other forms of relations in the Asia-Pacific region.

Historically, and during the Cold War in particular, the importance of the Northeast Asian and Northwest Pacific regions for both the United States and Russia rested primarily on security concerns. Since the end of the Cold War, Moscow-Washington cooperation has focused chiefly on nuclear weapons dismantlement, European politics, the United Nations, and the G-7 rather than on Asia-Pacific affairs. Moreover, despite having both an interest and a role to play in Northeast Asia, Russia has been largely ignored by past and present administrations in Washington, which seem to assume that Russia will play at best only a marginal role in Asia for a long time to come and can, therefore, be safely neglected.[4]

The sobering reality is that neither the dissolution of the USSR nor Russia's formal security and ideological accommodation with the United States has given Moscow a higher profile in Washington's Asia policy. U.S. analysts[5] and policymakers[6] tend to disregard Russia when they think of

Asia; in some recent publications, Russia is not even considered part of Northeast Asia.[7] Leading scholars advise the U.S. administration to deal in a more innovative way with all Asian players except Russia.[8] Very few defense analysts tend to see recent developments as positive and promising shifts; instead, they argue—in a rather contradictory fashion—that a resurgent Russia may represent a continuing source of security concerns for the United States in the region, while at the same time remaining a "distant third-tier state."[9]

The influence of this kind of analysis may well explain the nature of U.S. policy toward Russia, a policy which is nothing if not inconsistent. For example, the January 1993 White House report, *National Security Strategy of the United States,* declares: "More than anything else our encouragement of private trade and investment will help these [Commonwealth of Independent States and East European] countries integrate themselves into the free market economic system." Closer political relationships between the United States and Russia, the report notes, are expected to result from a "wide variety of exchange programs and other initiatives."[10] However, in the chapter dealing with the U.S. agenda on Asia, no mention is made of Russia.[11] A similar report, published in August 1991, was perhaps more "generous" insofar as it noted the Soviet occupation of Japan's Northern territories, Soviet military and economic aid to North Korea, Moscow's interest in improving relations with Seoul and Tokyo, and China's changing perception of the Soviet threat.[12]

Even though U.S. objectives in Asia are described in a 1992 presidential report to Congress as "strengthening the Western orientation of the Asian nations [and] fostering the growth of democracy and human rights,"[13] Russia is not identified in this context. Instead, the report mentions Russia in the section "Sources of East Asian and Pacific Regional Instability," indicating that the residual power projection capability of Russian naval and air forces in Siberia and Russian Northeast Asia, together with Russia's formidable nuclear arsenal, remains a major concern.[14]

Secretary of Defense Dick Cheney, in his January 1993 report *Defense Strategy for the 1990s: The Regional Defense Strategy,* does not mention Russia, only "the Soviet annexation of the Northern Territories of Japan."[15] In a statement issued in May 1993, Admiral Charles Larson mentions the Russian Far East but once, and then in the same line with North Korea as a source of instability.[16] In short, the typical view of Russia, when it *is* considered as a part of the North Pacific Rim, is linked to its military power and strategic nuclear weapons.

According to some analysts, Russia may return to a policy of imperial centralization under an authoritarian leadership intent on halting incipient anarchy. The authors of a RAND publication, for instance, warn of just such a prospect and argue against precipitate reductions in U.S. military power in the region absent major alterations in the military deployments of the former USSR.[17] Such views are by no means uncommon. They are, however, often exaggerated and inaccurate, and as such they are capable of undermining any prospects for Russia to join what James Goodby has called "the Western society of states."[18]

The Clinton administration's emerging list of priorities in Asia includes trade, constructive engagement with China, restyling cooperation with Japan, ensuring the stability of the Korean peninsula, preventing the proliferation of weapons of mass destruction, and supporting efforts toward more open democratic political systems. Attention also has been given to the formulation of a postcontainment strategy vis-à-vis the former socialist countries. What has emerged thus far has been described by U.S. National Security Advisor Antony Lake as a "strategy of enlargement." However, it is not clear whether this new concept could be the glue that holds together the United States' general policy toward Russia with its postcontainment policy in Northeast Asia. Ideally, U.S. regional leadership should be a key factor in helping Russia to define its new role in the region. However, a positive interaction with Russia on the Pacific seems to be a distant goal. In November 1993, Russia was not even mentioned by President Clinton during his address to the Asia Pacific Economic Cooperation group (APEC) meeting in Seattle.

The reality is that postcommunist Russia is neither a military adversary, like Iraq in the 1990s, nor a potential partner, like the People's Republic of China in the 1980s. The residual ability of Russian strategic forces to challenge the security of the United States, even after the START reductions are fully implemented, continues to cause Washington great concern and to inspire negative attitudes toward Russia. And the core of the problem is that Russian and U.S. defense policies can be harmonized only to the degree that harmony can be achieved between both countries' definitions of their national interests. It is also true that the partnership can only prosper within the wider context of economic cooperation, which has yet to be developed.

In addition, neither Russian membership in the regional community nor new relations with the United States in the region are achievable without solving the problems in Russia's relations with Japan. Every side of the Japan–United States–Russia triangle faces a challenge or dilemma of its own. For Russia, it is critically important to maintain a cooperative relationship with the United States and Japan. Moscow, however, has been slow to recognize Tokyo's growing political independence. For Japan, the challenge of dealing with Russia is to determine whether it is really in Japan's interest to assist Russia's transition to a market economy. Currently, Japan seems to see no advantages for itself in such a policy. Enduring mistrust of Russia narrows Tokyo's policy options. For the United States, the dilemma is even more difficult. Washington is interested in seeing a friendly regime in Moscow in full control of the Soviet nuclear arsenal. But with its own financial power limited, Washington seeks to encourage Tokyo to increase its economic support for Russia. Meanwhile, Washington supports Tokyo on the territorial dispute, but fears that any bold move toward its resolution might weaken the reformist government in Moscow.

The direction of Moscow-Tokyo relations remains uncertain. Russia is no longer a communist country, but for Japan it is still a source of security concerns and mistrust. In the seas that separate the Russian Far East, Japan, and the U.S. Pacific coast, Russian nuclear strategic submarines are deployed, and the waste from their nuclear reactors is dumped in the Sea of Japan. Whereas NATO has offered Russia a "Partnership for Peace," the U.S.-Japanese alliance has made no such overtures. Both Moscow and Tokyo have to think of how to build new bilateral bridges in a broader regional and global context, and how to coordinate their policies with the interests and goals of the United States. Moreover, the problem of the Northern Territories cannot be separated from the realities of the regional security environment. And this is the area where nothing can be accomplished without the participation of the United States, either directly or as a facilitator. Fortunately, opportunities do exist for the United States to facilitate better relations between Japan and Russia, and it is encouraging to note that despite neglecting Russia at the 1993 APEC meeting, President Clinton did urge Japan to provide greater assistance to Russia during the G-7 summit in Tokyo.

Both Washington and Tokyo are facing the same question: Why should Russia be included in the region? Answers are, in fact, not hard to find. Those same arguments for cooperative engagement with Russia in Europe could equally serve to justify Russia's inclusion in the Asia-Pacific region. A wide variety of nations—particularly the United States and Japan, the two leading Pacific powers—have interests in seeing Russia become an active and constructive member of the regional community. Much could be gained from cooperation with Moscow in areas ranging from nonproliferation of nuclear weapons to environmental protection, from conflict prevention on the Korean peninsula to the development of energy resources in Siberia. Most importantly, Russia's security and strategic posture and thinking, which are still in transition, could be influenced through this process of cooperation. A hesitation to address the "Russian problem on the Pacific" by the U.S. Department of State or the Department of Defense will not help Moscow shape its foreign or security policy along new lines of partnership and cooperative engagement with the United States and Japan.

The Clinton administration inherited a foreign policy that was inattentive to Asia, and the level of knowledge of the region among American politicians reportedly is not great.[19] A "Russian question" in Asian affairs is thus something of a novelty to U.S. policymakers. Those policymakers should consider the potential political advantages of closer cooperation with Russia and recognize the potential dangers of inattention to Russia. For instance, despite its cool relations with North Korea, Russia, simply because of the geography of the Russian Far East, remains a potentially useful ally of the United States in the event of severe domestic political crises in North Korea, such as the outbreak of civil war. Russia and the United States have already found good reasons to cooperate in the UN Security Council to contain North Korea's nuclear ambitions.

In the realm of the foreign policy, although Russia is unlikely to exert significant influence in Asia for some years to come, its potential impact on Japan should not be underestimated. Under extreme circumstances, Russian relations with Japan could spark nationalistic feelings on both sides, creating new security concerns and even new incentives for a military buildup.

Economically, because of the multiple crises caused by the dissolution of the Soviet Union and by Russia's transition to a market economy, as well as by the end of old alliance relations in Asia, Russia is currently becoming increasingly unimportant for Northeast Asia, except as far as trade with China is concerned. Eventually, however, market forces will inevitably orient Russian civilian manufacturing industry and military equipment producers toward the markets of Asia. In the future, industrial development in Northeast Asia—Korea and China in particular—will grow more dependent on Siberian and Far Eastern oil and gas resources, timber, and minerals. This may well create significant opportunities for American companies to invest in Russia.

The underutilized capacity of Russians to invent and produce manu-factured goods for civilian needs may also attract the interest of U.S. businesses. With low labor costs, abundant energy and mineral resources, and a well-established educational and research and development base, Russia has the capacity to become a significant economic competitor in some Asian markets. The question here is whether Russians and other former Soviets are capable of building dynamic and civilized capitalist systems on the foundation of a democratic civic society that is supported and promoted by the government as well as by the initiative and entrepreneurship of ordinary citizens.[20] Official and private U.S. assessments differ substantially on this question. Interest-ingly, an increasing number of U.S. experts on Asian affairs privately admit that the Chinese model of economic reform might be more helpful to Russia than the politically more liberal but economically more chaotic Western model.

However, whatever the degree and pace of economic development within Russia, the future of U.S.-Russian economic relations—and of any political closeness that such relations might generate—is highly depend-ent upon the vitality and dynamism of the U.S. economy and the readiness of the U.S. government to support its private sector in trade and economic relations with Russia, particularly with the Russian Far East and Siberia.

The emerging relationship between Russia and the other republics of the former Soviet Union is a special source of problems for Moscow-Washington relations and could indirectly influence their interaction in the North Pacific. Although a return to the situation that existed before the declaration of the Commonwealth of Independent States on December 7, 1992, is highly unlikely, even a process of gradual reintegration based on the idea of a larger economic union is regarded by many observers as an attempt to recreate the Russian sphere of influence and to resurrect some aspects of the former Soviet empire. In 1993, after Kozyrev's speech at the UN General Assembly, Western observers noted with concern that the foreign minister seemed to be enunciating a Russian version of the Monroe Doctrine.[21] "In a word, a new Russian empire is in the making," commented William Odom.[22]

How can Russian policy in the region change? How can the residual pattern of confrontational relations with the United States and Japan be erased? Under new circumstances, this is more a problem of fundamental changes in strategic relations than a problem of traditional military security. For Russia, without a breakthrough in this area it will be impossible to design a new policy of economic openness or to maintain a regional security posture that will not contradict Russia's long-term economic and political interests. The Russian leadership must gain access to the regional economy and link Russia with the key sources of economic and technological power. But unless the major security concerns of the United States and Japan are eliminated, it would be unrealistic to expect either country to give support to Russian reforms or be willing to cooperate in other areas.

For the United States, traditional American interests in the Asia-Pacific region and the chances of establishing a cooperative post–Cold War order could suffer if the democratic changes in Russia result only in Russia's continuing isolation, thereby diminishing the chances for the success of both Russian reforms in particular and political liberalization in Northeast Asia in general.

What price must Russia pay for its entry into the Asia-Pacific regional community and for improved relations with Japan and the United States? At the very least, Moscow must show itself sensitive to the security concerns and interests of its new partners. With economic and social development as its main priority, the Russian leadership has to display a readiness to propose steps, including unilateral ones, that will eventually permit a security reconciliation with the United States and Japan. But further changes in the Russian strategic posture should be combined with a multilateral approach to the security of the region that accepts Russia as a potential partner. The reduction of security-related tensions in the Moscow-Washington relationship and movement toward the de facto denuclearization of the North Pacific would greatly expand the options for U.S.-Russian constructive engagement.

Not only Russia but also the United States must reconsider the future of the strategic nuclear arsenals left in the North Pacific from the era of confrontation. The end of the Cold War presents an opportunity to change the entire pattern of regional relations. Self-restraint in defense efforts, transparency and cooperative adjustments in defense postures and military doctrines, and cuts in nuclear weapons and related forces in the Pacific would greatly ease the security environment in the vicinity of Japan and facilitate an improvement in Russo–Japanese relations.

It is clearly in the interest of the West to support current Russian leaders simply because President Yeltsin and his government are perceived to be interested in strategic reconciliation, nuclear disarmament, and security cooperation with the United States. However, Washington's lack of interest in dealing with Russia as a part of the Asia-Pacific region could be counterproductive to finding a solution for other key problems relevant to U.S. interests. The concept of Europe "from the Atlantic to the Urals" served well for the détente between NATO and the Warsaw Pact, but it is unlikely to be an adequate basis for the Russian Federation to deal with post–Cold War security issues. The North Pacific is no less important to the security of Russia than is Europe. Furthermore, the bureaucracy in Moscow is sensitive to the changing geostrategic position of Russia, which though it has improved in overall terms, has been weakened in a traditional military sense. The concept of a Partnership for Peace between NATO and former Warsaw Pact nations must be extended also to the North Pacific/Northeast Asia region. According to a joint Russian-American academic study, it is important that Russian-U.S. military cooperation eventually take the form of a security association involving Russia, Japan, Eastern Europe, and the United States and the other NATO members, with the possible inclusion of China at a later stage.[23]

The alternative to Russia's participation in regional cooperation is uncertainty and, potentially, misunderstanding and tension. If the current opportunity to foster some coordination between U.S. policy in Asia and Russia's regional interests is wasted, new problems may arise. As James Goodby has pointed out:

> Turning points in history have not been stories with happy endings. They have been seen as opportunities to overcome mistakes of the past and to lay down the foundations for a new international order. Historically, however, these have been the times when the seeds of future conflict have been planted. Probably this turning point will be no exception, and yet Kant's idea of a Pacific Federation, a zone of peace among democratic states, may be closer to broad realization in the Russian-U.S. world than ever before in history.[24]

The future of U.S.-Russian relations depends not just on Moscow's policies but also on the influence of Western attitudes and perceptions, many of which have been inherited from the Cold War. For many observers, the future of Russia appears to be highly unpredictable, and the shadows of the former Soviet Union and of Russia's strategic forces darken Washington's policy calculations. Nevertheless, even with a huge and demanding domestic agenda, Russia is bound to play a more active role in the coming restructuring of Asian relations and to exercise a considerable indirect influence in Central Asian, Chinese, and Middle Eastern subregional affairs. Any workable approach to Asia's future must, therefore, include Russia as an essential regional actor. Medium- and long-term prospects for peace, security, and the development of Asia depend, among other factors, on the type and degree of Russian involvement. Bilateral relations between major regional powers will also depend on the role and place of Russia in regional affairs. Furthermore, despite its present economic difficulties and other domestic problems, Russia will not break up into European, Siberian, and Far Eastern components. The hope is that the positive role that Russia has the potential to play in Asia will contribute to the peaceful evolution of the region in the 1990s and the resolution of bilateral and other disputes. Armed with a carefully conceived policy supported by carefully chosen policy instruments, Washington can materially assist the transformation of the former Soviet Union into a number of market democracies, enjoying harmonious relations among themselves and with the outside world.[25] But if Russia is isolated, it may well prove a formidable obstacle to the construction of a post–Cold War security order.

Not surprisingly, Moscow still finds it difficult to deal with the hard facts of its new international position and its uncertain relationship with Washington in Asia. Russian leaders regard the end of the Cold War as neither a victory nor a defeat, but rather as an escape from confrontation with the West. However, the Russian obsession with the quest for partnership with the United States on the basis of full equality does not correspond with the position of most U.S. politicians and analysts. The concept of a symmetrical and mutually beneficial partnership is likely to be difficult to put into practice. Also, as Moscow searches for a new national identity, the assertion (by reformers as well as hard-line nationalists) of the idea of Russia as a great power does not help Russia overcome the trauma it has suffered.

The simple truth is that Russia needs more from the United States than vice versa. Self-restraint and unilateral military reductions, at least on the conceptual level, could help to develop a new context for bilateral relations, one in which Russian reforms and democracy, not Russian nuclear weapons, become the basis for partnership. Economic prosperity, democratic stability, and new relations with the United States have to be earned by the skill of building compromises and avoiding wishful thinking, empty rhetoric, and narrow nationalism.

Notes

1. See, for example, the document drawn up by the Russian Federation Foreign Ministry, "Kontseptsiia vneshnei politiki Rossiiskoi Federatsii" (The Concept of Foreign Policy of the Russian Federation), p. 38.

2. Vladimir Lukin, "Our Security Predicament," *Foreign Policy,* no. 88 (Fall 1992), p. 71.

3. For instance, the authors of a 1992 RAND report point out "the significant military capability of former Soviet forces and the fact that superpower status of the former Soviet Union resulted from its military strength." They continue:

> Modern units, particularly nuclear submarines built in the 1980s, provide the greatest threat to U.S. naval operations in the western Pacific. . . . Removing the submarine threat in the western Pacific will require several CVBGs [air carrier battle groups], initially for open-ocean antisubmarine warfare (ASW) and eventually for strikes against submarine bases. The Russians could strike out, using land based air forces against naval forces approaching Russian territory.

John Y. Schrader and James A. Winnefeld, "Understanding the Evolving U.S. Role in Pacific Rim Security. A Scenario-Based Analysis" (Report prepared for the Commander-in-Chief, U.S. Pacific Command, by RAND, Santa Monica, Calif., 1992), pp. 37–38.

4. Ibid., p. 37.

5. See, for example, Robert Legvold, "Foreign Policy," in Timothy J. Colton and Robert Legvold, eds., *After the Soviet Union. From Empire to Nations* (New York: W. W. Norton & Company, 1992), p. 163.

6. See, for instance, Lonnie S. Keene, "New Dimensions in Political and Military Postures in Asia: Security Dialogue and Preventive Diplomacy" (Paper dated January 25, 1993, and prepared for delivery at the United Nations Office for Disarmament Affairs–sponsored conference, "National Security and Confidence Building among Nations in the Asia-Pacific Region," Katmandu, Nepal, February 1–3, 1993), pp. 6–10. To be precise, there is a brief mention of the territorial dispute between Russia and Japan (p. 5) and of Russia as a part of "a broader consensus on the nuclear issue" on the Korean peninsula (p. 8).

7. See, for instance, *America's Role in Asia, Interests & Policies,* Report of the Working Group convened by the Asia Foundation's Center for Asian Pacific Affairs (Washington, D.C.: Asia Foundation, January 1993).

8. Chalmers Johnson, "Where's Clinton on Asia?" *The New York Times,* February 8, 1993.

9. See, for example, Richard F. Ellings and Edward A. Olsen, "A New Pacific Profile," *Foreign Policy,* no. 89 (Winter 1992–93), pp. 123–124.

10. *National Security Strategy of the United States,* issued by the White House, January 1993, pp. 7–8.

11. Ibid., p. 6.

12. *National Security Strategy of the United States,* issued by the White House, August 1991, p. 9.

13. U.S. Department of Defense, Office of the Assistant Secretary of Defense for International Security Affairs (East Asia and Pacific Region), *A Strategic Framework for the Asian Pacific Rim,* Report to Congress (Washington, D.C.: Government Printing Office, 1992), p. 9.

14. Ibid., pp. 10–12 and 6.

15. Secretary of Defense Dick Cheney, *Defense Strategy for the 1990s: The Regional Defense Strategy* (Washington, D.C.: U.S. Department of Defense, January 1993), p. 22.

16. Admiral Charles R. Larson, United States Pacific Command, "Posture Statement 1993," issued in May 1993. See the section entitled "Key Judgements."

17. James A. Winnefeld, Jonathan D. Pollack, et al., *A New Strategy and Fewer Forces: The Pacific Dimension* (Santa Monica, Calif.: RAND, 1992), p. 13.

18. James Goodby, "Commonwealth and Concert: Organizing Principles of Post-Containment Order in Europe," *The Washington Quarterly* (Summer 1991), p. 88.

19. See *America's Role in Asia,* p. 14.

20. S. Frederick Starr, "A Year of Capitalism in Russia" (Paper presented at "America and Russian Future," a conference held at the Embassy of the Russian Federation, Washington, D.C., January 15, 1993), pp. 2, 5.

21. See, for example, Suzanne Crow, "Russian Federation Faces Foreign Policy Dilemmas," *RFE/RL Research Report* 1, no. 10 (March 6, 1992), p. 19. See also *The Washington Post,* September 29, 1993.

22. William E. Odom, "Yeltsin's Deal with the Devil," *The Washington Post,* October 24, 1993.

23. See "Harmonizing the Evolution of U.S. and Russian Defense Policies" (Draft paper, Center for Strategic and International Studies, Washington, D.C., and Council on Foreign and Defense Policy, Moscow, November 1993).

24. James E. Goodby and Benoit Morel, *The Limited Partnership: Building A Russian-U.S. Security Community* (London: Oxford University Press for SIPRI, 1993), p. 6.

25. See Alexander Dallin, "America's Search for a Policy toward the Former Soviet Union," *Current History: A World Affairs Journal* (October 1992), p. 326.

9

Russian-American Strategic Relations: Current Trends and Future Opportunities

Andrei V. Kortunov

Relations between the United States and Russia since the dissolution of the Soviet Union have been clearly influenced by nuclear issues. One can question the prospects for large-scale economic cooperation between the two countries in the foreseeable future or discard any similarities between the American and Russian psyches, but the nuclear interdependence between Washington and Moscow cannot be denied. Russia inherited from the USSR a vast nuclear complex; it is the only state in the world that has the technical capability to destroy the United States.[1] Russia also acquired the infrastructure of U.S.-Soviet nuclear arms control negotiations, along with the obligations, rights, and responsibilities associated with those negotiations. Finally, it inherited traditional Soviet nuclear doctrines, including basic concepts of "nuclear stability," "strategic parity," "unacceptable damage," and so on.

However, what Russia has not inherited from the USSR is no less important. First of all, it rejected the political foundation of the U.S.-Soviet nuclear interaction—the model of "confrontational-competitive-cooperative" relations that guided nuclear arms control negotiations between the two superpowers. Russian President Boris Yeltsin has stated on several occasions that Russia considers the United States to be an ally rather than a competitor or adversary.

Second, Russia did not preserve the secretive and centralized Soviet-style decision-making process in nuclear issues. The major decisions in the USSR, even during Mikhail Gorbachev's years as Soviet president, had usually been taken at the very top, boldly and promptly, without extensive consultations with legislative bodies, without major media interference, and without any public discussions. The Russian leadership obviously lost this advantage, and is today obliged to follow democratic and often cumbersome procedures of budgeting and ratification.

Finally, the Soviet Union had been an extremely stable—one could say "sterile"—environment for the production and deployment of nuclear weapons. Russia, from the very beginning of its independent existence, has had to face numerous regional instabilities, ethnic conflicts, and communication failures, not to mention rigid economic constraints and potential nuclear challenges from some of the former Soviet republics.

Given this ambiguous patrimony of Russia, the future of Russian-U.S. nuclear arms control depends largely on the ability of both sides to find a proper balance between continuity and change. To what extent should the experience accumulated during more than 20 years of Soviet-American nuclear arms control be preserved, revised, or discarded as obsolete and irrelevant in the post–Cold War world? How can old principles, old mechanisms, and old institutions of arms control be adapted to a radically different political environment? This essay addresses these questions with a special emphasis on three issues: one, the advantages and shortcomings of the START-2 Treaty, and the extent to which it can serve as a link between the Cold War and a new post–Cold War nuclear arms control model; two, the evolution of the global strategic balance and of new strategic agendas and strategic options for Russia and the United States; and three, the development of a "revisionist" model of strategic arms control for the post–Cold War world.

The START-2 Treaty and Its Critics[2]

The START-2 agreement, signed by U.S. President George Bush and Russian President Boris Yeltsin in January 1993, turned out to be the most comprehensive and, at the same time, the most radical document of the nuclear era. The agreement was something more than another arms control deal: it marked a phase in the history of arms control, rounded off 20 years of efforts in this sphere, and showed the implicit limitations of the traditional world military order. The START negotiations and the treaty itself (as well as the START-1 Treaty) reflected both the advantages and the shortcomings of the traditional Cold War arms control approach (which had always been, as a matter of fact, an American rather than a Soviet-American approach). At the same time, during the START negotiations some new, unorthodox methods and procedures were tested for the first time. It is important to note that START-2 triggered wide discussions on future strategic relations between Russia and the United States, as well as on the more general issues of Russia's strategic posture.

Most of the Russian public reacted with complete indifference to the signing of the START-2 Treaty. This response stemmed partly from the fact that the contents of the treaty were already well known from the Framework Agreement concluded by Bush and Yeltsin in Washington six months earlier. Partly too, popular indifference reflected the fact that, for the vast majority of the Russian population, nuclear competition with the United States belongs to the Cold War and has little, if anything, to do with present hopes and frustrations. The perceived American nuclear threat is gone, as is the public interest in nuclear arms control.

Therefore, if Yeltsin wanted to use the treaty to boost his popularity and take revenge for his evident defeat at the Seventh Congress of People's Deputies in December 1992, START-2 clearly fell short of the task. However, the conservative political opposition in the Russian Supreme Soviet, as well as outside of it, found greater success in using the treaty and its ratification process to launch yet another offensive against the president, his foreign minister, and the government as a whole. For the opposition, this attack represented a sort of revenge for events in the fall of 1992, when Yeltsin managed to push START-1 through the Russian Parliament with surprising ease, avoiding any amendments and any serious discussions of the arms control policies of the government.

Numerous arguments have been used against START-2 in the conservative media, the Supreme Soviet, and the military. They reflect the different levels of sophistication, competence, and integrity of the treaty's critics. The vast variety of views, ideas, and positions can, however, be reduced to seven main lines of criticism.

1. The first line of criticism was aimed not at the treaty itself, but at the way it was negotiated and signed. As Iona Andronov, deputy chairman of the Supreme Soviet's Committee on International Affairs and Foreign Economic Relations, put it: "I am bewildered as to why such an important document was prepared secretly without Parliament, the public, and the media being involved."[3] The ratification hearings, which began in the

committees of the Supreme Soviet in April of 1993, turned into a broader discussion of the relationship between the executive and legislature in the foreign and defense policy decision-making process. The Foreign Ministry, as well as Yeltsin himself, was openly accused of conducting the old "Soviet" style of foreign policy.[4]

This argument deserves serious consideration. Of course, it is not that easy to forge a new decision-making mechanism within two years of the birth of a new state. Furthermore, the heritage of the Soviet Union in arms control decision making was of little help to Yeltsin.[5] But after the Soviet disintegration, many hoped that arms control decision making would become an open procedure, involving not just top bureaucrats, but also parliament, leading political parties, the media, the public, independent experts, and lobbying groups. Unfortunately, nothing of the sort happened. Neither a clear chain of command nor an established procedure seemed to exist. The lack of open discussion, information feedback, and independent opinion was evident. The treaty is by no means perfect, and some of its deficiencies—in terms of the specific systems to be cut, the time frame established, and the procedures agreed for the elimination of weapons—are directly related to the absence of an effective decision-making body in arms control matters. Russia could surely have struck a better deal with the United States in the START-2 negotiations if only Yeltsin had been more persistent in institutionalizing the arms control process and more open to views from the outside.

Some of Yeltsin's statements also suggested that the president was himself ill informed. For example, his notorious statement of early 1992 that Russian missiles would no longer be targeted on U.S. cities clearly indicated that he had not been properly briefed on nuclear strategy issues. One simply cannot retarget thousands of nuclear missiles overnight; it is a time-consuming and extremely complicated procedure. Besides, if U.S. cities were no longer targets for Russian intercontinental ballistic missiles (ICBMs) and sea-launched ballistic missiles (SLBMs), what were their new targets? Chinese citizens? Ukrainian? U.S. strategic forces? Any radical change in the nuclear targeting of a strategic superpower could provoke dangerous instabilities.

2. The second, and probably the most common, argument used against START-2 is that its implementation would break the principle of parity established during the two decades of U.S.-Soviet strategic arms control negotiations. Considering the agreed subceilings for ICBM and SLBM warheads, and the relatively smaller number of deployable Russian bomber

warheads, the overall Russian total might be as low as 3,000, as compared to 3,500 for the United States. The United States will not, it should be noted, necessarily keep 3,500 warheads; Russia could also go lower than 3,000. But the two sides will have different "rights" because of different structures in their strategic forces. This numerical disadvantage is considered destabilizing not only strategically, but also politically because the "preservation of parity" is perceived as important for Russia's international status.

But Russia's numerical disadvantage, in the eyes of START-2 critics, is not the most serious problem with the treaty. After all, START-1 also gave an edge to the United States (the U.S. military was allowed to keep 8,556 warheads out of the 12,646 that it had accumulated by 1990, whereas its Soviet counterpart was entitled to only 6,161 warheads out of total of 11,012), and from an arithmetic point of view, START-2 should be regarded as a Russian diplomatic victory, not a defeat.[6] What really concerns conservatives in Moscow is the ban on the multiple independently-targetable reentry vehicle (MIRVed) ICBMs that have always been the core of the Soviet nuclear arsenal.

This problem cannot be discarded as artificial. The MIRVed ICBMs account for more than 60 percent of the former Soviet nuclear arsenal, and to eliminate them completely would mean reconsidering the very foundations of the traditional nuclear posture, moving away from ICBMs to SLBMs and strategic bombers.[7]

Even so, the interpretation of START-2 as Russian "unilateral disarmament," "a one-way street," and "capitulation" does not hold water. The total numbers prove that the reductions are balanced, not unilateral. True, Russia must cut more ICBMs and SLBMs than must the United States (1,500 and 900, respectively), but the United States must make considerably greater reductions in the number of its aircraft (approximately 250) than must Russia (50). In actual warheads, U.S. reductions (8,000) look more impressive than Russian reductions (7,000).

It is important to note that for the first time in arms control history, the United States agreed to substantial reductions in its sea-based strategic arms component. The subceiling of 1,700 to 1,750 SLBM warheads is one-third of what the United States already has and one-half of what the START-1 levels provided. The Trident II SLBMs will have half the number of warheads than at present (which, incidentally, will be one-third as powerful).

Another major U.S. concession is the decision to turn from "counting numbers" to "actual numbers" in calculating warheads. (The "counting numbers" approach of START-1 allowed both sides to keep more warheads on their aircraft than they were formally entitled to keep.) The difference between the former and the latter was especially significant in the case of bomber warheads, with the United States being able to keep 2,000 to 2,500 more such warheads than START-1 formally permitted.

Finally, the United States has agreed to eliminate some of its most modern and most destabilizing systems—the MIRVed MX (Peacekeeper) ICBMs, which have always been considered by the Russian military as a key first-strike weapon.

However, U.S. concessions do not mean that START-2 will have an absolutely symmetrical effect on Russian and American strategic forces. The United States will be able to preserve most of the current composition of its strategic triad and will be less affected in general by the treaty. All 500 Minuteman IIIs will be kept, though downloaded to one warhead each; 18 Ohio-class submarines will carry 960 warheads on Trident II missiles, with 768 warheads carried on Trident I missiles (all 432 U.S. SLBMs on Tridents will be downloaded from 8 to 4 warheads each); all B-1B strategic bombers will be "reconfigured" to conventional missions and will not be subject to the 3,500 warhead limit, while 1,272 warheads deployed on B-2s and B-52Hs will continue to possess a formidable nuclear potential.

Yet, the question can be asked: Do we really need parity to preserve stability? Even in the worst-case scenario, if Russian-U.S. relations were to dramatically deteriorate, Russia would have enough weapons to inflict "unacceptable damage" on the United States in its second strike. In fact, the second-strike capabilities of Russia increase with START-2, because the U.S. cuts will affect first and foremost the systems most suitable for the first (disarming) strike—such as MIRVed ICBMs, MXs (Peacekeepers), and SLBM Tridents.

3. The third argument against START-2 is both related to the second one and contradictory to it. The treaty is viewed as a decisive step on the road to the "Americanization" of the Russian nuclear potential, turning it into a carbon copy of U.S. strategic forces. By reducing dramatically the ground portion of the triad, Russia is doing what the Soviet Union resisted for four decades: it is following the U.S. lead in shifting to sea-based and air-based systems. Thus, the United States has imposed its own strategic structure on Russia and, from now on, will direct the evolution of Russian strategy, putting it in an unequal and, in some respects, dependent position.[8]

One has only to look at a map to see that U.S. submarines have better access to the high seas than Russian submarines have. The United States is, as it always has been, more advanced in the development of antisubmarine warfare, a fact which makes Russian SLBMs less survivable. Russian strategic bombers have always been inferior to American bombers, and most of the presently deployed craft are aging, with no major modernization programs under way. According to START-2, all the most modern and sophisticated Blackjack bombers are to be scrapped, while the obsolete Bear-H will be preserved. Revitalization of this portion of the strategic triad will require a great deal of time and money.[9]

This criticism of START-2 seems more to the point. Indeed, the Russian side was too receptive to American proposals, especially during the initial stages of the negotiations (later, the Russians tried to win back some of their concessions, but were only partially successful: they were allowed to keep 90 silos from the eliminated MIRVed SS-20 ICBMs and to keep 105 downloaded SS-19s). Still, within the general ceilings of the treaty, each side will be able to choose its preferences.

4. The fourth argument against START-2 is based on the assumption that Russia simply cannot afford it because the costs of implementation are too high. Russia does have serious problems with the treaties it has already signed and ratified (START-1 and the Treaty on Conventional Forces in Europe, in particular), because of insufficient funding and inadequate technical expertise. If Russia unintentionally fails to comply with the provisions of START-2, it might be interpreted in the United States as deliberate cheating and as a result could cloud the entire horizon of Russian-American relationships.

No doubt, the implementation of START-2, which requires the elimination of thousands of missiles, hundreds of launchers and aircraft, and dozens of submarines, will not be a cheap undertaking. According to some preliminary estimates, the costs for the Russian side will run as high as 40 billion rubles (in constant 1992 rubles) within the next 10 years.

But it can hardly be considered a convincing argument against the treaty. As a leading Russian arms control expert, Alexei Arbatov, has explained: "The implementation of START-1 only, which has met no opposition in Russia, would cost us not much less—about R30 billion. Besides, large savings on strategic modernization programs will be a substantial compensation for START-2 implementation expenses. Without cuts, the costs of maintenance of the already deployed forces for the next ten years would amount to no less than R200 billion."[10] Anyhow, within the next 10 to 12 years, Russia must replace almost all of the currently deployed MIRVed ICBMs because their lifetime expires. These ICBMs will become not only technologically obsolete but also highly unreliable and even dangerous; the chances of a major nuclear accident will grow dramatically, as will the cost of maintenance. The same can be said about cuts in Russian strategic bombers and submarines. At least half of them would need to be replaced by the end of this century, and it is hard to believe that under current economic, financial, and political constraints, Russia could carry out this replacement schedule. Furthermore, for the first time in the history of strategic arms control, the implementation timetable is linked to a future agreement on an assistance program promoting implementation. If such an agreement is reached, the financial burden on Russia will be considerably eased.

5. Yet another argument against START-2 is that its implementation will create an additional employment problem for the defense sector of the Russian economy. For instance, Evgenii Kozhokin, deputy chairman of the Committee on Defense of the Supreme Soviet, reportedly raised the issue of the treaty's impact on the military-industrial complex, emphasizing the negative impact on employment.[11]

This argument is not convincing. First, because they are more capital intensive than labor intensive, strategic arms production industries accounted for a relatively minor part of the Soviet military-industrial complex budget. While some 15 million people were engaged in the defense sector as a whole, strategic arms production enterprises employed only about 900,000. Second, as was noted earlier, the major facilities for MIRVed ICBM production that will be most affected by START-2 are located in Ukraine and not in Russia. Ukrainian officials have already declared their intention to close down these plants; such closures will not, therefore, create an additional problem. Finally, one should consider that disarmament, especially dismantlement, of sophisticated weapons can also create jobs.

6. The sixth argument is related to possible changes in the Ukrainian position on nuclear issues. In fact, one of the major reasons for Yeltsin to press for START-2 earlier in 1992 was that it would further guarantee the removal of all nuclear weapons from Ukraine and Kazakhstan. Because all of their remaining ICBMs are MIRVed, START-2 does not affect the ICBMs of Belarus, which are single-warhead SS-25s. However, Russia has never been particularly concerned about Belarus because its government has consistently advocated denuclearization.

When Yeltsin and Bush signed the Framework Agreement in June 1992, it seemed that Ukrainians had already made up their minds to "go nonnuclear." The implementation of START-2 would leave only the nuclear-capable bombers nationalized by Ukraine and Kazakhstan outside the scope of international arms control agreements. The Ukrainian position is still unclear. Opposition is mounting in the Ukrainian Parliament to denuclearization, and the Lisbon Protocol to START-1 has yet to be ratified. Russia should go no further with nuclear disarmament, critics maintain, until it is certain what will happen in its own backyard.

To some extent, Russia itself is responsible for this problem. Neither Ukraine nor other "nuclear" republics of the former Soviet Union were consulted when the treaty was negotiated, even though START-2 affects systems currently stationed on their territory. No wonder Ukrainians feel humiliated and pronuclear political groups are gaining momentum.

However, Ukrainian President Leonid Kravchuk strongly supported START-2 and confirmed the Ukrainian decision to become a nuclear-free state. He also stressed that the Lisbon Protocol of 1992 would be ratified if three conditions were met: that Ukrainian security be guaranteed by the West; that Ukraine receive assistance in dismantling and shipping the missiles from its territory; and that Ukraine retain ownership of all fissionable materials removed from the warheads.[12] In any case, START-2, as well as START-1, will not be implemented until Ukraine moves ahead.

7. The final argument against START-2 raises the possibility of a U.S. abrogation of the Anti-Ballistic Missile (ABM) Treaty by uploading Trident II missiles or arming the Strategic Defense Initiative (SDI) program. The first part of this argument seems fair (though it does not seem fatal), but the second part is irrelevant because the SDI program was officially closed by U.S. Secretary of Defense Les Aspin.

Because many of the reductions in the new agreement result from downloading and not from the dismantling of weapons, additional confidence-building measures (CBMs) are appropriate—these might include early deactivation of all warheads slated for eventual elimination; the central storage of all bomber weapons; and the institution of procedures to decrease the possibility of uploading ICBMs and SLBMs. Developing a package of CBMs could be done as a follow-up agreement.

To what extent are recent and current domestic political developments in Russia likely to influence the fate of START-2? As of early 1993, their immediate impact on foreign and arms control policies has been limited.

Although both the president and the opposition, during the preparation for the April 1993 referendum, tried to make use of the perceived triumphs or failures of the Yeltsin-Kozyrev policy abroad (including START-2), this area was clearly overshadowed by domestic issues. The constitutional debates in the summer of 1992 also distracted public attention from foreign and defense policies.

However, this does not mean that the confrontation between the executive and the legislative power in 1992 was irrelevant in terms of the future arms control policy of Moscow. In fact, some of the conse-quences are already visible.

Before the referendum and the break with Aleksandr Rutskoi, Yeltsin had to make sure that his foreign policy and arms control decisions would not lead to yet another conflict between the executive and legislative branches of the government, or to a dispute within the executive branch itself. This was particularly evident when he was choosing where to make concessions to the Supreme Soviet and to Rutskoi's group: Yeltsin often preferred to compromise on international rather than domestic issues, as exemplified in the abrupt and clumsy cancellation of Yeltsin's state visit to Japan scheduled for September 1992.

The president's hands are no longer tied. His final break with Ruslan Khasbulatov and Aleksandr Rutskoi has given Yeltsin the luxury of forging and implementing his own foreign and arms control policies regardless of how the opposition might react to them. At least two signs have been given that possible changes in Russian foreign policy might be more than shifts in rhetoric. First, after the spring constitutional crisis, Yeltsin clearly took a less ambiguous and more pro-Western position on the conflict in the former Yugoslavia, and on Bosnia in particular. Second, he announced that he would go to Tokyo in the fall of 1993, demonstrating a readiness to take additional steps to accommodate the Japanese on territorial issues. Both changes would have been unthinkable had Yeltsin still wanted to appease his domestic critics. One can also expect a more consistent and radical nuclear arms reductions policy from Moscow now that the supreme protector of the Russian military-industrial complex, Yurii Skokov, has left the presidential team.

The reaction of the Supreme Soviet is easy to predict: on Bosnia, it will take an even more openly pro-Serbian position (Evgenii Ambartsumov, chairman of the Committee on International Affairs and Foreign Eco-nomic Relations of the Supreme Soviet, has already called for the suspen-sion of economic sanctions); on Japan, it will watch closely all Yeltsin's moves, ready to declare any attempt to compromise on the territorial issue "unconstitutional" and "illegitimate." The Supreme Soviet may also seek to weaken Yeltsin politically by blocking the ratification of the START-2 Treaty under the pretext of concern at the Ukrainian position on nuclear disarmament.

The Changing Nuclear Landscape

When one tries to look beyond the START-1 and START-2 Treaties, the horizon of Russian-U.S. strategic relations becomes rather hazy. Many variables cloud the picture. Not only could domestic Russian politics dramatically affect these relations, but also the general global strategic situation could fluctuate considerably. Under different conditions, the same systems might appear stabilizing or destabilizing, the same programs could look economically affordable or unaffordable, the same strategies could turn out to be prudent and realistic or irresponsible and reckless.

However, no one doubts that the attention of the United States and Russia in nuclear matters will turn to the problem of nonproliferation.

Cooperation between Moscow and Washington on this problem has a long history. In a sense, it has been one of the major successes in superpower strategic relations. As early as the 1960s, at the height of the Cold War, the Soviet Union and the United States acknowledged that to limit the number of states that could have access to nuclear weapons was not only in the interest of international security at large but also in the national interests of both superpowers. The modern nonproliferation regime is largely the result of bilateral Soviet-American efforts. Their persistent pressure was a key factor in bringing 140 countries to join the Treaty on the Non-Proliferation of Nuclear Weapons (NPT) by 1990. Every year, despite very uneven political relations, the United States and the USSR held consultations aimed at coordinating their policies in this field. In 1989, the Soviet Union and the United States also launched a collaborative project on nuclear terrorism.

At the same time, all the accomplishments of nonproliferation efforts notwithstanding, by the beginning of the 1990s it became evident that within the general political framework of the Cold War, the Soviet and American efforts were not adequate to the level of danger that nuclear proliferation posed to international security. In fact, throughout the Cold War, there had been a slow but steady inflow of new members to the "nuclear club" outside of the nonproliferation regime. Today, there are at least three "underground" nuclear powers—India, Pakistan, and Israel. In March 1993, South African authorities confessed that during the 1970s and 1980s South Africa obtained six nuclear explosives. Neither Ukraine nor Kazakhstan has become a signatory nation to the NPT. Brazil and Argentina are rapidly developing their nuclear power–related industries without signing the NPT. Nowadays, it is difficult to say exactly how many nuclear states exist. The political ambitions of a few states—signatories as well as nonsignatories to the NPT—have fueled their pursuit of nuclear weapons. Their rapid mastering of the means of missile delivery and their accumulation of chemical weapons cannot but encourage suspicions that these states are on the road to developing nuclear bombs.[13]

It is not clear if the NPT will be preserved after 1995 or if it will be "revised" to give the green light for rapid and irreversible nuclear proliferation. The most dangerous step toward proliferation was taken by North Korea in March 1993, when it announced its intention to leave the NPT regime and thus escape its obligation not to develop nuclear weapons. Though later North Korea had to step back, its declaration set a precedent for other threshold states. As the Iraqi case suggests, some potential proliferators can efficiently use their "temporary" participation in the NPT to develop nuclear capabilities. If the NPT regime is eroded, the international system of the early 21st century will be shaped not by the United Nations, the G-7, or even the United States, but chiefly by a group of highly unstable Third World regimes brandishing nuclear arms. The potential dangers to international security posed by proliferation might well exceed those of the Soviet-American nuclear confrontation during the Cold War.

This is why the incentives for both the United States and Russia to concentrate on their bilateral nuclear equation will diminish. The age of nuclear rivalry between the superpowers has come to an end, but the age of the proliferation of weapons of mass destruction, including nuclear weapons, is just beginning. Apocalyptic visions of "nuclear pygmies" dominating world politics and blackmailing the whole of humankind may be exaggerated, but a new level of Russian-U.S. strategic cooperation is required to limit the risks of proliferation.

The future of such cooperation may be significantly influenced by two factors. One factor is whether a state's possession of nuclear weapons will continue to confer on it special status in the international system.

The current collapse of rigid bipolar structures could increase the relative military and political weight of the Third World's nuclear arsenals and, accordingly, bolster the overall international importance of the nuclear factor. Furthermore, the current shift in the balance of economic power in favor of nonnuclear states (notably, Germany, Japan, and the newly industrialized countries of Asia) could spur members of the nuclear club to rely on their unique assets to preserve their political positions.

If the end of the Cold War means greater nuclear multipolarity, then the accelerated modernization of nuclear arsenals, including both offensive systems and strategic defenses, will probably become an essential component of the defense postures of both the United States and Russia. The members of the nuclear club will, in this scenario, consider new generations of missiles and strategic defense systems not as a means to bring about a fundamental shift from "mutually assured destruction" to "mutually assured survival," but rather as an insurance policy to prevent their strategic potential from being devalued. The functions of the new generation of launchers and strategic defenses might thus be limited primarily to assuring second-strike capabilities if the numbers of nuclear warheads and means of delivery are not increased, and if the center of gravity is shifted from the arms race in its traditional form to competition in technology.

The other factor that will influence the future of Russian-U.S. strategic cooperation and the global nuclear balance is whether nuclear weapons can or will be used in the context of possible North-South conflicts. Is it feasible to use nuclear weapons to deter regional conflicts in Asia, Africa, and Latin America?

If the Northern countries do not choose to distance themselves from conflicts in the chronically unstable South, nuclear weapons will inevitably become an important factor in North-South relations. This prospect has special significance for Russia, which directly borders the most explosive regions of the Third World.

Growing economic tensions between the North and the South, with subsequent political implications (or even conflicts among the developing countries themselves), exacerbated by the accelerating arms race in the South, might lead to very serious strategic readjustments. The developed world could use against potential aggressors from the South the same strategy that the West employed against the USSR during the Cold War: the threat of a nuclear strike to deter a possible conventional offensive. Under these conditions, Russia would become an outpost of the North much like Germany was an outpost of NATO. If this scenario becomes reality, new command, control, communications, and intelligence (C3I) systems, guidance technologies, and ballistic missile defenses are sure to become part of the strategic picture.

Ballistic missile defense systems are often claimed to be necessary to guard against the accidental launch of ballistic missiles and the dangers of nuclear terrorism. Such claims, however, are dubious. First of all, ballistic missiles (both ICBMs and SLBMs) are the most reliable of all the various nuclear delivery systems. Equipped with technical and electronic locks, changing codes, and so forth, ballistic missiles can be fired only with the authorization of the top political leadership. Other systems (tactical missiles, gravity bombs, artillery shells, and nuclear mines) are much more vulnerable to unauthorized launch—and ballistic missile defenses can hardly reduce this vulnerability.

Similar reasoning can be applied to the dangers of nuclear terrorism. It seems highly unlikely that terrorists would use ballistic missiles against the North. The terrorists have too many other options—ranging from cruise missiles to a "bomb in a briefcase"—that are more reliable and less expensive. Ballistic missiles are extremely inconvenient for terrorist-type actions: they cannot be built and deployed secretly, and they can (as the Gulf War demonstrated) easily be destroyed at their launching sites even by conventional means.

This is not to say that the dangers of accidental launches and terrorist use of ballistic missiles do not exist. Still, they are not as serious as the dangers that might be posed by other systems. In short, the development of a large-scale and very expensive ballistic missile defense system cannot be realistically justified on these grounds. Better arguments will be needed to generate (or, rather, to maintain) broad public and political support for such an enterprise.

Chief among those arguments are the potential efficacy of ballistic missile defense systems in accomplishing a variety of "preventive" missions, including preventing Third World nations from striking developed nations. Accurate and powerful enough to destroy strategic ballistic missiles in flight, these systems could be used to hit other air, ground, and sea targets, including command posts, communication and control networks, large floating targets, and key economic facilities (for example, oil and gas refineries, chemical plants, and power stations).

Taking the U.S. program as a model for other nuclear countries, one can make several predictions. First, given the technical complexities and high costs of ballistic missile defenses, as well as new strategic offensive weapons, it is clear that not all the nuclear powers will be able to afford them. In fact, in one or two decades, we may see a distinct division within the nuclear club between first-class members with state-of-the-art C3I, high-precision delivery vehicles, and defense systems, and second-class members without them. It is very unlikely that China or India, even in 20 or 30 years, will be ready to launch their SDIs. Russia can afford such a program technically, but perhaps not financially.

Second, some nuclear powers (especially France and the United Kingdom) will probably be obliged to cooperate more closely with one another to develop a new generation of both offensive and defensive systems. Such an evolution of the global strategic balance may accelerate overall European military integration and the gradual disintegration of the Atlantic partnership (it should be noted that the Europeans have received few benefits from their cooperation with the United States in SDI-related areas).

Third, the general global strategic balance will become much more complex and much more fragile. Although ballistic missile defense systems will be created and deployed, the means of penetrating them by strategic offensive forces will rapidly improve. Reductions in the numbers of ballistic missiles in the arsenals of Russia and the United States will be slowed, and other nuclear countries may feel it necessary to enlarge their nuclear weapons stockpiles to compensate for improvements in defense systems. Ballistic missile defenses also can trigger potentially destabilizing shifts in the nuclear postures of major actors; for instance, nuclear powers may decide to increase the number of their long-range cruise missiles, including sea- and ground-based ones, the deployment of which is extremely difficult to verify by national technical means. Yet another danger is that, because ballistic missile defenses can be used as antisatellite weapons (ASAT), they may undermine the strategic balance, which largely depends on the degree of all sides' confidence in the reliability and security of the warning, control, and monitoring systems based on different types of satellites.

Fourth, introduction of ballistic missile defenses at national levels will complicate the entire process of arms control. A new component will be added to the strategic forces of the major nuclear powers, creating additional difficulties in estimating the balance of forces of partners in arms control talks. Furthermore, as was the case with strategic offensive arms, the development of ballistic missile defenses by leading nuclear powers will very likely follow different lines, and this will further increase the asymmetry of their strategic forces and make them even more difficult to compare.[14] This asymmetry may be even greater if one considers potential countermeasures taken to neutralize the ballistic missile systems of opponents.

Future nuclear arms control negotiators may well envy their predecessors: regulating a bilateral nuclear balance is child's play compared to the problems of regulating multilateral nuclear relations. New models and new institutions of arms control will be needed, and past experience will be of little use. Important as they are for the security of the United States and Russia, bilateral agreements on nuclear arms control have nothing to do with preventing nuclear proliferation. Ritual references in the texts of the SALT-I, SALT-II, Intermediate Nuclear Forces (INF), START-1, and START-2 Treaties to the effect that both sides will abide by their obligations according to the provisions of the NPT neither strengthen the treaties themselves nor slow the pace of nuclear preparations by the threshold states.

Fifth, nuclear proliferation is unlikely to be halted by the development of strategic defense systems. Possession of nuclear weapons will still confer prestige and status. At the global level, however, proliferators will face an insuperable technological barrier. Many proliferators will have to limit their ambitions to a regional level, where the ballistic missile defenses of the developed countries will be, in most cases, irrelevant. For example, Pakistan will have no nuclear leverage against the United States, but it may well have such leverage against India. (Of course, a Northern policy perceived in the South as nuclear blackmail might provoke the South to respond with much less expensive, but almost equally destructive, chemical weapons. For Russia, yet another problem might emerge: the need to provide nuclear, as well as strategic defense, guarantees to other members of the CIS.)

Finally, the gap between nuclear "haves" and "have-nots," as well as the gap within the nuclear club itself, will widen, leading to new dividing lines in international politics. Nuclear states might form a new "Holy Alliance" aimed at preserving the existing structures of world politics. Nonnuclear actors, for their part, will try to restructure international relations according to new parameters of state power. In practical terms, it will mean a long and destructive struggle over who will have permanent membership in the UN Security Council—the current "big five" or countries like Germany, Japan, India, and Brazil. It could also mean that Ukraine, for example, will try to keep nuclear weapons at any cost in order to get the same attention from the West as nuclear Russia enjoys.

With the Cold War over, it is no longer possible to combine, for any extended time, the mutually exclusive goals of preserving the nuclear club and preventing others from joining it. If the nuclear club is not to grow, it must be disbanded or, at the least, moves must be made in this direction via the nuclear test ban and a formal ban on the production of enriched uranium and plutonium.

One could argue that to stop or slow down the nuclear programs of the threshold states it is first necessary to upgrade the existing international nonproliferation regime by creating additional disincentives for states to cross the nuclear threshold. But the paradox of the nonproliferation policy lies in the fact that to halt the drive of the majority of threshold states to nuclear status, they should be treated as de facto nuclear powers. Most measures to restrain nuclear proliferation in South Asia, the Middle East, Africa, and Latin America or on the territory of the former Soviet Union can be accepted by threshold countries if those measures assume not only a regional but also a global character. For example, to secure a pledge from these states to abstain from nuclear testing would be realistic only under the Comprehensive Test Ban Treaty, which has as yet been neither signed nor ratified.

The only radical alternative to the post–Cold War "nuclear renaissance" is gradual internationalization of nuclear weapons. Proposals to put nuclear weapons outside of national control are as old as nuclear arms themselves. The first U.S. initiative of this kind, the so-called Baruch plan, proposed that nuclear responsibilities be delegated to the United Nations. In the divided world of the Cold War, however, such an idea could not be implemented. Now, although the Cold War is over, this process still cannot develop under the aegis of the United Nations—the members of the nuclear club are too sensitive to any steps that can be interpreted as interference in their defense planning. A deepening of bilateral and multilateral interaction of nuclear states appears to be a more promising route to gradual internationalization.

In this respect, the development of strategic defense systems might become a valuable pilot project if pursued as a truly international venture and not as just another cycle of the arms race. Politically and psychologically, nuclear powers might find it easier to cooperate in developing strategic defenses than in modernizing strategic offensive weapons.

The feasibility of this option depends to a large extent on the position of the United States, which is the only remaining military superpower in the world. The collapse of the Soviet superpower and of the post–World War II international security system has led to increasing anarchy in world politics. No central authority exists in modern global politics beyond a rudimentary set of international institutions with no practical power to enforce law and order. One can only hope that, in some distant future, institutions such as the United Nations will become powerful enough to create and maintain international stability.

Meanwhile, conventional and, especially, nuclear power remain important and legitimate factors in world politics, and will continue to play significant roles in different regions of the globe. Neither the arms race nor international conflict is about to come to an end. Facing a highly unstable and sometimes dangerous world, the United States will have to define a new security policy, one which will have a major influence on the future of ballistic missile defenses.

One option for the United States would be to define its security policy along highly "nationalistic" lines, with priority being given to the protection of short-term U.S. security interests, even at the expense of international stability. This policy need not mean a return to isolationism and the "Fortress America" concept; it could try instead to exploit the multipolar balance in Eurasia and play one power center against another, in the manner of the Nixon-Kissinger approach. Under such a policy, the United States would continue to regard the SDI as entirely its own program, and would refuse to share technology with other nuclear powers.

The main consequences of adopting this kind of policy would be further disintegration of the global security system, extreme fragility of the multilateral strategic balance, and the decline of the global political standing of the United States. A number of unresolved regional tensions would reemerge from the ruins of the bipolar Cold War system. Arms control would have limited importance for all the participants of the international system. Although military conflicts between major actors in world politics would be unlikely to erupt, threats to use conventional military force might well increase at lower levels of interstate relations, as the great powers disengage from local conflicts, leaving mid-level countries free to pursue the role of regional hegemon.

Already, the preparedness of the leading military powers to reduce their arsenals is far greater than their willingness to cooperate in creating international political institutions capable of filling the power vacuum that progress in Russian-U.S. disarmament threatens to produce. The threat of war may even increase as the possibilities of a planetary nuclear conflagration diminish.

A narrowly defined, nationalistic U.S. security policy is also likely to accentuate the destabilizing effects of different economic challenges, varying from instability in the international financial system to foreign trade wars and fierce conflicts in the area of technology transfer. Economic interests, processes, and forces already transcend nations and regions and exert a potent influence on political and military-technical ties throughout the world. World and regional economic imbalances are likely to produce tremendous upheavals in the international system, creating very considerable difficulties for the weakest members of the community. Such upheavals could provoke national economic crises and cause unpredictable social and political shifts that will have a direct impact on the level of international stability, including its military component.

How would these things affect Russian-U.S. strategic relations? One can imagine that, losing its superpower status and facing American egotism in Geneva, Russia would also lose much of its interest in conducting a bilateral arms control process with the United States. Instead, Russia might opt for a kind of "nuclear isolationism," which would mean complete independence in the strategic sphere ("asymmetrical response") and the rejection of American strategic culture (including unacceptable damage criteria, the concept of strategic stability, and so forth). In a way, this choice would be very similar to the choice made by Gaullist France in the 1960s. Unable to play with the nuclear superpowers according to their rules, France made sure that it would not obey those rules. If Russia follows the French path in the mid-1990s, the United States may find itself with no nuclear power with which to negotiate arms control agreements.

The likelihood that Russia would adopt such a post–Cold War nuclear posture seems even greater in light of the profound political and strategic changes of recent years that have gradually undermined the whole notion of parity as the basis of strategic stability. The huge nuclear arsenals of the United States and Russia themselves, even if relatively equal, have begun to pose a greater threat to stability, rendering it less secure. Consequently, the so-called statistical threat of conflict resulting from an error or a technical malfunction in ever more numerous and intricate automated systems has grown. Therefore, many criteria other than parity are now taken into account in Russian defense decision making, the main criterion probably being the preservation of a sufficient quantity and quality of nuclear forces to assure a devastating counterstrike—enough nuclear weaponry to inflict "unacceptable damage" on a would-be aggressor and thus deter it. If Russia opts for nuclear isolationism, it will represent a retreat to the strategic situation of the 1950s and, especially, of the 1960s, when the United States and the Soviet Union already possessed the potential for mutually assured destruction, but were not engaged in any meaningful negotiations and had no mechanisms to ensure strategic stability.[15]

Presently, both the Russian and the U.S. strategic arsenals are militarily redundant. In the current situation, Russia has the opportunity to unilaterally lower the level of its forces and change their structure. The latter step would involve making an independent decision as to the future development of strategic forces and refusing to duplicate U.S. weapons systems.

A second option for the United States as it redefines its foreign and defense policies is altogether more "globalistic" and less nationalistic in character. If the United States adopts this global approach, it will not separate its own security interests from those of the world as a whole. Instead of promoting another version of a multipolar system in Eurasia, the principal American goal will be to establish a kind of international security structure based on "Greater Europe," a structure able to repulse numerous destabilizing impulses from the South. The SDI in this context might become the first really multilateral strategic program based not only on the mutual trust of the participants, but also on their perceptions of a common threat.

Of course, future U.S. security policy will not be a clear-cut choice between the first and the second options. Rather, U.S. policy will fluctuate between them, depending on U.S. domestic political and international developments. If the United States pursues a course closer to the second option, which seems both more feasible and preferable, ballistic missile defenses might become a key factor in the creation of the new world security order.

Conclusion: Nuclear Arms Control in the Post–Cold War Era

Nuclear arms control can no longer be confined to bilateral Russian-American relations. Perhaps the last bilateral accord will be START-2 or the "START-2 follow-up" (the later being a number of specific agreements not included within the START-2 package but already within reach of negotiators in Geneva). It would be highly impractical to dismantle the existing mechanism of negotiations, which can still produce a number of positive results.

In the very near future, the effectiveness of arms control will depend directly on the ability of the United States and the Russian Federation to engage other nuclear powers in this process. Clearly, the United States should play a more important role here than should the Russian Federation. It remains up to the Americans to bring their allies to the negotiating table. The difficulties of this multilateral approach—not only political, but also technical—should not be underestimated, however. Indeed, multilateral nuclear arms control talks certainly cannot be conducted according to the old bilateral model. In the first place, traditional principles of parity, equal capabilities, and mutual concessions must give way to new, incomparably more complex principles and criteria. Furthermore, geopolitical, geostrategic, and other factors will have to be taken into account to an even greater degree than in the talks hitherto conducted.

It is tempting to imagine that future strategic arms control talks between nuclear powers (at least the nuclear powers of the Northern Tier) will resemble current NATO discussions on defense burden-sharing.[16] Such a scenario, however, is too optimistic for the foreseeable future. Nuclear arms will undoubtedly remain an important symbol of political status for relatively weaker countries like France, Russia, and Great Britain. Besides, the security concerns of the various nuclear powers will differ even if they find complete accommodation among themselves. For example, Russia might find it indispensable to have an "extended deterrence" strategy to counter a potentially overwhelming conventional threat from the south or from the east.

In all likelihood, it will be easier to make progress in multilateral nuclear arms control if its goals are specified as strictly arms control, and not as involving disarmament. Multilateral arms control should not be directed primarily at reducing and rigidly limiting the existing forces, but rather at coordinating their modernization and instituting CBMs.[17] The engagement of third powers in bilateral Russian-American strategic interaction in this case can occur in a very gradual and flexible fashion—as a first step, for example, multilateral risk reduction centers could take the place of the existing bilateral ones. Each nuclear power should be able to choose its own level of participation in the arms control process based on its own analysis of related costs and benefits.

The aims of multilateral arms control should be realistic, but they should not be confined to the pursuit of stability and a controlled nuclear arms race. Leaders of nuclear powers will not be able to afford such a pragmatic approach: they will have to negotiate arms control not just among themselves but also with their powerful domestic antinuclear constituencies. There are no reasons to believe that these constituencies will soon disappear in the United States, Europe, or the Russian Federation. They will prevent arms control from becoming too "professional" and bureaucratic.

It is clear that the time for comprehensive arms control deals has already passed. Many experts favor the "bite-after-bite" model, in which the sides try to reach agreement on a range of issues addressed in a certain order, in the process not only resolving specific problems but also advancing the entire front of the talks. Such an approach will not necessarily facilitate arms control negotiations, however. After all, in the 1970s and 1980s, the United States and the USSR tried persistently to reach comprehensive agreements, and not just because of their political significance (though that was, of course, a major factor). The larger the package of agreements was, the easier it was to find a compromise, trading concessions in one sphere for concessions in another. Given the existing asymmetries in the structure of Russian and American forces, to say nothing of French and British forces, it would appear to be extremely difficult to find an acceptable solution on only one system without touching others, and the bite-after-bite model will not work.

The answer to this problem might be to keep packages but to limit their size—to make them just as large as is needed to allow concessions to be exchanged and compromises reached.

Another problem with the bite-after-bite approach is that it can rationalize, but not retard, the arms race by closing off avenues of little real military potential or significance. For instance, the Soviet Union and the United States tried to redirect their arms race away from overly expensive paths (through the ABM treaty, for instance), to limit the ecological damage of nuclear arms development (by limiting nuclear tests), and to prevent other countries from acquiring nuclear capabilities (through the NPT regime). In other words, negotiators were inclined to solve easy questions without trying to address more fundamental problems. A lot of loopholes exist in arms control agreements. Even the START-1 agreement contains such loopholes, despite the fact that it was initially designed as a comprehensive treaty.

There seem to be no solutions to this problem. Yet, it has to be said that the quest for comprehensive treaties typical of the traditional arms control approach was itself a result of deep mistrust and suspicion between the superpowers. Perhaps in a cooperative, rather than a confrontational post–Cold War political environment, the sides will not try to use any legally unresolved issues to secure unilateral advantages and undermine the security of their partners.

The sides should adjust themselves to a new balance between negotiated agreements and unilateral actions. If current political developments in Russian-U.S. relations continue, unilateral restraints in the strategic sphere will outpace even a revised and accelerated arms control process. To avoid Russian-American strategic decoupling, it becomes extremely important to ensure that these unilateral steps are taken in a parallel and, when possible, coordinated fashion.[18]

This is not to say that negotiated agreements are of no significance. When meaningful, they create a political and psychological impediment for the side that leads in the arms race, hindering it from building up its advantages in the most favorable areas. They also strengthen opposition to the arms race and have a positive effect on the general international situation. Existing treaty regimes and the very prospect of reaching further accords not only check the arms race in certain areas, but also influence developments in defense-related efforts and intensify political strife around them. In parallel, dialogue on arms limitations enhances one side's knowledge of the other side's capabilities and intentions and creates greater confidence.

Nevertheless, the early 1990s have shown that the arms control process simply cannot catch up with political changes, and it should not be used to prevent unilateral steps from being taken.

Coordinated unilateral actions will avoid the delays associated with the ratification process. In the record of Soviet-American relations, one can find several examples (SALT-II springs to mind) of such unilateral steps that had no legal power but were nonetheless politically binding and played an important role in curbing the arms race.

Such "soft" arms control might be more attractive to the third nuclear powers, none of which appears ready to participate in any traditional arms control negotiations, even as an observer. Nonbinding coordinated actions will not compromise the nuclear independence of third powers, yet such actions will create additional reliability and predictability in general nuclear balance.

The format of negotiations should also be changed. The following four-stage model is one option that seems to merit consideration.

At the first stage, a permanent forum of military, political, and technical experts from all the participating sides would exchange information on strategic systems and technologies in the process of development. The forum would discuss the possible impact of specific programs on strategic stability and the arms control process. The forum would not be directly linked to any negotiations—its functions would not be to trade one system for another, but to coordinate future strategic postures on both sides. Because the participants would discuss programs that exist only in blueprints, they would find it easier to avoid current political considerations than do the participants in the START process.

After a more or less prolonged period of consultations at the level of experts, the forum would present its recommendations on the most dangerous trends in nuclear technologies and possible ways to block these trends to the governments of the nuclear powers. At the second stage, each government would either respond unilaterally and inform its partners of its decision, or participate in high-level consultations (at the level of foreign ministers or even heads of state) designed to reach a common accord.

At the third stage, detailed directives would be issued requiring the accord to be translated swiftly by professional negotiators and lawyers into a legally binding agreement. Once such an agreement had been drawn up, the negotiators would disperse. If the agreement dealt chiefly with technical issues, it could be signed by high-ranking officials and take the form of an executive agreement not subject to subsequent ratification.

However, if the accord touched upon vital issues, a fourth and final stage would be needed. A summit would be held at which a document could be signed by political leaders, and then submitted to national legislatures for their consideration and ratification.

Thus, at every stage of the arms control process there would be a chance to solve a problem. The best way of dealing with a problem, of course, would be to avoid it altogether by discussing potential threats to stability at the forum of experts. The second-best option would be to solve the problem by parallel unilateral actions, especially if such actions included adequate verification mechanisms. A third option would be to reach an executive agreement without the involvement of top-level politicians. As a last resort, the sides could turn to the traditional arms control mechanism.

Today, conditions are being created for the dismantling of the post–World War II system of military confrontation. The arms control negotiation process has been given a powerful impetus, with the groundwork laid for its reconfiguration into a new pattern that would combine multilateral, bilateral, parallel, and unilateral measures.

Notes

1. On Western assessments of the Russian "share" in the total Soviet nuclear arsenal, see Kurt M. Campbell, Ashton B. Carter, Steven E. Miller, and Charles A. Zraket, "Soviet Nuclear Fission: Control of the Nuclear Arsenal in a Disintegrating Soviet Union," *CSIA Studies in International Security*, no. 1 (Cambridge, Mass.: Center for Science and International Affairs, Harvard University, November 1991), pp. 1–34.

2. This section of the essay is based on a report prepared by the author for the Center for Post-Soviet Studies, Washington, D.C., January 1993.

3. *Rossiia*, January 6, 1993. Andronov is not exactly right. The Foreign Ministry did try to involve the Supreme Soviet and, in particular, the heads of the related committees in the process of finalizing the treaty. However, this attempt was made at the very last stage of negotiations in Geneva, thus raising legitimate suspicions that the Foreign Ministry was trying to buy the support of the Supreme Soviet for the treaty's ratification with the pretense of real parliamentary participation.

4. One should bear in mind that Foreign Minister Andrei Kozyrev was not confirmed by the Russian Parliament, and that, because of this, he is perceived by many parliamentarians as a "semi-legal" foreign minister.

5. In fact, during the 1970s and 1980s, there were no attempts on the part of the top political leadership to share a solid constitutional or even a bureaucratic framework for arms control decision making. General political statements usually had very little to do with specific negotiating positions, and the latter were primarily the responsibility of the so-called Inter-Agency Commission (which included representatives from the military, the defense industry, diplomats, the KGB, and the International Department of the Central Committee of the Communist Party of the Soviet Union) that reported directly to the Politburo. All the participating institutions defended their interests, and the final position depended on the very delicate balance of power that existed in the top Soviet political establishment at any given moment.

6. In reality, U.S.-Soviet strategic parity never meant quantitative equality. The United States always had more warheads on its delivery vehicles, with the disparity being occasionally quite substantial. For example, in the mid-1970s, when parity, by mutual recognition, was firmly set, the United States had twice as many warheads as the USSR (8,000 and 4,000, respectively).

7. Theoretically, Russia could, of course, replace its MIRVed ICBMs with 1,200 to 1,400 single-headed ICBMs of the SS-25 (or further modified) type to preserve its present strategic structure intact. But there are two reasons to believe that this cannot happen soon. First, the SS-25 ICBMs are road mobile, and given regional instability and potential disintegration trends within Russia, the military is concerned about the missiles' physical security. The military clearly prefers silo-based missiles over mobiles—all reservations about survivability notwithstanding. Second, such an ambitious redeployment program would be prohibitively expensive (costing more than 400 billion 1993 rubles). A more modest program—to deploy a limited number of additional single-headed ICBMs—will not make much difference.

8. History suggests that this state of affairs was sought by American strategic planners. For example, in the late 1950s and early 1960s, the United States went to great efforts to drag the Soviet Union into competition in building strategic bomber aircraft, expecting that the U.S. geostrategic advantage (in particular, the dense network of military bases scattered around the borders of the USSR), as well as America's technological and industrial superiority, would enable Washington to dictate terms in that competition. Later, the United States tried persistently to "push the Russians into the water," that is, to ensure that the Soviet strategic potential would be reinforced through SLBM deployments rather than through the development of land-based ICBMs. In this case, too, geostrategic advantages were prevalent (the United States had unimpeded access to the world's oceans—something that the Soviet Union could not boast of). Besides, the United States has always had a substantial edge in antisubmarine warfare. Emphasis has also been put on maximizing economic costs for the USSR (an SLBM costs seven to ten times more than an ICBM).

9. To be more specific, this line of criticism assumes that the Russian side made a strategic mistake by accepting a complete ban on all MIRVed ICBMs, including mobile ones. Mobile MIRVed ICBMs are not more destabilizing than MIRVed SLBMs; they are relatively survivable and not as accurate as ICBMs in silos. Russia has an advanced program of MIRVed ICBMs deployed (railroad-based SS-24s) that has not been affected by the START-1 Treaty. Instead of trying to keep, or at least download, this force of 360 warheads, Yeltsin simply surrendered them to the United States.

10. Alexei Arbatov, "Dogovor dorozhe deneg," *Novoe vremia,* nos. 2–3 (January 1993), p. 24.

11. *Rossiia,* January 6, 1993.

12. *Nedelia,* January 5 and 6, 1993.

13. Recently, public opinion in Russia and abroad was stirred by the potential emigration of Russian nuclear and ballistic specialists to North Africa, the Middle East, and East Asia. However, the rumors about Russian nuclear scientists flooding Third World countries seem exaggerated, at least for the time being. For example, according to information released by the Institute of Atomic Energy in late January 1992, only two nuclear experts have left the former USSR to work on contracts not approved by the government. However, their countries of destination were Germany and Israel, not Libya or Iraq; besides, neither expert is working on serious nuclear arms-related projects. See *Rossiiskaia gazeta,* January 28, 1992.

As far as government-approved contracts are concerned, the Soviet Union assisted in launching the nuclear programs of Libya, Iraq, Egypt, Cuba, and Vietnam (it also prepared blueprints for Syria and Morocco). After the Gulf War of 1991, Soviet cooperation with Iraq was terminated, although it continued in the case of the other countries.

Rough estimates indicate that 900,000 people within the CIS are currently working, or have worked, in nuclear industries. But only 10,000 to 20,000 of these are experts who could make a difference in a nuclear program of a Third World country. See Elaine Sciolino, "U.S. Report Warns of Risk in Spread of Nuclear Skills," *The New York Times*, January 1, 1992, p. 1; and Gerald F. Seib and John J. Fialka, "Scientists of Former Soviet Union Find the U.S. Slow in Putting Out the Welcome Mat for Them," *The Wall Street Journal*, February 3, 1992, p. A14.

Further political turmoil and the collapse of former Soviet nuclear research programs could encourage many of these people to emigrate. According to Deputy Minister of Atomic Power and Industry Victor Mikhailov, who heads the nuclear arms production program of the Russian Federation, there are more than 100,000 employees in the ministry. Of these, between 2,000 and 3,000 have top-secret expertise. In an interview with *Newsweek International* magazine, Mikhailov said that the major problem was not a leak of top nuclear experts from Russia, but rather emigration of nuclear specialists from other republics of the former Soviet Union. Mikhailov stated that "all members of the former Soviet Union need to approve laws preventing nuclear proliferation and the spread of advanced technology, including laws governing the emigration of people involved in nuclear weapons development" (*Newsweek International*, February 24, 1992, p. 58). The best solution to this problem is probably to engage Soviet nuclear experts in an internationally sponsored program addressing such subjects as controlled nuclear synthesis, annihilation of nuclear warheads, or nuclear power plant safety.

14. The asymmetries are certain to increase because of the different strategic needs of the major nuclear powers. For example, Russia, with its lengthy borders and potentially unstable neighbors to the south and east, will demand the right to deploy not 1,000, but rather 3,000 missile interceptors. Moreover, being unable to compete with Washington in modern guidance systems, Moscow might choose to deploy missile interceptors with nuclear warheads.

15. This problem is analyzed at length in V. Zhurkin, S. Karaganov, and A. Kortunov, *Reasonable Sufficiency and New Political Thinking* (Moscow: Nauka Publishers, 1989).

16. On the possible integration of Russia and other former Soviet republics into NATO, see Hans Binnendijk, "NATO Can't Be Vague about Commitment to Eastern Europe," *International Herald Tribune*, November 8, 1991, p. 6; and Jay P. Kosminsky and Leon Aron, "Transforming Russia from Enemy to Ally," *The Heritage Foundation Backgrounder* (March 19, 1992), p. 11.

17. On "operational" priority of post–Cold War arms control, see Fred Charles Iklé, "Comrades in Arms: The Case of a Russian-American Defense Community," *The National Interest*, no. 26 (Winter 1991–92), pp. 18–32; and Ashton B. Carter, William J. Perry, and John D. Steinbruner, *A New Concept of Cooperative Security*, Brookings Occasional Papers (Washington, D.C.: The Brookings Institution, 1992).

18. An interesting analysis of this approach can be found in Carl Kaysen, Robert S. McNamara, and George W. Rathjens, "Nuclear Weapons After the Cold War," *Foreign Affairs* 70, no. 4 (Fall 1991), pp. 95–110.

10

On Western Perceptions of the New Russian National Security Doctrine

Evgenii S. Volk

Unlike Russia's economic development, ethnic turmoil, and domestic politics, the emerging national security doctrine of the new, democratic Russia does not seem on the surface to be a top priority with Western political scientists and mass media. However, a close and constant monitoring of foreign publications and the activities of various fact-finding missions reveals a deep and genuine—albeit not always explicit—interest in the West in this problem and its practical aspects.

Even so, little is know in the West about the dynamics of the process of formulating Russian national security doctrine. Only a few in the Western political research establishment follow the problem scrupulously. Leon Aron is among them, and I am grateful to him and his colleagues for their academic interest and practical efforts designed to assist this process.

It has already become commonplace to refer to a deep crisis in American Soviet studies, which appeared to be unable to predict the rapid and drastic disintegration of the communist system and of the former USSR as its main stronghold. A similar failure of prediction seems to exist in respect of the emergence of new Russian concepts of national security. In fairness, however, researchers—even as recently as the 1980s—could hardly have been expected to imagine a radically new paradigm for a Russian strategic posture in the world.

As Michael McGwire put it in his 1987 book, *Military Objectives in Soviet Foreign Policy,* alluding to a well-known Churchill epigram, "The image of Russia as a riddle, wrapped in a mystery, inside an enigma is immensely compelling to the West."[1] This is no less true today than it was in the 1970s and 1980s. The crucial problem for the Western scholar has always been selecting and interpreting the available information. It was difficult to do this during the Cold War, when an overwhelming majority of the publications on security and military issues were subject to a centralized propaganda and censorship effort designed to conceal the real strategic goals of the totalitarian regime.

Some Western analysts have apparently fallen victim to that deceptive campaign. I would disagree with Michael McGwire's contention that "the Soviets' overarching objective" was "to promote the long-term well-being of the Soviet State."[2] McGwire neglects the expansionist dimension of communist ideology and its implementation in the international affairs of the USSR. Furthermore, the "well-being of the state" had often been understood by the ruling elite in terms of their personal well-being, an interpretation that had many practical repercussions for foreign and defense policy concepts, planning, and practice.

On the other hand, I am inclined to caution some Western analysts against exaggerating the role of communist ideology in Soviet security and defense thinking and conduct. This point is important to understanding better the debate around Russian national security doctrine. Baker Spring of the Heritage Foundation puts the following question in his 1991 study, *Five Questions Facing the Soviet Military:* "Will the Soviet military abandon its commitment to Communist ideology?"[3] In practice, however, such a commitment hardly existed in recent decades, either in the armed forces or in the civilian establishment, except perhaps for a few among the old guard. Communist ideology was regarded rather as a code of conduct to comply with—regardless of the blatant contradictions between its theoretical content and its implementation in the reality of "socialist society." Everyone in the military knew perfectly well that without a demonstrative loyalty to the Communist Party's "ideals," one would be deprived of the opportunity to pursue a successful military career.

The disappearance of Communist Party cells in the armed forces went unnoticed and caused no negative reaction among the military; indeed, it was as if these organizations had never existed. This fact eloquently indicates the deep indifference and the purely pragmatic approach of most officers toward communist ideology. The same could be said of officials in other security-related agencies. However, it is important to note that communist ideology supplied them all with a precisely defined image of the enemy. This image served a necessary military purpose insofar as it discouraged members of the armed forces from undertaking an independent and nonpartisan study of the international situation. Today, many people in the armed forces feel the want of such clearly defined national defense priorities and have become vulnerable to anti-Western, neocommunist demagoguery. A remnant of the totalitarian mentality still survives within the national security sector, and it is extremely difficult to eliminate once and for all.

Dramatic domestic and external changes have accelerated the process of reevaluating Soviet security priorities and needs on the level of both government and public opinion. As is pointed out in the U.S. Department of Defense study, *1991 Military Forces in Transition,* among the most prominent events and factors prompting this reevaluation were the Chernobyl disaster, the war in Afghanistan, arms control agreements, economic decline, revolution in Eastern Europe, separatist challenges to the USSR from the republics, the Persian Gulf War, and changes in the national security decision-making process itself.[4] I would add to this list increased domestic instability and the politicization of public opinion.

Adequate research and accurate interpretation of national security developments have been severely undermined by the collapse of the official mechanisms of political research conducted by and for the Communist Party, and by the subsequent entry of incompetent politicians and amateur scholars into the field. Basic national security notions, including the general definition of national economy, the concept of national vital interests, the understanding of existing threats and challenges, and the search for available and feasible resources and allies, have become elements in the domestic political struggle. The pervasive character of that struggle—flagrant disinformation, manipulation of carefully selected facts and figures, and deliberate subversion of the sense of various key terms—influences the debate on national security matters.

It seems helpful, therefore, to look back to Russian national security doctrine as it started to emerge under the new geopolitical and strategic conditions after the collapse of communism and totalitarianism became evident in 1989–90. Until then, as almost all Western scholars acknowledge, Soviet approaches toward national security identity remained extremely militarized. National security was treated as a subject of military interest rather than as a matter of national defense more broadly construed.

The civilian establishment and academic research system were actually prevented from participating in the formulation of distinct views on the national security problem. Nevertheless, the problem was of great interest to many scholars in both the social and the natural sciences, Academician Andrei Sakharov among them. Their efforts were often concentrated on the examination of the Western (first and foremost, the U.S.) experience of constructing a legislatively shaped national security system after World War II.

Overcoming the strongly militarized approach to the problem and drafting a fundamentally new national security concept became one of the priorities (although not the top one) for the group of democratically oriented intellectuals that emerged unexpectedly as an influential political force at the First Congress of People's Deputies of the USSR and in the Supreme Soviet which was elected by the Congress in 1989.

The efforts of these intellectuals were encouraged by two major sociopolitical trends outside and inside the country. The first was a substantial decrease in the role of the military in the newly emerging system of international relations. This new item was based on a sophisticated combination of checks and balances, including a complex approach to the balance of power and the balance of interests, as well as reciprocity in relaxing the degree of military and political confrontation. As Harry Gelman remarks in his study, *Gorbachev and the Future of the Soviet Military Institution,* of all the revolutionary changes begun under Gorbachev, "probably one of the most encouraging implications for the rest of the world was the trend towards the gradual demilitarization of Soviet society and the Soviet ethos."[5]

The understanding of the complex nature of security—both national and international—as an entity possessing political, economic, strategic, ecological, demographic, and other relevant aspects of societal life was spreading in the West and the East. It began to create in Russia a qualitatively new intellectual and sociopolitical infrastructure for the shaping of national security.

The second significant trend that influenced both political thinking and conduct was the active involvement of competent civilians in such critical national security spheres as arms control and disarmament negotiations. Under Gorbachev, the monopoly of the Ministry of Defense and its General Staff as the principal actor in defining strategic goals, priorities, and guidelines in the arms control process (this unconditionally approved by the Politburo) appeared to be undermined. The Piatiorka

(The Five)—a Politburo commission that included key figures from the Central Committee of the Communist Party of the Soviet Union, the Ministry of Foreign Affairs, the KGB, the Ministry of Defense, and the VPK (Military-Industrial Commission of the Council of Ministers), as well as experts from other agencies—started to play a leading role in decision making on arms control issues and appeared to pose a serious challenge to the claims of the military to know "the truth in the last instance." The time had passed when Soviet military negotiators at arms reduction talks, when passing official data on Soviet strategic forces to their American counterparts, would warn them against sharing this information with other Soviet representatives who had no security clearance (*dopusk*) for such highly classified data. Harry Gelman remarks that the new arrangement represented "an evolution of Soviet practice in a direction unwelcome to the military":

> At the working level the proliferation of institutions and individuals authorized to participate in the inner discussion about negotiations in progress inevitably put pressure on the General Staff to widen access to classified military information which it had long sought rigidly to restrict, so as to protect its own monopoly on advisory use of such information.[6]

The breakthrough in this informational monopoly stimulated the appearance of conceptually mature and democratically oriented approaches toward arms control and disarmament priorities. A high-level representation of the advocates of Gorbachev's "new thinking" meant that a wide circle of lower-ranking officers (who shared nontraditional views) from all the nonmilitary agencies concerned became involved—directly or indirectly—in shaping the national security process. As Gelman correctly observes: "The make-up of the Politburo Commission itself was almost certainly unwelcome to the General Staff since the inclusion of Aleksandr Yakovlev as well as Eduard Shevardnadze substantially increased the political weight of the forces likely to endorse negotiating concessions in the Commission discussions."[7]

Although the Piatiorka never managed to assume the function of a forum for a broad national security debate, its existence and manner of operation certainly contributed to achieving this goal. What is less well known is that some of the collective decisions of the Piatiorka, stipulated by the Politburo as "directives" for Shevardnadze's talks with his Western counterparts, including Secretary of State James Baker, were successfully circumvented by the joint efforts of Gorbachev, Yakovlev, and Shevardnadze himself. To my mind, this is not an insignificant fact. It indicates that the differences in approaches to the disarmament negotiations were deeply rooted in conceptually different understandings of national security interests and priorities in various layers of the Soviet establishment. The growing polarization of views and positions on this issue strongly influenced decision making in the field of foreign and military policy.

Between 1989 and 1991, a great number of new and interesting ideas on various aspects of national security doctrine originated in various political circles, and they found their expression in a number of official, semiofficial, and informal draft documents. The intense political and intellectual struggles waged around these ideas and concepts is a matter yet to be adequately explored in Russia and, especially, in the West, despite the fact that those struggles typified that particular stage of the disintegration of the USSR and the emergence of a new, independent Russian state.

My guess is that some Western scholars are prone to underestimate the significance of the initiative taken in 1990 by the chairman of the Committee on Science and Education of the Supreme Soviet of the USSR, Yu. M. Ryzhov, to start drafting a national security concept. This idea originally appeared when work on the concept of military reform began and the necessity of a more general basis for such reform became evident.

This effort represented a new kind of challenge—not that of civilian politicians and experts to the military within the framework of the old nomenklatura, but that of nonpartisan democratic figures to the communist (and neocommunist) establishment in the field of national security, which the latter considered to be its holy of holies. The activities of this initial group of democratically oriented parliamentarians and intellectuals under Academician Ryzhov's guidance naturally faced powerful resistance from Communist Party officials, the military, and the KGB. What is typical of the Gorbachev era is that none of those challenged took the responsibility to oppose these activities openly or to assert that they were futile. The tactics of bureaucratic delay, filibustering, and neglect were covertly applied. Gorbachev himself, having formally approved the start of the group's activities in his capacity as chairman of the Supreme Soviet, did practically nothing to support it when he became president.

One of Ryzhov's main ideas was that priority be given to the "human dimension" of security (that is, social security, human rights, the rights of refugees, minorities, and members of the armed forces) over all other dimensions, including the security of the state and society. This innovation undermined the Communist Party and state monopoly on regulating this vital sociopolitical sphere of national security.

Ryzhov's activities also constituted a challenge to the internal parliamentary nature of one of the most influential and conservative committees of the Supreme Soviet—the Committee of Defense and State Security Issues—which was packed with party apparatchiks, military-industrial bosses, and high-ranking generals from the armed forces and the KGB. The views of the committee's members could be summarized as follows: A national security concept is a bourgeois, Western notion unnecessary and inapplicable to the Soviet condition; and the military doctrine to be formulated by the military in accordance with Communist Party guidelines, approved by the Politburo, and rubber-stamped by the docile Supreme Soviet is quite sufficient. The committee preferred the term "state security" to "national security," the former implying that counterintelligence and political surveillance were the key elements in the protection of national interests.

The committee's approach was essentially bureaucratic and lacked political and strategic dimensions. This was reflected, for example, in the draft version of the "Concept of Military Reform," which was made public as a response to Gorbachev's appeal for urgent political reforms in the military field. The limited and reactionary nature of the draft was immediately identified by Western analysts. For example, David E. Colton remarked that the "complicated task of balancing the reforms being conducted in the society by the requirements of the military science—the most difficult task for the Soviet Armed Forces since the Civil War—was not dealt with in the Draft."[8] As Colton emphasized, the main drawback of the draft was its lack of any provision or mechanism for civilian control over the military, either in an administrative or political sense.[9]

At the same time, Ryzhov's group was actually prevented from undertaking further work on its version. In spring 1991, the chairman of the Supreme Soviet of the USSR, Anatoly Lukyanov, dismissed the Ryzhov group under the pretext that the elaboration of a national security concept was a prerogative of the president of the state, not of a parliamentary commission.

The situation around the national security doctrine seemed deadlocked. On the one hand, the traditional establishment was unable to generate and advance constructive ideas capable either of receiving any kind of political support from the dissident Union republics (most notably, the Baltic ones) or of winning a consensus in Moscow through a compromise between the central government and Russian authorities, especially the Russian Parliament, which under its chairman (and, since

June 1991, president of the republic) Boris Yeltsin presented open opposition to the Union's line on the majority of political issues.

On the other hand, the democratic forces were active in applying their intellectual powers to the question of national security, shaping and drafting a number of interesting versions of a national security concept. But they were too weak politically and organizationally to put their ideas into governmental practice within the USSR, facing, as they did, enormous political and bureaucratic resistance. The absence of a state agency or public institution that could have reconciled new ideas with the old establishment—thereby giving birth to a new concept backed by a new, responsible organizational structure with an extended consultative mandate in the field of national security—impeded the process of introducing a new pattern of national security deliberation on a state level. As a Western analyst, who privately clarified this situation for me, said, "The quality of the final product cannot be higher than the quality of the political process itself."

This is only a partial explanation of the difficulties that existed in 1991 and still remain. Indeed, by the end of 1990, as soon as Russia started to pursue independent policies and to create new structures in the field of national security, positive results came rather quickly. A first draft of the law "On Security" and a general concept of Russia's national security were prepared at the end of 1990 by a group of highly qualified experts from various institutions, both governmental and public. (The law itself, however, was only finally adopted on March 3, 1992.) Embryonic versions of a national security council were conceived almost simultaneously (for some time, two draft bills—"On Security" and "On Security Council"—had a parallel existence and even competed to a certain extent until they were finally integrated by the Supreme Soviet at the end of 1991).

The law "On Security" was a breakthrough in Russian political thinking and conduct on national security issues. It incorporated a number of revolutionary democratic ideas that went far beyond the existing state of affairs in Russia, including a special emphasis on the human dimension of security. National security was understood in the broadest sense of the term as a highly dynamic process of the safeguarding of the security of the person, the society, and the state. (If a careful and exhaustive analysis of this law has ever been undertaken in the West, I have not succeeded in finding it. This may, though, simply reflect the dearth of current Western scholarly periodicals in Russia.)

Despite this law, however, many national security problems and questions remain unresolved and unanswered. The law first defines security on the level of the highest concerns of the state: vital national interests; the nature and scale of threats and challenges; and the resources needed to protect interests and rebuff threats. Some answers to the question of how these things are defined seem clear enough. For example, maintaining stable political and economic development appears to be a universally acknowledged national interest, while threats such as those posed to territorial integrity or by the proliferation of weapons of mass destruction constitute a blatant challenge to the security of every civilized state. Beyond them, however, many specifics require clarification and remain topics of heated argument.[10] Such clarification greatly depends on reaching general agreement on unambiguous answers to some profound and complex questions: What is Russia? What kind of state do Russians live in and expect to live in? What is Russia's place and role in the modern world?

In almost every country it is the constitution that provides the answer to these questions. In Russia, however, the political and economic instability of recent years has prevented it from modernizing its constitution on the basis of popular consensus in accordance with the principles of democracy and rule of law. This situation has produced a whole chain of problems in the formation of Russian national statehood: without a new constitution, it is difficult to adopt a comprehensive national security doctrine; without the latter, no efficient military doctrine seems possible; the failure of defining doctrinal guidelines in the military sphere becomes a stumbling block on the way to the restructuring of defense industries toward civilian production within the framework of defense conversion; and so forth.

The absence of definite solutions to particular problems because of the lack of general guidelines has further accelerated the deteriorating political, economic, and social situation in the country and prevented the creation of a domestic climate in which fundamental state decisions can be made. This vicious circle has seemed to satisfy various political forces and social groups because it provides them with a perfect excuse for idleness in the course of radical reforms and gives them sufficient space to pursue their vested interests. To foster a rational and civilized national security perspective among the Russian public—a perspective that could supplant the chauvinist communist legacy—common sense would seem to suggest the need for an active policy on the part of democratic leaders of the country. It is no accident that at the meeting of the National Security Council of Russia on March 2, 1993, President Yeltsin called for an acceleration of the work on the formulation of foreign policy and military doctrines. This effort is important for countering the attempt of the opposition to exploit uncertainty in these fields.

Contrary to some Western expectations, Russia has thus far survived an unsettled period of transition to a new political and economic system. As new statehood develops, neither national security interests nor priorities have been finalized; they are, however, undergoing dynamic evolutionary changes. Translating these conceptual changes into practice in its external and military policies is no easy task for the Russian government, which needs sympathetic help from the West to overcome these difficulties.

In this respect, Western analysts might usefully display a greater readiness to examine the remaining contradictions and antagonisms (schematically speaking, between conservatives and democrats, civilians and the military) inside the Russian political establishment as far as national security doctrine is concerned. Encouragingly, it seems that Western analysts are at least aware of the ambivalent nature of the advisory and decision-making processes through which national security issues are addressed. Harry Gelman's observation about the trend to gradual demilitarization "wavering, being bitterly contested," with "its future far from certain"[11] seems a partial acknowledgment of contemporary Russian conditions.

A line still separates the democratically oriented political forces from the majority of the armed forces. As Christopher Bluth remarks in his study, *New Thinking in Soviet Military Policies*, "Some ambiguities do remain. This is because Soviet [let us admit, Russian—E.V.] military doctrine derives from rather disparate sources such as development of military science by military experts, on the one hand, and the radical departure of the new political thinking by the political leaders, on the other."[12] We have certainly not yet witnessed the elimination of such ambiguities. It should be remembered that many versions of the military doctrine (in all, 12 were examined by the Supreme Soviet of Russia) originate from military institutions that have by no means yet accepted the new security concepts, and their work still bears the imprint of a militarized internal and a confrontational external policy of the past.

What is the typical Western perception of, and response to, the emerging Russian national security doctrine? It would seem to be distinguished by a preoccupation with practical steps and actions and a disregard for the underlying theoretical and conceptual debate that is so important to Russians. Among dozens of Western fact-finding missions visiting Russia, I recall only Jay Kosminsky, then working for the Heritage Foundation, who asked the direct question: How is the Russian national security doctrine being conceptualized?

This lack of understanding of the Soviet/Russian national security mentality and its specifics has on occasion delayed and distorted Western appreciation of the momentous scale of the changes that have occurred in the former Soviet Union. Paul Goble, a former U.S. State Department expert on the non-Russian nationalities of the former Soviet Union, has been quoted as characterizing the pro-Gorbachev, Union-oriented policy of the Bush administration as follows: "We desperately want the world not to change. This administration and the Soviet studies fraternity got it wrong."[13] This observation seems equally applicable to the official U.S. attitude toward the effort by Russian democrats to formulate a civilized national security concept: the Bush administration did not seem too enthusiastic about it and was reluctant to encourage the reformist wing inside the Russian national security establishment.

Naturally, U.S. and NATO efforts to explore the Soviet/Russian security situation focused on the problems of nuclear weapons control and proliferation. Even so, the West provided useful advice to Russian democrats regarding civil/military relations. In this connection, one cannot underestimate the political significance of the missions to Russia and other members of the Commonwealth of Independent States (CIS) by Senators Nunn, Lugar, Exon, and Levin, Representatives Aspin and Solarz, and Special Advisor to the Secretary General of NATO Donnelli. Their clear views on the necessity of effective civilian control and parliamentary oversight of the military (as well as their explanations of U.S. and NATO defense strategy) were illuminating and valuable to Russian parliamentarians and political experts. The problem remains, however, of how to adapt Western experience to the specific conditions and traditions of Russia.

Western analysts and politicians find it difficult to appreciate the width of the historical and cultural gap that separates Russia from the West. Excessive Western pressure on sensitive issues—such as national security—could slow the process of closing that gap by heightening anti-Western sentiment within the military and defense-related industries, sectors of Russian society that are generally skeptical about rapprochement with the West and the extent of Western contributions to Russian reforms.

As foreign scholars sometimes acknowledge, although the danger of superpower conflict has receded, the potential threat to the West from the East remains. For example, Francis Miko of the Congressional Research Service has remarked that "the greatest long-term danger is that Russia and the other former Soviet Union states might prove unable to make a successful transition to political pluralism and functioning free markets and then take a path of undermining international stability."[14] As such a development is not impossible, the obvious response by the United States and the international community should be to contribute to the success of the political and economic transition in the former Soviet Union by all the means at their disposal.

I will not try to elaborate within this short essay a sophisticated scheme for the most efficient means by which the West can assist reforms in Russia. I am sure that the U.S. government and its advisors from the world of political studies excel in what they do. I also sympathize with a statement on U.S. national security policy made recently by one of my American colleagues: "We should stop looking for new answers to old questions. The essence is to find new questions and answer them." I would like to share my perceptions of some of these new problems.

One of the major achievements of international political thought in recent years has been to bring about an almost universal understanding of the fact that no state can safeguard its national security entirely by itself; international cooperation is essential. The rapprochement between Russia and the United States, which might lead to a genuine convergence of interests at some future date, suggests new directions, forms, and methods of international cooperation that could advance the interests of the world community as a whole. That is why some Russian scholars were attracted to a 1992 study published by the Brookings Institution, *A New Concept of Cooperative Security*.[15]

As we understand this study in Moscow, looking at the authors involved, it can be regarded as a kind of national security policy manifesto of the Clinton administration. Some of the study's ideas are particularly important for bilateral and multilateral confidence-building in the framework of the new system of international relations: "The central purpose of cooperative security arrangements is to prevent war and to do so primarily by preventing means for successful aggression from being assembled."[16] This is a goal that has never been accomplished before—as the history of the world wars and recent regional conflicts testifies.

For Russia, as well as for the United States, the conclusion that countries should move from preparing to counter threats to preventing threats—in other words, from deterring aggression to taking measures to make it more difficult—might encourage the reshaping of the entire political, economic, and military infrastructure designed to protect national security interests and sovereignty.

It is imperative to achieve harmony in understanding the threats and challenges facing Russia and America. This requires, at the least, a joint Russian-American effort; a broader Euro-Atlantic, or even global effort, might also be considered. The establishment of a joint Russian-U.S. research commission, or some similar move to institutionalize cooperation in the field of political and national security research, is the best way to contribute to better political decision making and bridge-building. Bilateral institutions that enhance the contacts between Russian scholars and their counterparts in other CIS countries and CSCE member states could lead to the formation of a new, reliable security structure in the Euro-Atlantic sphere.

At the same time, precautions should be taken to neutralize the impact of factors that could endanger Russian-U.S. cooperation. The threat of the uncontrolled disintegration of the former Soviet Union's military establishment is prominent among these factors. Like some of my colleagues in the West, I do not have a ready remedy for this potential disaster. In Russia, many people are skeptical about measures recommended from abroad. In particular, they are doubtful about the Nunn-Lugar legislation providing denuclearization assistance because its implementation, "which was originally so lethargic and unimaginative,"[17] is still subject to bureaucratic procedures and obstacles. Information about Western measures to prevent the proliferation and uncontrolled use of nuclear weapons is virtually unavailable to members of the Russian military, reinforcing their doubts about the sincerity of Western intentions and pledges. In light of this, and given widespread disillusionment with Western assistance, one cannot exaggerate the importance of establishing greater contacts between the Russian and U.S. militaries as a short-term confidence-building measure. For the same reasons, I disagree with Fred Iklé's assessment that better Russian-U.S. relations can only be built on influential, stable, and reliable institutions, and that in modern Russia only military structures meet these requirements.[18] The Russian military is certainly influential, but its stability and reliability are altogether less assured.

What is appealing to the influential *and* stable political and academic establishment in Russia is active U.S.-Russian cooperation in preventing

wars and threats at the earliest, critical stages of their development—
before the military has any professional role to play. In pursuit of this end
(and in addition to the above-mentioned scheme for harmonizing national
security concepts and interests), it might soon be feasible to develop a
joint system of strategic warning and intelligence gathering, processing,
and evaluation as part of a comprehensive international system of crisis
prevention and management.

One cannot help but be attracted by Iklé's general concept of a
Russian-U.S. "brotherhood in arms."[19] Indeed, prospects for a Russian-
American defense community seem favorable, considering the reality of
common threats and interests. Nevertheless, one should candidly recognize the existence of profound differences between the two countries'
historical, economic, political, military, intellectual, and spiritual traditions; their geostrategic positions; and their worldviews, philosophies,
and mores. Such differences do nothing to advance the trend towards
establishing an allied defense community. Fulfilling the goal of a brotherhood in arms is, in short, probably a task for future generations.

My impression is that Iklé is overly optimistic in his assumption that
"the military are less hostile towards their former Cold War adversaries
than are other groups of the population."[20] Unfortunately, the long-term
anti-Western and anti-American indoctrination of the armed forces of the
former USSR has left its legacy in the Russian army. Conflict and competition between Russia and the United States regarding the conventional
arms trade in the Third World (and maybe even in the NATO zone in the
future) could cause serious political repercussions. New approaches are
thus required, including perhaps a resumption of the bilateral consultations on arms transfers that occurred during the Carter administration.

Let me close this good-natured debate with Iklé by challenging, at least
partially, his statement that the majority of Russia's military commanders
want their country to be a model state, with the armed forces under
effective civilian control. Civilian control neither exists today nor accords
with Russia's historical traditions. Free of Communist Party control, the
army is directly or indirectly involved in a political struggle in an unstable
society where each institution is seeking a more influential role for itself.

Perhaps the most important element of contemporary U.S. approaches
to the question of national security is the recognition that the disarmament
process by itself does not necessarily lead to a more secure world. Iklé's
reference to the period between the two world wars, when agreements on
naval disarmament failed to protect peace, is pertinent.[21] Disarmament

cannot prevent war; moreover, it might encourage a potential aggressor to bolster its military strength while its neighbors grow weaker. What is needed is a complex network of agreements regulating all aspects of the national security of Russia and the United States, and thereby enhancing their ability to cooperate in their roles as the chief guarantors of international security. American studies on the emergence of a new Russian national security doctrine, and the responses of Russian scholars and politicians to this research, contribute to this goal. We in Russia certainly look forward to more research on this crucial matter, as it will help us to understand better our achievements and failures.

Notes

The views expressed in this essay are the author's own and should not be construed as representing the official positions of either the Russian Institute for Strategic Studies (of which the author is deputy director) or the Committee on Defense and Security Issues of the Supreme Soviet (to which the author is an advisor).

1. Michael McGwire, *Military Objectives in Soviet Foreign Policy* (Washington, D.C.: The Brookings Institution, 1987), p. 1.

2. Ibid., p. 37.

3. Baker Spring, *Five Questions Facing the Soviet Military,* The Heritage Lectures, no. 328 (Washington, D.C.: The Heritage Foundation, 1991), p. 8.

4. *1991 Military Forces in Transition* (Washington, D.C.: Department of Defense, 1991), p. 8.

5. Harry Gelman, *Gorbachev and the Future of the Soviet Military Institution,* Adelphi Papers, no. 258 (London: International Institute for Strategic Studies, Spring 1991), p. 3.

6. Ibid., p. 22.

7. Ibid.

8. David E. Colton, "The Constitutional Basis of Consolidating the Armed Forces of the USSR," *Voennaia mysl'* (Moscow), no. 5 (1991), pp. 72–73.

9. Ibid., p. 76.

10. As an example, I would point to the discussion on the role of the Moslem factor in Russia's national security. In 1991, before the attempted coup, the statement of this problem in respect of the USSR—that "historical brotherhood of free nations"—was regarded by communist ideologues as heretical. Subsequent tragic developments in a number of Islamic regions of the former USSR proved the validity of the apprehensions shared by some scholars, both in Russia and in the West.

11. Gelman, *Gorbachev and the Future of the Soviet Military Institution,* p. 3

12. Christopher Bluth, *New Thinking in Soviet Military Policies* (London: Chatham House Papers, 1990), p. 20.

13. See Christopher Madison, "Catch-up Diplomacy," *National Journal* 24, no. 8 (February 22, 1992), p. 448.

14. Francis T. Miko, *Post-Soviet Transformation: Implications for U.S. Policy*, CRS Issue Brief (Washington, D.C.: Congressional Research Service, January 8, 1992), p. 5.

15. A. B. Carter, W. J. Perry, and J. D. Steinbruner, *A New Concept of Cooperative Security* (Washington, D.C.: The Brookings Institution, 1992).

16. Ibid., p. 7.

17. Ibid., p. 14.

18. *New Time* (Moscow), no. 8 (1992), p. 38.

19. *New Time*, nos. 7–8.

20. *New Time*, no. 7, p. 27.

21. *New Time*, no. 8, p. 40.

Contributors

Leon Aron is E. L. Wiegand Fellow at the American Enterprise Institute (AEI) in Washington, D.C. Before joining AEI, he was a senior political analyst at the Heritage Foundation. During 1992–93, he was a Jennings Randolph Peace Fellow at the United States Institute of Peace, where he researched Russia's emerging foreign policy. Born in Moscow, Aron came to the United States as a refugee; he received his doctorate from Columbia University, where he concentrated on Soviet political sociology and U.S.-Soviet relations. He is a frequent guest on U.S. television and radio talk shows and a regular participant in a weekly discussion of current Russian politics and U.S.-Russian relations broadcast by the Voice of America. A contributor to many newspapers and magazines, Aron is currently working on a biography of Boris Yeltsin.

Mikhail E. Bezrukov is director of the Russian Science Foundation, where he conducts economic research. He is also a senior fellow at the Institute of the USA and Canada of the Russian Academy of Sciences.

Susan L. Clark is research staff member for political-military affairs at the Institute for Defense Analyses based in Alexandria, Virginia, with a special focus on former Soviet security policy as it relates to Western Europe, Japan, and Latin America, as well as on ethnic and environmental issues within the Commonwealth of Independent States. Before joining the Institute in 1986, Clark worked at the Center for Naval Analyses. She is the author of several books, including the forthcoming *Security in Russia and Eurasia: The New National Militaries and Emerging Defense Policies,* and numerous articles and chapters on Soviet foreign policy and related issues.

Charles H. Fairbanks, Jr., is a research professor of international relations at the Johns Hopkins University School of Advanced International

Studies (SAIS) and a fellow in the SAIS Foreign Policy Institute. After teaching political science at Yale University from 1974 to 1981, he worked as a member of the policy planning staff and as a deputy assistant secretary in the Department of State until 1984. Fairbanks also served as an adviser to the Bush campaign in 1988. He was guest editor of the spring 1993 issue of *The National Interest,* which focused on the collapse of communism, and has published extensively on such diverse issues as arms control and arms races, Soviet bureaucratic politics, and Anglo-German naval competition before World War I.

Vladimir Ivanov is currently an Abe Fellow working at the East-West Center in Honolulu. He is also chairman of the Asia-Pacific Region Studies Department at the Institute of World Economy and International Relations in Moscow. In 1992–93, Ivanov was a Jennings Randolph Peace Fellow at the United States Institute of Peace. Prior to his tenure at the Institute, he had been an advanced research fellow with the Program on U.S.-Japan Relations at the Harvard University Center for International Affairs. A noted expert on relations between Russia and its Asian neighbors, he has published books and numerous articles on the political economy and security concerns of the Asia-Pacific region, and is currently working on a book tentatively titled *Russia on the Pacific: A Missing Nation.* A native of Russia, Ivanov received a doctorate in political economy from the Institute of Oriental Studies of the Academy of Sciences of the USSR and served as science attaché at the Soviet embassy in New Delhi.

Kenneth M. Jensen is director of Special Programs at the United States Institute of Peace, where he was previously director of the Research and Studies Program and the Grants Program. In his present position, Jensen directs a variety of Institute programs, including its projects on the former Soviet Union and the Balkans. He holds degrees from the University of Colorado, University of Wisconsin, and Moscow State University. Jensen's doctoral research and subsequent scholarship has focused on Russian Marxist social and political thought. He is the author of *Beyond Marx and Mach: A. A. Bogdanov's Filosofiia zhivogo opyta,* as well as numerous articles, papers, and reviews in the Russian, Soviet, and East European field. Jensen is also editor (with Fred Baumann) of three books on U.S. policy issues: *American Defense Policy and Liberal Democracy; Crime and Punishment: Issues in Criminal Justice;* and *Religion and Politics.* His numerous edited publications produced under the auspices of the United States Institute of Peace include *The Origins of the Cold War: The Novikov, Kennan, and Roberts 'Long*

Telegrams' of 1946; A Look at "The End of History?"; The Professionalization of Peacekeeping; (with Patricia Carley) *Civil War in Tajikistan;* and (with W. Scott Thompson and others) *Approaches to Peace: An Intellectual Map.*

Igor' Kliamkin is senior researcher at the Institute of International Economic and Political Studies (IMEMO) and senior fellow at the Public Opinion Foundation in Moscow. He is also the former editor-in-chief of *Democratic Russia.*

Andrei V. Kortunov is currently the head of the Department of Foreign Policy of the Institute of USA and Canada of the Russian Academy of Sciences. He is also president of the Russian Science Foundation.

Martin Malia is a professor in the Department of History at the University of California at Berkeley. Malia has written numerous works on the nature of Soviet ideology, including the article "To the Stalin Mausoleum," which appeared under the pseudonym "Z" in the fall 1989 issue of *Daedalus.* Malia's latest book, released in the spring of 1994 by Free Press, is *The Soviet Tragedy.*

Elizabeth Teague is adviser on ethnic affairs to Max van der Stoel, High Commissioner on National Minorities of the Conference on Security and Cooperation in Europe. For many years, she was senior research analyst at Radio Free Europe/Radio Liberty in Munich. She has written many articles and reports on labor and domestic political issues in the former Soviet Union, including in-depth examinations of economic and political restructuring. Teague received her doctorate from the University of Birmingham Centre for Russian and East European Studies. As a Jennings Randolph Peace Fellow at the United States Institute of Peace from September 1992 to August 1993, she worked on a survey of minority groups in Russia and neighboring republics of the former Soviet Union, identifying factors that may encourage or ameliorate conflicts.

Evgenii S. Volk is head of the Heritage Foundation's Moscow office. He was previously deputy director of Russia's Institute for Strategic Studies. In the course of a distinguished academic and diplomatic career with the Russian Academy of Sciences (Institute of International Economic and Political Studies, 1981), the Ministry of Foreign Affairs (1976–90), and the Committee on Defense and Security Issues of the Supreme Soviet of the Russian Federation (1991–92), Volk has served as an expert on European security, NATO, and disarmament.

THE EMERGENCE of RUSSIAN FOREIGN POLICY

The text and display types of this book are Berkeley
Old Style and Avenir. Cover design by Richard Lee
Heffner; interior design by Day Wilkes Dosch and
Joan Engelhardt; page makeup by Helen Y. Redmond
of HYR Graphics.